KW-338-641

Criminal Appeals

A Practical Guide to Appeals
to and from the Crown Court

AUSTRALIA
The Law Book Company Ltd.
Sydney : Melbourne : Brisbane

CANADA AND U.S.A.
The Carswell Company Ltd.
Agincourt, Ontario

INDIA
N. M. Tripathi Private Ltd.
Bombay
and
Eastern Law House Private Ltd.
Calcutta
M. P. P. House
Bangalore

ISRAEL
Steimatzky's Agency Ltd.
Jerusalem : Tel Aviv : Haifa

MALAYSIA : SINGAPORE : BRUNEI
Malayan Law Journal (Pte.) Ltd.
Singapore

NEW ZEALAND
Sweet & Maxwell (N.Z.) Ltd.
Auckland

PAKISTAN
Pakistan Law House
Karachi

90 0705832 8

WITHDRAWN
FROM
UNIVERSITY OF PLYMOUTH
LIBRARY

Criminal Appeals

A Practical Guide to Appeals to and from the Crown Court

Ian McLean

Metropolitan Stipendiary Magistrate

London
Sweet & Maxwell
1980

Published in 1980 by
Sweet & Maxwell Limited of
11 New Fetter Lane, London
Computerset by MFK Graphic Systems (Typesetting) Ltd.,
Saffron Walden, Essex
and printed in Great Britain by
Fletcher & Son Ltd, Norwich

British Library Cataloguing in Publication Data

McLean, Ian
    Criminal appeals.
    1. Criminal procedure – England
    2. Appellate procedure – England
    I. Title
    347'.42'08   KD8420

    ISBN 0-421-24760-6

PLYMOUTH POLYTECHNIC
LEARNING RESOURCES CENTRE

ACCN. No.   121233

CLASS No.   347.4208 MAC

©
Ian McLean
1980

PREFACE

MANY questions encountered by practitioners in relation to appeals in criminal cases can be resolved only by time-wasting research in a number of different books, some now obsolete, many out of print. In order to provide a convenient guide to the subject, collecting all the relevant material in a single volume, Peter Morrish and I wrote *A Practical Guide to Appeals in Criminal Courts* in 1970. Sadly, it was itself obsolete almost as soon as published. The years 1970–1973 saw a great deal of upheaval in the criminal courts' system and the Beeching Report was published shortly before our book. A deal of water has flowed under the bridges of the court system since then, and quarter sessions and assizes, which formed the core of that earlier book, are known to many practitioners only by name.

Since the original book proved useful to many, the publishers felt it right to take a new look at the subject. This present volume is in no sense a second edition of the first; indeed it covers different ground. First, the material relating to appeals to magistrates' courts has no place in this volume. Useful though it may have been, for it was not, I think, to be found elsewhere in that form, it makes up a very small part of a practitioner's experience. The same is true of appeals to the Crown Court in quasi-criminal matters under regulatory legislation ranging from firearms certificates to highways. Licensing, in particular, is a wholly specialised field. This material has also been removed. Secondly, it has been necessary to "tighten" the style. The earlier volume, while informative, had a narrative style which led to at least one member of the Bar claiming that he took it on holiday with him in the summer for light reading!

The present volume seeks to present, in a number of separate but linked parts, all aspects of appeals from magistrates' courts and the Crown Court in criminal cases, up through the Divisional Court and the Criminal Division of the Court of Appeal, to the rarefied regions of the House of Lords. The word "appeal" is used in its broadest sense of challenging the decision of the court below and the practice on an application for judicial review under the new Order 53 is included, as are references by the Home Secretary under section 17 of the Criminal Appeal Act 1968, and by the Attorney-General under section 36 of the Criminal Justice Act 1972. Appendix H contains a copy of the statutory instrument providing for appeals against taxation of costs out of central funds. While not strictly an avenue of appeal, the procedure for applying to a judge in chambers for bail is clearly a method of challenging the decision of the lower court, and for completeness' sake is also included. Some line has to be drawn, however, and appeals under special extradition or immigration procedures are not included, nor are appeals in contempt cases by persons other than the defendant in a criminal case, nor are references to the European Court.

Appendix A is a diagram of the appellate system in criminal cases.

Costs and legal aid are two of the prime concerns of most practitioners these days, and this volume sets out to deal with both. Many of the procedures in relation to taxation, however, are of an administrative nature and it has not been possible to deal with all of this in a work of this size.

A number of forms and precedents are included for convenience' sake in Appendices C to G.

By its very nature, a volume of this kind contains little material that is wholly original. Some of the text is necessarily derived from the earlier work in which Peter Morrish and I collaborated, and this I readily acknowledge. The views of a Stipendiary Magistrate on the workings of the Criminal Division of the Court of Appeal are likely to be of limited interest. For the part dealing with those matters I owe an enormous debt to working with Peter Morrish and Cyril Horsford, both former officers of that court, on volume 11 of the new Halsbury, and even more to collaborating with Peter Morrish and Master Thompson, the Registrar of Criminal Appeals, on our recent book on the subject. Anything that is original and valuable in the text dealing with that court is to be attributed to knowledge derived from them.

I would like to acknowledge also the great assistance I have received from the staff of the Inner London Crown Court. The Administrator, Mr. J. G. O'Smotherly gave me considerable encouragement, and Mr. O. A. Hunt, now the Deputy Administrator, gave me invaluable help in providing the forms for Appendix C. Mr. A. R. Edwards gave me his advice on appeals from the Crown Court. As I completed the manuscript, I heard with great sadness of the death of Mr. C. W. W. "Chalky" White, of the Metropolitan Police Solicitors' Department, who, when running the appeals section of the old "London Sessions," gave us such great encouragement in that earlier volume.

IAN MCLEAN

CONTENTS

PART II. APPEALS TO THE HIGH COURT BY WAY OF CASE STATED

A: APPEAL FROM MAGISTRATES' COURTS

B. APPEAL FROM THE CROWN COURT

PART III. JUDICIAL REVIEW: THE PREROGATIVE ORDERS OF MANDAMUS, CERTORARI AND PROHIBITION

PART IV. APPLICATION TO THE HIGH COURT FOR BAIL

PART V. APPEALS FROM THE CROWN COURT TO THE CRIMINAL DIVISION OF THE COURT OF APPEAL

PART VI. APPEALS TO THE HOUSE OF LORDS FROM THE DIVISIONAL COURT AND THE CRIMINAL DIVISION OF THE COURT OF APPEAL

PART VII. APPENDICES

TABLE OF CASES

TABLE OF STATUTES

APPEALS FROM MAGISTRATES' COURTS TO THE CROWN COURT

1. General Provisions

(1) The Crown Court as an appellate court

The Crown Court primarily exists, in its appellate jurisdiction, to deal with disputed questions of fact.[1] An appeal takes the form of a rehearing of the whole case, with the prosecutor proving his case afresh. Either party is within his rights in calling any relevant and admissible evidence in support of his case, whether or not that evidence was called by him in the court below.[2] On determining an appeal, whether against conviction or sentence, the Crown Court may award any punishment, whether more or less severe than that awarded by the magistrates' court whose decision is appealed, if that is a punishment which that magistrates' court might have awarded.[3]

(2) Rights of appeal: general

A person convicted by a magistrates' court[4] has, by statute[5] a right of appeal to the Crown Court: (a) if he pleaded guilty,[6] against his sentence; (b) if he did not plead guilty, against both his conviction and sentence.[7]

A person sentenced by a magistrates' court for an offence in respect of which a probation order, or an order of conditional discharge, has been previously made has a statutory right of appeal to the Crown Court against his sentence.[8]

A person sentenced in a magistrates' court for a breach of the requirements of a community service order has a statutory right of appeal to the Crown

---

[1] *R. v. Wandsworth Justices, ex p. Read* [1942] 1 K.B. 281, at p. 285, *per* Humphries J.
[2] See pp. 19–21, *post.*
[3] See p. 21, *post.*
[4] A "magistrates' court" is defined for the purposes of the Magistrates' Courts Act 1952, in *ibid.* s. 124 (1). See also the Interpretation Act 1978, Sched. 1. As to juvenile courts, see p. 2, *post.*
  An executive act, such as an order made by a justice of the peace under the food and drugs legislation, condemning food as unfit for human consumption, is not an order made by a court of summary jurisdiction: *R. v. Cornwall Quarter Sessions, ex p. Kerley* [1956] 1 W.L.R. 906.
[5] It is most elementary that no appeal from a court lies to another court unless there is a statutory provision which gives a right of appeal: *R. v. West Kent Quarter Sessions, Appeals Committee, ex p. Files* [1951] 2 All E.R. 728, at p. 730 *per* Lord Goddard C.J.; also *R. v. Durham Justices, ex p. Laurent* [1945] 1 K.B. 33, at p. 37, *per* Humphries J. As to the control of inferior courts by prerogative order, see pp. 39–53, *post.*
[6] As to equivocal pleas of guilty, see pp. 3–5, *post.*
[7] Magistrates' Courts Act 1952, s. 83 (1); Courts Act 1971, s. 56 (2), Sched. 9, Pt. I.
  Where a person is convicted in a magistrates' court of a "schedule offence," to which the Criminal Law Act 1977, s. 23 relates, it is not open to him to appeal to the Crown Court against the conviction on the ground that the magistrates' court's decision as to the value involved was mistaken: *ibid.* s. 23 (8).
  A convicted person remitted to another magistrates' court for sentence in accordance with the Criminal Law Act 1977, s. 45, has no right of appeal against the remittal: *ibid.* s. 45 (2).
[8] Magistrates' Courts Act 1952, s. 83 (2); Courts Act 1971, s. 56 (2), Sched. 9, Pt. I.

Court against the sentence,[9] as has a person in respect of whom a community service order is revoked by a magistrates' court and another sentence substituted.[10]

Where, under the Justices of the Peace Act 1361 or otherwise, a person is ordered by a magistrates' court to enter into a recognisance, with or without sureties, to keep the peace or to be of good behaviour, that person has a statutory right of appeal to the Crown Court.[11]

A parent or guardian[12] ordered by a magistrates' court, under section 55 of the Children and Young Persons Act 1933, to pay a fine, compensation or costs in respect of a juvenile offender may appeal to the Crown Court[13] as may a parent or guardian ordered[14] by a magistrates' court to enter into a recognisance to ensure that a juvenile offender pays outstanding sums in respect of fines, etc., or ordered[15] by a magistrates' court to pay such sums himself or herself.

There is no right of appeal to the Crown Court against the dismissal of an information or complaint before a magistrates' court unless expressly conferred by statute.[16]

Where examining justices determine not to commit a defendant for trial on the ground that the evidence is not sufficient, and, being of opinion that the charge was not made in good faith, they order the prosecutor to pay the whole or any part of the costs incurred in or about the defence,[17] the prosecutor has a statutory right of appeal to the Crown Court, if the amount ordered exceeds £25.[18]

A juror may appeal to the Crown Court against the order of the proper officer declining to excuse him from service.[19]

(3) Rights of appeal: juvenile courts

A juvenile court is a magistrates' court[20] to which certain matters are assigned by statute. It has all the jurisdiction and powers of a magistrates'

---

[9] Powers of Criminal Courts Act 1973, s. 16 (6).
[10] *Ibid.* s. 17 (4).
[11] Magistrates' Courts (Appeals from Binding Over Orders) Act 1956, s. 1 (1); Criminal Justice Act 1967, Sched. 7; Courts Act 1971, s. 56 (2), Sched. 9, Pt. I. As to bail pending such an appeal, see *ibid.* s. 1 (2) (*b*).
[12] As to the expression "guardian" in relation to local authorities, see *R.* v. *Croydon Juvenile Court JJ. ex p. Croydon London Borough Council* [1973] 1 Q.B. 426; *Somerset County Council* v. *Brice* [1973] 1 W.L.R. 1169; *Lincoln Corporation* v. *Parker* [1974] 1 W.L.R. 713; *Leicestershire County Council* v. *Cross* [1976] 120 S.J. 299; *Nottinghamshire County Council* v. *Cox* (1976) 140 J.P.N. 10; also *Somerset County Council* v. *Kingscott* [1975] 1 W.L.R. 283.
[13] Children and Young Persons Act 1933, as amended, s. 55 (5).
[14] In accordance with the Criminal Law Act 1977, s. 36, see *ibid.* s. 36 (7).
[15] In accordance with *ibid.* s. 34, see *ibid.* s. 34 (4) (*a*).
[16] *Benson* v. *Northern Ireland Road Transport Board* [1942] A.C. 520 (H.L.); also *R.* v. *London County Keepers of the Peace and London Justices* [1945] K.B. 528; also *ante*, p. 1, n. 5. Such rights are conferred by, *e.g.* Customs and Excise Act 1952, s. 283 (4) and the Diseases of Animals Act 1950, s. 81. The dismissal of an information may, however, be challenged by way of case stated, see p. 24, *post.* An unsuccessful prosecutor may challenge the refusal of justices to commit for trial by fresh committal proceedings or by voluntary bill, see *R.* v. *Manchester City, ex p. Snelson* [1977] 1 W.L.R. 911.
[17] *i.e.* under the provisions of the Costs in Criminal Cases Act 1973, s. 2 (4).
[18] *Ibid.* s. 2 (5).
[19] Crown Court Rules 1971, r. 20.
[20] As to which, see *ante*, p. 7, n. 4.

court subject to any statutory provisions or restrictions. In addition to the general right of appeal against conviction and sentence conferred upon persons convicted before a magistrates' court by section 83 of the Magistrates' Courts Act 1952,[21] a juvenile has a statutory right of appeal to the Crown Court: (a) against a finding or order made by the juvenile court in care proceedings[22]; (b) against the finding in such proceedings that the offence condition is satisfied, where the offence was not admitted by him before the court[23]; (c) against the making of, or the dismissal of an application to discharge, a supervision order[24]; and (d) against the making of, or the dismissal of an application to discharge, a care order.[25]

A juvenile remitted from a magistrates' court to a juvenile court for sentence[26] has the same rights of appeal against any order of the court to which he is remitted as if he had been found guilty by that court.[27]

(4) Appeal after plea of guilty; equivocal plea

The Crown Court has no jurisdiction to hear an appeal against the conviction of a person who has unequivocally pleaded guilty in the magistrates' court.[28] Where, however, it appears to the Crown Court that a person is seeking to appeal against his conviction on the basis that his plea before the magistrates' court was equivocal, the court is not only entitled,[29] but is bound[30] to dispose of that issue as a preliminary point.

Any such enquiry made by the Crown Court involves an examination of what happened in the magistrates' court.[31] If the Crown Court is satisfied on the evidence of what happened in the magistrates' court that the plea tendered there was ambiguous or equivocal and should never have been accepted as a proper plea of guilty,[32] then it is bound to treat the plea as a nullity and remit the case to the magistrates' court with an expression of the court's opinion to that effect.[33]

---

[21] See *ante*, pp. 1, 2.
[22] Children and Young Persons Act 1969, as amended, s. 2 (12).
[23] *Ibid*. s. 3 (8).
[24] *Ibid*. s. 16 (8).
[25] *Ibid*. s. 21 (4). See *ibid*. s. 21 (5) as to appeal by the local authority.
[26] Under the provisions of the Children and Young Persons Act 1933, s. 56.
[27] *Ibid*. s. 56 (2). He has no right of appeal, however, against the order of remittal: *ibid*.
[28] Magistrates' Courts Act 1952, s. 83 (1); *R.* v. *West Kent Quarter Sessions Appeal Committee, ex p. Files* [1951] 2 All E.R. 728. See also *R.* v. *Durham Quarter Sessions, ex p. Virgo* [1952] 2 Q.B. 1; *R.* v. *London Sessions Appeals Committee Deputy Chairman, ex p. Borg* [1958] 1 Q.B. 43 (explaining *Mittelmann* v. *Denman* [1926] 1 K.B. 519; *R.* v. *Tottenham JJ., ex p. Rubens* [1970] 1 W.L.R. 800; *Woodhall* v. *Christal* [1961] Crim. L.R. 315.
[29] *R.* v. *Durham Quarter Sessions, ex p. Virgo, supra*, applied in *S (An Infant)* v. *Manchester City Recorder* [1971] A.C. 481 (H.L.) See also *R.* v. *London Sessions Appeals Committee Deputy Chairman, ex p. Borg, supra*, at p. 47 *per* Lord Goddard C.J.
[30] *R.* v. *Marylebone JJ., ex p. Westminster City Council* [1971] 1 W.L.R. 567; see also *R.* v. *Tottenham JJ., ex p. Rubens, supra*.
[31] *R.* v. *Marylebone JJ., ex p. Westminster City Council, supra*; *P. Foster (Haulage) Ltd.* v. *Roberts* [1978] R.T.R. 302. Unless the Crown Court is told something which raises the issue, however, it should not set about making an enquiry: *R.* v. *Coventry Crown Court, ex p. Manson* (1978) 67 Cr. App. R. 315.
[32] See p. 4, *post*.
[33] See Courts Act 1971, s. 9 (2) (*b*) and p. 4, *post*. Where the Crown Court properly remits a case in this manner the magistrates are under a duty to give effect to that "expression of opinion": *R.* v. *Tottenham JJ., ex p. Rubens, supra*. It is, of course, otherwise where the Crown

It is important to draw a clear distinction between the duties of a magistrates' court faced with a plea that is equivocal at the time it is made, and the exercise of the magistrates' discretion to permit a defendant to change an unequivocal plea of guilty into a plea of not guilty at a later stage of the proceedings.[34] In order to amount to a binding and effective plea of guilty to a criminal charge, the plea must be unambiguous and unequivocal. "A court cannot accept an equivocal plea of guilty; it has no discretion in the matter; faced with an equivocal plea the court must either obtain an unequivocal plea of guilty, or enter a plea of not guilty."[34] For a plea to be equivocal, however, the defendant must have added to the plea of guilty a qualification which, if true, might show that he was not guilty of the offence charged.[35]

What the Crown Court cannot do, on an appeal against conviction,[36] where the defendant unequivocally pleaded guilty in the magistrates' court, is to embark upon an enquiry as to whether that plea was entered by mistake or under a misapprehension.[37] Where an unequivocal plea of guilty is entered in the magistrates' court, that court has an inherent power, in a proper case,[38] to permit that plea to be changed to one of not guilty, and this power obtains up to final adjudication,[39] but the exercise of this power is a matter for the magistrates' discretion, and it is a power which should only be exercised in clear cases, and very sparingly.[40] There is no statutory provision enabling a person who has pleaded guilty unequivocally in the magistrates' court to go to the Crown Court and ask that court to enquire into whether he intended to

---

Court exercises its power improperly, see R. v. Marylebone JJ., ex p. Westminster City Council, supra and see text to note 42a on p. 5, post.

Where a case is remitted to the magistrates' court in this manner it is remitted for trial de novo. Such trial commences when the evidence is called and the preliminaries may be taken as read. The justices are not bound to put his election to the defendant afresh, nor to entertain an application to do so, but are entitled, if they see fit, to permit a change of election, depending upon how they see the "broad justice of the situation": R. v. Southampton City Justices, ex p. Briggs [1972] 1 W.L.R. 277; R. v. Bradfield and Sonning JJ., ex p. Jones [1975] (1975) 119 S.J. 679.

[34] P. Foster (Haulage) Ltd. v. Roberts [1978] R.T.R. 302, at p. 310 per O'Connor J.

[35] Ibid. An example of this type of qualification is found where a person charged with handling a stolen motor car pleads "guilty to handling but I didn't know it was stolen." It is not, of course, every qualification which makes a plea equivocal; for example, the burglar charged with stealing spoons, forks and a camera, who pleads "guilty but I didn't take the camera" is making an unequivocal plea of guilty to burglary: ibid.

The material before a court which may indicate that a plea is equivocal includes not only what was said in court after the plea, in mitigation or otherwise by or on behalf of a defendant, but also any statement made by the defendant prior to the plea and presented to the court as part of the prosecution's case: see, e.g. R. v. Blandford JJ., ex p. G (An Infant) [1967] 1 Q.B. 82; Leahy v. Rawlinson [1978] Crim. L.R. 106, also R. v. Tottenham JJ., ex p. Rubens [1970] 1 W.L.R. 800, at p. 804, per Bridge J.

[36] As opposed to a committal under the Magistrates' Courts Act 1952, ss. 28 and 29: see R. v. Mutford and Lothingland JJ., ex p. Harber [1971] 2 Q.B. 291; R. v. Fareham JJ., ex p. Long [1976] Crim. L.R. 269; R. v. Camberwell Green JJ., ex p. Sloper [1979] Crim. L.R. 264. See also p. 7, post.

[37] R. v. Durham Quarter Sessions, ex p. Virgo [1952] 2 Q.B. 1, at pp. 6, 7, per Lord Goddard C.J.

[38] If the defendant pleads guilty and later makes a statement which, if true, would amount to a defence to the charge, the magistrates should enter a plea of not guilty: R. v. Durham Quarter Sessions, ex p. Virgo [1952] 2 Q.B. 1, at p. 7.

[39] S (An Infant) v. Manchester City Recorder [1971] A.C. 481; see also R. v. Midhurst JJ., ex p. Thompson [1974] Q.B. 137; P. Foster (Haulage) Ltd. v. Roberts [1978] R.T.R. 308.

[40] S. (An Infant) v. Manchester City Recorder, supra, at p. 507 per Lord Upjohn.

plead guilty or whether he did not.[41] Where the magistrates accept an un-equivocal plea of guilty, the Crown Court has no power on the hearing of an appeal to remit the case to them, and they are right to refuse to entertain any such purported "remittal."[42] It is otherwise, of course, where a defendant is committed to the Crown Court for sentence.[42a]

(5) Meaning of "sentence"

In relation to an appeal against sentence, the expression "sentence" is defined to include "any order made on conviction" by a magistrates' court,[43] not being a probation order, or an order for conditional discharge,[44] an order for the payment of costs,[45] an order under section 2 of the Protection of Animals Act 1911 (which enables a court to order the destruction of an animal)[46] or an order made in pursuance of an enactment under which the court has no discretion as to the making of the order or its terms.[47] It does not include a committal in default of payment of a sum of money or for want of sufficient distress to satisfy any sum of money or for failure to do or abstain from doing anything required to be done or left undone.[48]

The definitive characteristic of orders made "on conviction" is that they are orders made as a consequence of the conviction of the particular offence of which the defendant stands convicted.[49] An order of examining justices committing a defendant for trial on indictment is not an order "made on conviction" since there has been no conviction, and that order is not therefore the subject of a right of appeal to the Crown Court.[50] Again an order of a magistrates' court committing a defendant to the Crown Court for sentence under section 29 of the Magistrates' Courts Act 1952 is not an order made "on

---

[41] R. v. West Kent Quarter Sessions Appeals Committee, ex p. Files [1951] 2 All E.R. 728 at p. 732, per Lord Goddard C.J., who pointed out that the line of cases following R. v. Forde [1923] 2 K.B. 400 (for which see p. 61, post) are applicable only to appeals to the Criminal Division of the Court of Appeal, being decided under the Criminal Appeal Acts 1907 and 1968. They have no application to appeals to the Crown Court.

[42] R. v. Marylebone JJ., ex p. Westminster City Council [1971] 1 W.L.R. 567. In R. v. West Quarter Sessions Appeals Committee ex p. Files, supra, Lord Goddard C.J. was of opinion that certiorari might lie in the case of a person who pleaded guilty in the magistrates' court under a genuine misapprehension although, he added, it would require a strong case. See also R. v. Kings Lynn JJ., ex p. Fysh [1964] Crim. L.R. 143.

[42a] R. v. Camberwell Green JJ., ex p. Sloper [1979] Crim. L.R. 264.

[43] "Magistrates' court" is defined in the Magistrates' Courts Act 1952, s. 124 (1) and the Interpretation Act 1978, Sched. 1, see ante, p. 1, n. 4.

[44] Magistrates' Courts Act 1952, s. 83 (3) (a). A person subsequently sentenced in the magistrates' court for an offence for which he was previously placed on probation or conditionally discharged may appeal to the Crown Court against that sentence; see ante, p. 1.

[45] Magistrates' Courts Act 1952, s. 83 (3) (b). Certiorari lies to quash an order for costs made in excess of, or without, proper jurisdiction (R. v. Highgate JJ., ex p. Petrou [1954] 1 W.L.R. 485); mandamus lies to compel a proper taxation (R. v. Bow Street Magistrate, ex p. Palmer [1969] Crim. L.R. 658).

[46] Magistrates' Courts Act 1952, s. 83 (3) (c).

[47] Ibid. s. 83 (3) (d). As to disqualification under the Road Traffic Acts, see p. 7, post.

[48] Magistrates' Courts Act 1952, s. 126.

[49] R. v. London Sessions Appeals Committee, ex p. Beaumont [1951] 1 K.B. 557, at p. 561, per Hilbery J. Cf. the definition of "sentence" as defined in the Criminal Appeal Act 1968, s. 51 (1), considered in R. v. Hayden [1975] 1 W.L.R. 852, and see p. 92, post.

[50] It is submitted that the proper course to take where the committal proceedings are challenged is to move to quash the indictment. The prerogative orders (see pp. 39–53, post) may lie in a proper case, see e.g. R. v. Epping and Harlow JJ., ex p. Massaro [1973] 1 Q.B. 433.

conviction" since the whole tenor of that section is that the defendant is treated as though he had just been convicted before the Crown Court.[51]

An order made "on conviction" includes a restitution order, or an order of forfeiture, for example, of firearms, an order for the endorsement of a driving licence and an order of disqualification for holding or obtaining a driving licence, or an order of forfeiture under the customs legislation.[52] It does not include an order to enter into recognisances to be of good behaviour imposed in addition to a fine[53] or an order estreating recognisances for non-appearance[54] or a sentence of imprisonment imposed in default of payment of estreated recognisances.[55]

A recommendation for deportation made under section 6 of the Immigration Act 1971, is treated as a sentence for the purpose of any enactment providing an appeal against sentence.[56]

It has been held[57] that a compensation order made under the provisions of section 4 of the Forfeiture Act 1870, is not an order made "on conviction"[58] but there seems to be no doubt that a compensation order made under the provisions of section 35 of the Powers of Criminal Courts Act 1973, is such an order, and therefore liable to be the subject of an appeal to the Crown Court[59]; indeed the Act makes special provision, where such an order is made against a person in respect of an offence taken into consideration in determining his sentence, for appealing against that order as if it were part of the sentence imposed in respect of the offence, or any of the offences, of which he was convicted.[60]

Where, on the trial of an information charging a person with an offence, a magistrates' court makes a hospital order or a guardianship order in respect of

---

[51] See *ibid*. s. 29 (3), and the observations of Lord Goddard C.J. in *R.* v. *London Sessions, ex p. Rogers* [1951] 2 K.B. 74 at pp. 76, 77; also *R.* v. *Middlesex JJ., ex p. Director of Public Prosecutions* [1950] 2 K.B. 589.
   A committal for sentence is properly challenged by means of the prerogative orders (see pp. 39–53, *post*. The Criminal Division of the Court of Appeal has no jurisdiction in such a matter: *R.* v. *Warren* [1954] 1 W.L.R. 531; *R.* v. *Brown* [1963] Crim. L.R. 647; *R.* v. *Jones* [1969] 2 Q.B. 33; *R.* v. *Birtles* [1975] 1 W.L.R. 1623.
[52] *R.* v. *London Sessions Appeals Committee, ex p. Beaumont* [1951] 1 K.B. 557, *per* Hilbery J. at p. 561.
[53] *R.* v. *London Sessions Appeal Committee, ex p. Beaumont* [1951] 1 K.B. 557, but see now the Magistrates' Courts (Appeals from Binding Over Orders) Act 1956, *ante*, p. 2.
[54] Under the Bail Act 1976, a person who has been released on bail in criminal proceedings and who either (a) without reasonable cause fails to surrender to custody, or (b) having reasonable cause for his failure to surrender, fails to surrender as soon after the appointed time as is reasonably practicable, commits an offence punishable on summary conviction with three months imprisonment or a fine of £400 or both (see Bail Act 1976, ss. 4, 6 (1), (2), (5), and (6)). Appeal lies in the ordinary way against conviction or sentence for that offence.
[55] See Magistrates' Courts Act 1952, s. 126; also *R.* v. *Harman* [1959] 2 Q.B. 134, a decision on the Criminal Appeal Act 1907, applying *R.* v. *London Sessions Appeal Committee, ex p. Beaumont, supra*.
[56] Immigration Act 1971, s. 6 (5) (*a*).
[57] *R.* v. *Dorset Quarter Sessions, ex p. Randall* [1967] 2 Q.B. 222.
[58] The reasoning seems to be based on the ground that there had to be an application for compensation by the aggrieved person to found the order. See the observations of Lord Parker C.J. *ibid*. pp. 225–226.
[59] See the provisions for suspending an order pending the possibility of an appeal contained in the Powers of Criminal Courts Act 1973, s. 36 (2). As to an alternative means of review by way of application to the magistrates' court, see *ibid*. s. 37.
[60] Powers of Criminal Courts Act 1973, s. 35 (1), (5).

him without convicting,[61] that person has the same right of appeal against the order as if it had been made on his conviction, and on such appeal the Crown Court has the like powers as if the appeal were against both his conviction and sentence.[62]

In relation to orders for disqualification from holding or obtaining a driving licence, a discretionary disqualification is treated as an order made "on conviction"[63]; a mandatory or obligatory disqualification[64] though an order made "on conviction" cannot be appealed to the Crown Court in view of the express exclusion contained in section 83 (3) of the Magistrates' Courts Act 1952.[65]

An order for the payment of costs made by a magistrates' court, while clearly an order made "on conviction," is, like an obligatory disqualification, a conditional discharge and a probation order, expressly excluded from the ambit of section 83 (3) of the Act.[66]

A legal aid contribution order made by a magistrates' court, is not an order made "on conviction"[67] and cannot be appealed to the Crown Court.[68]

(6) Persons committed for sentence

A person convicted in a magistrates' court and committed to the Crown Court for sentence has no right of appeal as such[69] against that committal, although, of course, he is not debarred from appealing against the conviction on which the committal was founded.[70]

Where a person appears before the Crown Court on committal for sentence from the magistrates' court, the Crown Court should satisfy itself that the time for appealing against the conviction has expired. If it has not, the court should enquire whether the offender intends to appeal against the conviction. If he says that he does, the Crown Court should adjourn the question of sentence until the appeal has been heard or otherwise disposed of.[71]

(7) Effect of appealing

Apart from any special enactment[72] there is no general rule of law which

---

[61] *i.e.* under the Mental Health Act 1959, s. 60 (2).
[62] Mental Health Act 1959, s. 70 (1).
[63] See *R.* v. *Surrey Quarter Sessions, ex p. Commissioner of Metropolitan Police* [1963] 1 Q.B. 990.
[64] *i.e.* a disqualification under the Road Traffic Act 1972, s. 93 (1).
[65] *Ibid.* s. 83 (3) (*d*); and see *ante*, p. 5.
[66] See *ibid.* s. 83 (3) (*b*) and also *ante*, p. 6. See also the Crown Court Business Circular No. 10/77 dated July 22, 1977, and annexed to the judgment in *R.* v. *Bunce* (1978) 66 Cr. App. R. 109.
[67] By analogy with the position under the Criminal Appeal Act 1968, s. 51 (1). See *R.* v. *Hayden* [1975] 1 W.L.R. 852, and p. 92, *post.*
[68] The Crown Court has no power to revoke an order made by a magistrates' court even if a conviction is quashed, the order not being dependent on the conviction. The Crown Court may, of course, make a further contribution order relating to the appeal proceedings; see Crown Court Business Circular No. 10/77 referred to in note 66, *infra.*
[69] As to challenging the committal by prerogative order, see *ante*, p. 6.
[70] Provided that he is otherwise within the provisions of the Magistrates' Courts Act 1952, s. 83, as to which see *ante*, pp. 1–5.
[71] *R.* v. *Faithful* [1950] W.N. 550.
[72] See the Betting, Gaming and Lotteries Act 1963, s. 11 (2); Licensing Act 1964, s. 189; Obscene Publications Act 1964, s. 1 (4), proviso; Gaming Act 1968, ss. 25 (1), 39 (3); Road Traffic Act 1972, s. 94 (2); Powers of Criminal Courts Act 1973, s. 36; Costs in Criminal Cases Act 1973, s. 2 (5).

requires that execution of an order or sentence of a court should be stayed pending an appeal.

While a magistrates' court has power to grant bail pending an appeal hearing[73] there is no obligation on the justices to do so, and the general right to bail contained in the Bail Act 1976,[74] does not apply in relation to proceedings on or after a person's conviction.[75]

2. INITIATING AN APPEAL; BAIL; LEGAL AID

(1) Initiating an appeal

An appeal to the Crown Court from a decision of a magistrates' court, under the general provisions of section 83 of the Magistrates' Courts Act 1952, is initiated by the appellant's giving notice of appeal within 21 days[76] after the day on which the decision appealed against was given.[77] The notice must be in writing[78] and must be given to the clerk of the magistrates' court[79] and to any other party to the appeal.[80] In the case of an appeal arising out of a conviction by a magistrates' court, the notice must state whether the appeal is against conviction or sentence or both.[81]

(2) Grounds of appeal

It is clear from the Crown Court Rules 1971, that no special form of notice is prescribed, and the appellant is not required to submit grounds of appeal as such (at least in the sense that such grounds are understood, for instance, in the Criminal Division of the Court of Appeal[82]) when appealing from a magistrates' court to the Crown Court in a criminal matter. It has long been the practice, since the appeal is by way of a rehearing, to submit some general formula such as "the conviction is against the weight of the evidence" or "the sentence is excessive."[83]

[73] See p. 10, *post*.   [74] *Ibid.* s. 4 (1), (2).
[75] An application may be made to the Crown Court (see pp. 10–12, *post*) or to the High Court (see pp. 54–57, *post*). As to an appellant in custody for failure to comply with an order, whether under the Justices of the Peace Act 1361, or otherwise, to enter into a recognisance with or without sureties, to keep the peace or be of good behaviour see the Magistrates' Courts (Appeals from Binding Over Orders) Act 1956, s. 1 (2) (*b*).
[76] Excluding the day of the decision but including the 21st day: see the line of cases: *Stewart* v. *Chapman* [1951] 2 K.B. 792; *Cartwright* v. *McCormack*, etc. [1963] 1 W.L.R. 18; *Re Figgis, Roberts* v. *MacLaren* [1969] 1 Ch. 123.
[77] For this purpose, where the court has adjourned the trial of an information after conviction, that day shall be the day on which the court sentences or otherwise deals with the offender: Crown Court Rules 1972, r. 7 (2), (3); Crown Court (Amendment) Rules 1976, r. 4. It is submitted therefore that where sentence is deferred under the powers conferred by the Powers of Criminal Courts Act 1973, s. 1 appeal does not lie until sentence is imposed. As to the Crown Court's power to extend the time for giving notice, see p. 9, *post*.
[78] As to what is meant by "in writing" see the Interpretation Act 1978, Sched. 1.
[79] Crown Court Rules 1971, r. 7 (2) (*a*); Crown Court (Amendment) Rules 1976, r. 4. As to a form of procecedent, see Stones' Justices Manual, Precedent 192 and Appendix B, *post*, No. 1.
[80] Crown Court Rules 1971, r. 7 (2) (*a*); Crown Court (Amendment) Rules 1976, r. 4.
    In certain "third party" proceedings, as those under the Food and Drugs Act 1955, s. 113 (1), notice must be given by an appellant to the prosecutor and the third party, also by an appellant third party to both the prosecutor and the defendant: see *R.* v. *Derby Recorder, ex p. Spalton* [1944] K.B. 611; *Elkington* v. *Kesley* [1948] 2 K.B. 256; *Oxo Ltd.* v. *Chappell* [1966] 2 Q.B. 228.
[81] Crown Court Rules 1971, r. 7 (4).   [82] See p. 58, *post*.
[83] *Cf.* the position in the Criminal Division of the Court of Appeal, see p. 64, *post*.

It seems that the Crown Court, like its predecessor quarter sessions,[84] is the sole judge of the sufficiency of any notice, and the adequacy of any grounds, of appeal. It has been held[85] that where notice of appeal against sentence was given, quarter sessions had no jurisdiction to give leave for the notice to be amended so as to treat the appeal as one against conviction, but there seems no reason today, in view of the wide discretion given to the Crown Court to extend the time within which notice of appeal must be given,[86] why the Crown Court should not permit notice of appeal against conviction to be given out of time in a proper case.

On an appeal against conviction to the Crown Court, the powers of that court in relation to sentence are at large.[87]

(3) Extension of time

The time for giving notice of appeal to the Crown Court[88] may, on application, be extended by the Crown Court either before or after the prescribed time expires.[89]

In practice if a notice of appeal served on the Crown Court is out of time, the appellant will be informed that the appeal cannot be entertained, and he will be informed of the action which it is open to him to take to apply for an extension of time.[90]

The application for an extension of time must be made in writing,[91] specifying the grounds of the application and must be sent to the appropriate officer of the Crown Court.[92]

Where the Crown Court extends the time for giving notice of appeal, the appropriate officer of the court will give notice of the extension to the appellant and to the clerk to the magistrates' court.[93] The duty of giving notice of the extension to any other party to the appeal[94] is on the appellant.[95]

---

[84] See *R.* v. *Durham Justices* (1891) 7 T.L.R. 453; also *Province Motor Cab Co. Ltd.* v. *Dunning* (1909) as reported in 23 T.L.R. 646, at p. 647.

[85] *Paprika Ltd.* v. *Board of Trade* [1944] 1 K.B. 327.

[86] *Paprika Ltd.* v. *Board of Trade* was decided before the introduction, in the Magistrates' Court Act 1952, s. 84 (3), of the powers to extend the time: see *R.* v. *Pembrokeshire J.J., ex p. Bennell* [1969] 1 Q.B. 386. See now the Crown Court Rules 1971, r. 7 (5).

[87] See Courts Act 1971, s. 9 (4), and p. 21, *post.*

[88] See *ante*, p. 8.

[89] Crown Court Rules 1971, r. 7 (4); Crown Court (Amendment) Rules 1976, r. 4 (*b*). As to the court's discretion in the matter and the factors to be taken into consideration, see *R.* v. *Middlesex Quarter Sessions Chairman, ex p. M. (An Infant)* [1967] Crim. L.R. 471.

[90] Crown Court Manual, para. 9.6.1. A form as used in the Inner London Crown Court for this purpose is set out in Appendix C, *post*, No. 2. See also No. 3 sent to the court below.

[91] See *ante*, p. 8, n. 78. A form of questionnaire, as used by the Inner London Crown Court, is shown in Appendix C, *post*, No. 2 as an attachment.

[92] Crown Court Rules 1971, r. 7 (6).

[93] Crown Court Rules 1971, r. 7 (7). A form of notice, as used in the Inner London Crown Court, is set out in Appendix C, *post*, No. 5. If this notification is not made, magistrates' courts are seriously hampered in the institution of enforcement proceedings or consideration of applications for bail or suspension of disqualification pending appeal: see Crown Court Business Circular No. 10/77 dated July 22, 1977, and annexed to the judgment in *R.* v. *Bunce* (1978) 66 Cr. App. R. 109.

[94] As to "third party" appeals, see *ante*, p. 8, n. 80.

[95] Crown Court Rules 1971, r. 7 (7). In practice, the appropriate officer of the Crown Court will confirm, as far as is possible, that the other parties to the appeal are aware of the extension granted.

(4) Bail pending appeal: powers

Where a person has given notice of appeal[96] to the Crown Court against the decision of a magistrates' court, then, if he is in custody[97] the magistrates' court may[98] grant him bail[99]; the Crown Court[1] has a general power to grant bail to any person who is in custody pursuant to a sentence imposed by a magistrates' court, and who has appealed to the Crown Court against his conviction or sentence.[2]

(5) Bail pending appeal: the application

Where an application to the Crown Court relating to bail is made otherwise than during the hearing of proceedings there, notice in writing[3] of intention to make such an application must be given, at least 24 hours before it is made, to the prosecutor and to the Director of Public Prosecutions if the prosecution is being carried on by him, or, if the application is to be made by the prosecutor or a constable under section 3 (8) of the Bail Act 1976, to the person to whom bail was granted.[4] A person who makes an application must inform the Crown Court of any earlier application, whether to the High Court or the Crown Court, relating to bail in the course of the same proceedings.[5]

On receiving notice, it is the duty of the prosecutor or the Director of Public Prosecutions, or as the case may be, the person to whom bail was granted, to notify the appropriate officer of the Crown Court, and the applicant, of his intentions, namely either that he wishes to be represented at the hearing of the application or that he does not oppose the application, or to give to the

---

[96] *i.e.* where notice of appeal is given within the time prescribed by the Rules. Where notice of appeal is given out of time, it is submitted that the magistrates' court has no power to grant bail until the notice is validated by an extension granted by the Crown Court, as to which, see *ante*, p. 9.

[97] A circuit judge sitting in the Crown Court has held that a young person committed to the care of a local authority under s. 7 (7) of the Children and Young Person's Act 1969, following conviction in a magistrates' court, and placed in an assessment centre, is not a person "in custody" within the meaning of section 13 (4) of the Courts Act 1971, and there is accordingly no power in the Crown Court to grant him bail pending the determination of his appeal: *R.* v. *K.* [1978] 1 All E.R. 180.

[98] There is no general right to bail in respect of proceedings on or after a person's conviction, see Bail Act 1976, s. 4 (1), (2) and *ante*, p. 8.

[99] Magistrates' Courts Act 1952, s. 89 (1); Bail Act 1976, s. 12, Sched. 2, para. 22. This provision does not apply where the appellant has been committed for sentence under the Magistrates' Courts Act 1952, s. 28 or s. 29.

The time at which he is to appear is the time appointed for the hearing of the appeal and any recognisance taken from him (in a non-criminal matter), or from any surety for him, will be conditioned accordingly: Magistrates' Courts Act 1952, s. 89 (1); Bail Act 1976, s. 12, Sched. 2.

[1] As to the powers of the High Court to grant bail, see pp. 54–57, *post*.

[2] Courts Act 1971, s. 13 (4) (*b*); Bail Act 1976, s. 12, Sched. 2, para. 48.

[3] A form of notice is prescribed by the Crown Court Rules, 1971, Sched. 2, substituted by the Crown Court (Amendment) Rules 1978, see Appendix C, *post*, No. 4. See also Form 5023 in the Appendix to the Crown Court Manual included in Appendix C, *post*, No. 6.

The Crown Court Manual, para. 17 indicates that a solicitor acting for the appellant may inform the Crown Court, by telephone if necessary, of his intention to make the application, and ask for a date and time for the hearing of the application. Notice to the prosecutor or the D.P.P. in Form 5023 will then specify the time and place fixed for the hearing.

[4] Crown Court Rules 1971, r. 17 (1), (2) substituted by the Crown Court (Amendment) Rules 1978, r. 2. The Crown Court may dispense with these formalities where the Official solicitor is assigned, see below.

[5] Crown Court Rules 1971, r. 18 (1) substituted by the Crown Court (Amendment) Rules 1978, r. 3.

appropriate officer, for the consideration of the court, a written statement of his reasons for opposing the application, at the same time sending a copy of that statement to the applicant.[6]

Where a person, whether he is in custody or has been released on bail, desires to make an application relating to bail, and has not been able to instruct a solicitor to apply on his behalf,[7] he may give notice in writing to the Crown Court[8] of his desire to make an application relating to bail, requesting that the Official Solicitor act for him on the application, and the court may, if it thinks fit, assign the Official Solicitor to act for him accordingly.[9] Where the Official Solicitor is assigned in this manner, the Crown Court may, if it thinks fit, dispense with the requirements of giving notice before the application and deal with the application in a summary manner.[10]

An application for bail may be heard by a judge of the Crown Court in chambers.[11] Where a person has given notice in writing that he wishes to make an application and requests that the Official Solicitor act for him, the application will be heard by a judge of the Crown Court in London; all other applications are heard at that location of the Crown Court where the proceedings in respect of which the application arises took place or are due to take place.[12]

Except in the case of an application made by the prosecutor or a constable under section 3 (8) of the Bail Act 1976, the applicant is not entitled to be present on the hearing of his application unless given leave to be present by the court.[13]

(6) Bail pending appeal; recognisances; security

Where bail is granted,[14] the recognisance of any surety required as a condition of bail[15] may be entered into before an officer of the Crown Court or, where the person bailed is in a prison or other place of detention, before

[6] Crown Court Rules 1971, r. 17 (3) substituted by the Crown Court (Amendment) Rules 1978, r. 2.
[7] A legal aid order granted for the purpose of proceedings in the Crown Court covers an application to that court for bail: see the Crown Court Manual, para. 17.
[8] Where a person is in custody, the prison governor will in practice arrange for the application to be sent direct to the Crown Court.
[9] Crown Court Rules 1971, r. 17 (6) substituted by the Crown Court (Amendment) Rules 1978, r. 2.
[10] Crown Court Rules 1971, r. 17 (7) substituted by the Crown Court (Amendment) Rules 1978, r. 2.
[11] Crown Court Rules 1971, r. 22.
[12] *Practice Direction* [1971] 1 W.L.R. 1535.
[13] Crown Court Rules 1971, r. 17 (5), substituted by the Crown Court (Amendment) Rules 1978, r. 2.
[14] For forms, see Forms 5102 (Bail; record of decision—conditional or unconditional grant) and 5102A (Bail; record of decision—bail witheld) in the Appendix to the Crown Court Manual: also at Appendix C, *post*, Nos. 7, 8.
[15] The record required by the Bail Act 1976, s. 5, together with any note of reasons required by *ibid*. s. 5 (4) is made by way of an entry in the file relating to the case in question, and the record will include the effect of the decision, a statement of any condition imposed, indicating whether it is to be complied with before or after release, and where conditions are varied a statement of the conditions varied, and where bail is witheld, a statement of the relevant exception to the right to bail on which the decision is based: Crown Court Rules 1971, r. 17 (8) inserted by the Crown Court (Amendment) Rules 1978, r. 2. See Forms 5102, 5102A, 5102B, set out in Appendix C, Nos. 7, 8 and 9.

the governor or keeper of the prison.[16] Where the court imposes a requirement[17] to be complied with before release on bail, the court may give directions as to the manner in which, and the person or persons before whom, that requirement is to be complied with.[18]

A person who proposes to enter into a recognisance or give security in pursuance of an order made by the Crown Court for the grant of bail in criminal proceedings, must, unless the court otherwise directs, give notice to the prosecutor at least 24 hours before he enters into the recognisance or gives the security.[19] Where a recognisance is entered into or a requirement imposed[20] is complied with, being a requirement to be complied with before a person's release on bail, in pursuance of an order of the Crown Court, before any person, it is the duty of that person to cause the recognisance, or a statement of the requirement, as the case may be, to be transmitted forthwith to the appropriate officer of the Crown Court.[21]

Where a recognisance has been entered into in respect of a person granted bail to appear before the Crown Court, and it appears to the court that a default has been made in performing the conditions of the recognisance, the court may order the recognisance to be estreated.[22] The appropriate officer of the court will give notice to the person by whom the recognisance was entered into indicating the time and place at which the matter will be considered.[23] No order will be made before the expiry of seven days after the notice has been given.[23]

Where security has been given[24] in respect of a person granted bail with a duty to surrender to the custody of the Crown Court and either that person surrenders to the custody of the court, or having failed to surrender, the court decides not to order the forfeiture of the security, the appropriate officer of the court will, as soon as practicable, give notice of the surrender to custody, or as the case may be, of the decision not to forfeit the security, to the person before whom the security was given.[25]

---

[16] As well as before the persons specified in the Bail Act 1976, s. 8 (4). Crown Court Rules 1971, s. 18 (2) substituted by the Crown Court (Amendment) Rules 1978, r. 3. See Forms 5048, 5048A in the Appendix to the Crown Court Manual, set out at Appendix C, *post*, Nos. 10 and 11.

[17] *i.e.* under the Bail Act 1976, s. 3 (5) or (6).

[18] Crown Court Rules 1971, r. 13 (3); Crown Court (Amendment) Rules 1978, r. 3.

[19] Crown Court Rules 1971, r. 18 (5); Crown Court (Amendment) Rules 1978, r. 3.

[20] *i.e.* under the Bail Act 1976, s. 3 (5) or (6).

[21] Crown Court Rules 1971, r. 18 (6); Crown Court (Amendment) Rules 1978, r. 3.
    A copy of the recognisance or statement must at the same time be sent to the governor or keeper of the prison or other place of detention in which the person named in the order is detained, unless the recognisance was entered into, or the requirement was complied with before such governor or keeper: *ibid*.

[22] Crown Court Rules 1971, r. 18A (1); Crown Court (Amendment) Rules 1978, r. 4.

[23] Crown Court Rules 1971, rr. 18A (2); Crown Court (Amendment) Rules 1978, r. 4. See Form 5027 in the Appendix to the Crown Court Manual, set out for convenience in Appendix C, No. 12, *post*.

[24] In pursuance of the Bail Act 1976, s. 3 (5).

[25] Crown Court Rules 1971, r. 18 (7); Crown Court (Amendment) Rules 1978, r. 3. See Form 5028 in the Appendix to the Crown Court Manual, set out for convenience, at Appendix C, *post*, No. 13.

(7) Legal aid

A legal aid order made for the purpose of proceedings in the magistrates' court is authority for the solicitor assigned by that court to give advice on the question whether there appear to be reasonable grounds of appeal from any determination in those proceedings and assistance by him in the giving of a notice of appeal[26] provided that that notice is given within the ordinary time for doing so.[27] Once notice has been given, or the ordinary time for doing so has expired, it is necessary to make an application for legal aid in relation to the appeal, or any further steps to be taken in the appeal.

Where a person convicted or sentenced in the magistrates' court desires to appeal to the Crown Court, either the magistrates' court or the Crown Court may order that he be given legal aid for the purpose of the appeal, and where such person gives notice of appeal, either court may order the other party to the proceedings to be given legal aid for the purpose of resisting the appeal.[28]

An application for a legal aid order in respect of an appeal to the Crown Court is made in the prescribed form, either to the appropriate officer of the Crown Court[29] or to the clerk of the magistrates' court,[30] or it may be made orally to the Crown Court, or orally to the magistrates' court at the conclusion of the proceedings in that court.[30]

If a statement of the means of the applicant, and in the case of an applicant who has not attained the age of 16 years, a statement of the means of an appropriate contributor[31] was not submitted in pursuance of a previous application in respect of the same case,[32] the appropriate officer of the Crown Court, or the clerk to the magistrates' court, may require the appropriate statements to be furnished.[33] A legal aid order ought not to be made until the court, a judge of the court, the proper officer, or, where the application is made to the magistrates' court, the clerk or a justice entitled to sit as a member of the court, has considered those statements of means.[34]

The power of the court to determine an application for a legal aid order may be exercised, in so far as the Crown Court is concerned, by a judge of the court or the proper officer of the court,[35] and where the application is made orally to the court, it may be referred by the court to the proper officer.[36] Where the application is made to the magistrates' court the powers of determining it may be exercised by a justice.[37]

[26] Legal Aid Act 1974, s. 30 (5).
[27] See *ante*, p. 8.
[28] Legal Aid Act 1974, s. 28 (1), (5).
[29] The form is Form 2, prescribed in the Schedule to the Legal Aid in Criminal Proceedings (General) Regulations 1968, or if the application is made by a parent or guardian on behalf of a person who has not attained the age of 17 years, Form 2A: *ibid*. reg. 2 (1) (*b*).
[30] *Ibid*. reg. 2 (2).
[31] See the Legal Aid Act 1974, s. 40 (1).
[32] *i.e.* the proceedings in the magistrates' court.
[33] Legal Aid in Criminal Proceedings (General) Regulations 1968, regs. 4 (3), (4). The form prescribed is Form 4 set out *ibid*. Sched.
[34] *Ibid*. reg. 2 (4).
[35] *Ibid*. reg. 2 (5). An application determined otherwise than by the court may be determined in private and in the absence of the applicant: *ibid*. reg. 32.
[36] *Ibid*. reg. 2 (6).
[37] *Ibid*. reg. 2 (5).

The proper officer of the court[38] considering an application for a legal aid order is entitled (a) to make an order or (b) to refuse to make an order unless the applicant, or where the applicant has not attained the age of 16, an appropriate contributor, or both, first makes a down payment on account of any contribution towards costs which they or either of them may be ordered to make. Otherwise he must refer the application to a judge of the Crown Court, or a justice, as the case may be.[39] Where the proper officer refuses to make an order unless on a down payment, the applicant is entitled, on request, to have the application determined by a judge of the Crown Court, or a justice, as the case may be.[40] Where the Court, or a judge of the court, or a justice, refuses to make a legal aid order, the proper officer is not entitled thereafter to make an order, except where the refusal was on the basis that a down payment be made, and that down payment has been made.[41]

When a legal aid order is made, the proper officer of the Crown Court, or the clerk to the magistrates' court, as the case may be, will notify the applicant, and will deliver or send a copy of the order to the solicitor or counsel assigned. He will also notify the applicant if the application for legal aid is refused.[42]

On application by the solicitor assigned to the appellant, or the respondent, on whose application a legal aid order is made, copies of any notes of evidence taken in the proceedings in the magistrates'court will be supplied by the clerk of that court.[43]

In general, legal aid in criminal proceedings includes representation by a solicitor and counsel assigned by the court, including advice and assistance on the preparation of the person's case for those proceedings.[44] In relation to appellate proceedings, however, the Crown Court may, in cases of urgency, where it appears to the court that there is no time to instruct a solicitor, order that the legal aid given consist of representation by counsel only.[45] Again, where a magistrates' court, or the Crown Court, makes a legal aid order for such proceedings in the Crown Court, being proceedings at which solicitors have a right of audience,[46] the court may order that the legal aid consist of representation by solicitor only.[47]

Where the Crown Court on appeal confirms a person's conviction or sentence, any legal aid order in force for those proceedings is authority for counsel or the solicitor assigned to him to give advice on the question whether there appear to be reasonable grounds of appeal from the court's decision, and if such grounds appear to exist, assistance in making an application for a case to be stated for the opinion of the High Court.[48]

---

[38] Including the clerk to the magistrates' court: see Legal Aid in Criminal Proceedings (General) Regulations 1968, reg. 31.
[39] *Ibid.* reg. 2 (7).
[40] *Ibid.* reg. 2 (8).
[41] *Ibid.* reg. 2 (9).
[42] *Ibid.* reg. 6 (2), (3).
[43] *Ibid.* reg. 16.
[44] Legal Aid Act 1974, s. 30 (1).
[45] *Ibid.* s. 30 (3).
[46] See p. 19, *post.*
[47] Legal Aid Act 1974, s. 30 (3).
[48] Legal Aid Act 1974, s. 30 (6).

3. PREPARATION OF APPEAL; ABANDONMENT

(1) Appeal documents

It is the duty of the clerk to the magistrates' court to send, as soon as practicable, to the appropriate officer of the Crown Court:

(a) any notice of appeal given to him[48a];

(b) a statement of the decision from which the appeal is brought[48b];

(c) a statement of the last-known or usual place of abode of the parties to the appeal[48b];

(d) copies of the notes of the proceedings, where notes were kept[48c];

(e) where the appellant has entered into a recognisance (in non-criminal proceedings) conditioned for his appearance at the hearing of the appeal, that recognisance[48d];

(f) where notice of appeal is given in respect of a hospital or guardianship order made under sections 60 or 61 of the Mental Health Act 1959, any written evidence considered by the court[48e];

(g) where notice of appeal is given in respect of conviction, any admissions of fact made under section 10 of the Criminal Justice Act 1967, for the purposes of the trial in the magistrates' court.[48f]

(2) Entry of appeal; notice of hearing

On receiving notice of appeal, the appropriate officer of the Crown Court, after confirming that the notice is given in time, enters the appeal and gives notice of the time and place of the hearing to the appellant, to any other party to the appeal[49] and to the clerk of the magistrates' court.[50] If an appeal is adjourned without fixing a date for the resumption of the hearing, the appellant and any other party to the appeal must be notified in the same manner as of the original hearing.[51]

(3) The respondent; appearance of justices

Although it is the invariable practice for the prosecutor in the proceedings in the court below to take upon himself the duty of conducting the case for the

---

[48a] *i.e.* in Form 5012 in the Appendix to the Crown Court Manual. Magistrates' Courts Rules 1968, r. 62 (1); Magistrates' Courts (Amendment) Rules 1973. This procedure should be followed even where notice of appeal is given out of time; it is for the Crown Court to decide whether to treat the notice as given within time.

[48b] Magistrates' Courts Rules 1968, r. 62 (2).

[48c] This will assist the administration of business at the Crown Court, and in a proper case the court may be referred to them to ascertain what transpired in the magistrates' court: see *Practice Note* [1956] 1 Q.B. 451, explaining *R.* v. *Recorder of Grimsby, ex p. Fuller* [1956] 1 Q.B. 36. See also p. 20, *post.*

[48d] Magistrates' Courts Rules 1968, r. 62 (4).

[48e] *i.e.* under the Mental Health Act 1959, s. 60 (1) (*a*): Magistrates' Courts Rules 1968, r. 62 (5).

[48f] *Ibid.* r. 62 (6).

[49] See *ante*, p. 8, n. 80.

[50] Crown Court Rules 1971, r. 8. See Form 5011 in the Appendix to the Crown Court Manual, set out at Appendix C, *post*, No. 15, also No. 16. For the position where the appeal is out of time, see *ante*, p. 9.

[51] *R.* v. *County of London Quarter Sessions Appeals Committee, ex p. Rossi* [1956] 1 Q.B. 682; applied in *Beer* v. *Davies* [1958] 2 Q.B. 187.

respondent on an appeal to the Crown Court,[52] the justices whose decision is questioned have in law an absolute right to appear on the appeal, instruct counsel and call evidence in support of the decision at which they arrived which is under consideration at the Crown Court.[53] If they do,[54] they do not thereby make themselves a party to the appeal and no order for costs may be made against them.[55]

In appeals under the Magistrates' Courts (Appeals from Binding Over Orders) Act 1956, the other party to the proceedings which were the occasion of the making of the order is the respondent.[56]

(4) Abandonment before the hearing

An appellant who has given notice of appeal to the Crown Court may abandon his appeal by serving notice in writing[57] not later than the third day[58] before the day fixed for the hearing of the appeal, on the clerk to the magistrates' court against whose decision the appeal is brought, and on any other party to the appeal[59]; he must also send a copy of the notice to the appropriate officer of the Crown Court.[60]

No court can, in the absence of express statutory authority, deal with an appeal once it is abandoned. The jurisdiction of an appellate court is statutory and in the absence of being seised of an appeal it has no discretion at all.[61] It sometimes happens that an appellant, having given notice of abandonment, seeks at a later stage to "withdraw" his notice. A notice of abandonment, deliberately given, without fraudulent inducement or material mistake cannot subsequently be "withdrawn." All that an appellate court can do in the circumstances is to look at the position and see whether there has been an abandonment. Once the court finds that there has been an abandonment it can do nothing further in the matter.[61] If, on looking into the matter, however, the court finds that there has been in fact no real abandonment because the notice has been given under a mistake or fraudulent inducement, then it is open to the court to say so. The purported abandonment is, in such circumstances, a nullity and being a nullity, the court remains seised of the appeal.[62]

---

[52] See n. 55, *infra*.
[53] *R. v. Kent JJ., ex p. Metropolitan Police Commissioner* [1936] 1 K.B. 547. The Review of Justices Decisions Act 1872 (for which see pp. 36, 51, *post*) does not apply to proceedings in the Crown Court on a rehearing, and the justices have no power to file affidavits.
[54] In practice, few justices avail themselves of the right.
[55] *R. v. Kent JJ., supra*, at p. 562, *per* Humphries J., who expressed the view that where the respondent does not intend to appear on the appeal, the clerk of the magistrates' court should bring the matter to the attention of his justices who may wish to instruct counsel to appear on their behalf, or to ask the police authority or the D.P.P. to take up the appeal.
[56] *Ibid.* s. 1 (2) (*a*).
[57] See *ante*, p. 8, n. 78. As to the service of documents, etc., see Crown Court Rules 1971, r. 23.
[58] Saturday, Sunday and any day which is, or is to be observed as, a bank holiday under the Banking and Financial Dealings Act 1971, in England or Wales, is to be disregarded in determining whether a notice of abandonment was given in time: Crown Court Rules 1971, r. 9 (3).
[59] See *ante*, p. 8, n. 80.   [60] Crown Court Rules 1971, r. 9 (1), (2) (*a*), (*d*).
[61] *R. v. Essex Quarter Sessions Appeals Committee, ex p. Larkin* [1962] 1 Q.B. 712, at p. 717 *per* Lord Parker C.J.
[62] *R. v. Essex Quarter Sessions Appeals Committee, ex p. Larkin, supra*, applied in *R. v. Medway* [1976] Q.B. 779. See, as to the "kernel of the nullity test," *R. v. Medway, supra*, and p. 79, *post*. The powers of the Crown Court and the Criminal Division of the Court of Appeal are probably identical: see *Larkin's Case*, at p. 717, *per* Lord Parker C.J.

Where notice to abandon an appeal has been given in this manner,[63] the magistrates' court against whose decision the appeal was brought may proceed to issue process for enforcing its decision.[64] On the application of the other party to the appeal[65] the magistrates' court may order the appellant to pay such costs as appear to be just and reasonable in respect of any expenses properly incurred by such party in connection with the appeal before notice of the abandonment was given to him.[66] Such costs are recoverable as a civil debt.[67] If notice of abandonment is not given in time the case will be left in the list and if the appellant does not pursue his appeal it will be dismissed.

Where notice of abandonment is given after the time prescribed by the Crown Court Rules[68] any application for costs must be made to the Crown Court.[69] If no application is made, the appeal will be treated as if it had been dismissed without costs. Costs awarded by the Crown Court are recoverable as a civil debt.[70]

4. THE HEARING AT THE CROWN COURT

(1) Rules governing practice

The jurisdiction and powers of an appellate court are statutory and the practice governing appeals to the Crown Court against conviction or sentence in a magistrates' court is regulated principally by statute. Where a person appeals to the Crown Court from a magistrates' court in accordance with section 83 of the Magistrates' Courts Act 1952, the procedure is governed by the Act, the Rules made thereunder, the Courts Act 1971 and the Crown Court Rules 1971. Courts of quarter session were empowered to formulate their own rules of practice and procedure and were entitled to decide questions relating to the observance of such rules, and questions relating to the sufficiency of any notice of appeal and the adequacy of any grounds put forward, subject always to the supervisory jurisdiction of the High Court, exercised by means of the prerogative orders, where any particular rule involved a failure of justice.[71] The transfer of the appellate jurisdiction of quarter sessions to the Crown Court by the Courts Act 1971[72] is expressed not to affect the practice or procedure on any appeal,[73] other than by the provisions of the Act, but in view of the power to give administrative directions[74] and the provisions of the Crown Court Manual, it would seem that any power

---

[63] *i.e.* within the three days prescribed by the Crown Court Rules 1971.
[64] Subject to anything already suffered or done by the appellant: Magistrates' Courts Act 1952, s. 85 (2) (*a*), (2A); Attachment of Earnings Act 1971, Sched. 11; Courts Act 1971, Scheds. 8, 11.
[65] See *ante*, p. 8, n. 80.
[66] Magistrates' Courts Act 1952, as amended, s. 85 (2) (*a*), (2A).
[67] Under the Administration of Justice Act 1970, s. 41, Sched. 9.
[68] *i.e.* later than the third day before the day fixed for the hearing of the appeal.
[69] See p. 22, *post.*
[70] Under the Administration of Justice Act 1970, s. 41, Sched. 9.
[71] See Halsburys Laws of England (4th Ed.), Vol. 11, para. 680.
[72] *Ibid.* s. 8, Sched. 1.
[73] *Ibid.* s. 8 (6).
[74] Under the Courts Act 1971, ss. 4 (5), 5 (4). See, *e.g. Practice Note* [1971] 3 All E.R. 829; *Practice Direction* [1972] 2 All E.R. 1057; *Practice Direction* [1973] 1 All E.R. 182.

of the former courts of quarter session to formulate new rules of procedure on a customary basis should be considered obsolete.[75] Perhaps the sole survival of the customary procedure is the position by which an appeal to quarter sessions was a rehearing, which is expressly preserved by the Courts Act 1971.[76]

(2) Location of appeal

The hearing of an appeal from a magistrates' court takes place at that location of the Crown Court designated by a presiding judge as the appropriate location for such proceedings originating in the areas concerned.[77] The Crown Court may give directions for the transfer of appeals from one location of the Crown Court to another.[78] Any party who is dissatisfied with a direction of this nature given by an officer of the Court may apply to a judge of the Crown Court who may hear the application in chambers.[78]

(3) Constitution of Crown Court

On the hearing by the Crown Court of an appeal, the court consists of a judge of the High Court or a circuit judge or a recorder sitting with not less than two nor more than four justices.[79] On the hearing of an appeal from a juvenile court the court consists of a judge sitting with two justices, each of whom is a member of the juvenile court panel and who are chosen so that the court includes a man and a woman.[80] The Crown Court may, however, enter on an appeal notwithstanding that the court is not constituted as above[81] if it appears to the judge presiding that the court cannot be so constituted without reasonable delay, and the court includes one justice, or in so far as an appeal from a juvenile court is concerned, one justice who is a member of the juvenile court panel.[82] The Crown Court may at any stage continue with any proceedings with a court from which any one or more of the justices initially comprising the court has withdrawn or is absent for any reason.[83]

A justice must not sit in the Crown Court on the hearing of an appeal in a matter on which he adjudicated,[84] although a justice is not disqualified for the reason that the proceedings are not at a place within the area for which he was appointed a justice, or because the proceedings are not related to that area in any way.[85]

[75] See Halsbury's Laws of England (4th Ed.), Vol. 11, para. 680. As to the position on a case stated, see p. 32, *post*, n. 96.
[76] See s. 9 (6).
[77] *Practice Direction* [1971] 1 W.L.R. 1535, para. 10. Appeals will normally be listed for hearing by a court presided over by a circuit judge or a recorder: *ibid.* para. 12 (v); but may be allocated to a court comprising justices, if suitable: Courts Act 1971, s. 5 (1). *Practice Direction* [1971] 1 W.L.R. 1535, para. 13.
[78] *Ibid.* para. 14 (1). Directions may be given in a particular case by an officer of the court or generally, in relation to a class or classes of case, by the presiding judge or a judge acting on his behalf.
[79] Courts Act 1971, s. 5 (1).
[80] Crown Court Rules 1971, r. 3 (4).
[81] *i.e.* in accordance with the Courts Act 1971, s. 5, or r. 3.
[82] Crown Court Rules 1971, r. 4 (1).
[83] *Ibid.* r. 4 (2).
[84] Crown Court Rules 1971, r. 5.
[85] Courts Act 1971, s. 5 (9).

A decision of the Crown Court cannot be questioned on the ground that the Court was not properly constituted[86] unless objection is taken on that ground, by or on behalf of a party to the proceedings, not later than the time when the proceedings are entered on, or when any alleged irregularity begins.[87]

(4) Rights of audience

A solicitor may appear in, conduct, defend and address the court in criminal proceedings in the Crown Court on appeal from a magistrates' court if he, or any partner of his, or any solicitor in his employment or by whom he is employed, appeared on behalf of the defendant in the magistrates' court.[88]

(5) Preliminary matters; appearance

At the hearing of an appeal at the Crown Court, the conviction or order appealed against will be produced and the appellant may be called upon to prove that notice of appeal has been duly given.[89]

If, when the appeal is called for hearing, neither of the parties appears personally or by advocate, it is the practice for the appeal to be struck out.[90] If the appellant alone fails to appear, and he is not represented, and the court is satisfied that he has received due notice of the hearing, it may dismiss the appeal.[91] Where the appellant alone appears, then, upon proof of service of the notice of appeal and other formalities, the court may quash the order or conviction of the court below. If the appeal is against sentence only, however, the Crown Court has no power to quash the conviction.[92]

If there is insufficient evidence before the Crown Court to enable it to determine an appeal, the hearing should be adjourned until there is satisfactory representation by both parties.[93]

(6) Appeal by way of rehearing

An appeal to the Crown Court under section 83 of the Magistrates' Courts Act 1952 is, like an appeal to the former courts of quarter session, a rehearing of the whole case.[94] The case is heard afresh and the prosecutor proves his case

---

[86] *i.e.* under s. 5 (1) or (2).
[87] Courts Act 1971, s. 5 (7).
[88] *Administrative Directions* [1972] 1 All E.R. 608 made under the Courts Act 1971, s. 12. Special provisions apply to sittings of the Crown Court at Caernarvon, Barnstaple, Bodmin, Doncaster and Lincoln, see *Administrative Directions* [1972] 1 All E.R. 144.
[89] The conviction or other order is often read by the appropriate officer of the court, although this formality is generally dispensed with, particularly where both parties are represented.
[90] Whether or not such an appeal is later reinstated is a matter for the discretion of the Crown Court; it will not generally be reinstated without the consent of the other party to the appeal, or satisfactory evidence as to the circumstances of the non-appearance. A form of notice as used in the Inner London Crown Court is shown in Appendix C, *post*, No. 17.
[91] *R.* v. *Spokes, ex p. Buckley* (1912) 76 J.P. 354; *R.* v. *Lancashire Justices* (1838) 2 Jur. 468.
[92] *R.* v. *Kent JJ., ex p. Metropolitan Police Commissioner* [1936] 1 K.B. 547; see also *R.* v. *London County Quarter Sessions Appeals Committee, ex p. Rossi* [1956] 1 Q.B. 682.
[93] *R.* v. *Kent JJ., ex p. Metropolitan Police Commissioner, supra.* Where it is known that a party to the appeal does not intend to appear at the hearing, the clerk to the magistrates' court should bring that fact to the attention of the Crown Court and should endeavour to ensure that the Crown Court is aware of the reasons for the magistrates' decision: *ibid.*
[94] The position by which an appeal to quarter sessions was a rehearing is expressly preserved by the Courts Act 1971, s. 9 (6).

over again.[95] Either party is within his rights in calling any relevant and admissible evidence in support of his case, whether that evidence was called by him in the court below or not.[96] The Crown Court takes the place of the magistrates who heard the case originally and may substitute its opinion for that of the original tribunal.[97]

Where there is an appeal against conviction it has been said[98] that no documents should be placed before the court except the conviction, the notice of appeal, and copies of the exhibits if they are going to be proved and no objection has been taken as to their admission. Care must be taken to see that the police report is not given to the court until the decision is announced.[98] The safe rule to apply is that on an appeal against a summary conviction nothing should be placed before the appellate court which should not be given to a jury.[99]

Where, on the hearing of an appeal, a judge or recorder sits with justices, the judge or recorder presides. The decision of the court may be by a majority and, if the members of the court are equally divided, the judge has a second or casting vote.[1] It should be remembered, however, that the justices are themselves judges of the Crown Court and must play a full part in all decisions of the court, whether on interlocutory matters or on sentence. In matters of law they must take a ruling from the presiding judge in precisely the same way as a jury is required to take his ruling when it retires to consider its verdict.[2]

On an appeal against sentence only, the same strictness of proof is not required as in the case of an appeal against conviction.[3] An appeal against sentence is a rehearing from conviction onwards[4]; the practice in such cases being similar to that after a plea of guilty at first instance.[4] The Crown Court should take the matter up at the stage when conviction is announced and then proceed to fix the sentence.[5] The Court should go through the sentencing procedure on a rehearing basis without regard to the existing order in the magistrates' court. The Crown Court must ask itself "Should this man be

[95] *Drover* v. *Rugman* [1951] 1 K.B. 380.
[96] *R.* v. *Hall* (1866) L.R. 1 Q.B. 632.
[97] *Sagnata Investments Ltd.* v. *Norwich Corporation* [1971] 2 Q.B. 614. The Crown Court ought to consider the appeal in the light of the circumstances obtaining at the time when the order appealed from was made: *Drover* v. *Rugman, supra*; *Northern Ireland Trailers* v. *Preston Corporation* [1972] 1 W.L.R. 203.
    The ordinary rules governing such a rehearing apply, see, *e.g. R.* v. *Middlesex Crown Court, ex p. Riddle* [1975] Crim. L.R. 731, applying *R.* v. *Great Marlborough St. Magistrates' Court, ex p. Fraser* [1974] Crim. L.R. 47, *Cf. R.* v. *Knightsbridge, ex p. Martin* [1976] Crim. L.R. 463.
[98] *R.* v. *Recorder of Grimsby, ex p. Fuller* [1956] 1 Q.B. 36, (explained in *Practice Direction* [1956] 1 Q.B. 451), *per* Lord Goddard C.J. at p. 43.
[99] *Ibid.* The notes of the hearing below may also be referred to for the purpose of ascertaining the likely length of the hearing, or during the hearing of the appeal, if a specific part of the evidence in the magistrates' court is put to a witness, to clarify what he is saying in evidence as against that which was said in the court below: *ibid.*
[1] Courts Act 1971, s. 5 (8).
[2] *R.* v. *Orpin* [1975] Q.B. 283. Thus, where in the course of a hearing, the issue of the admissibility of a confession is raised, it is proper for the judge or recorder to retire with the justices and for them together to reach a decision on the facts within the framework of the law explained by the presiding judge: *ibid.*
[3] *Paprika* v. *Board of Trade* [1944] 1 K.B. 327.
[4] *Dyson* v. *Ellison* [1975] 1 W.L.R. 150, at p. 153.
[5] In a proper case, therefore, the Crown Court should order disqualification or endorsement as appropriate.

sentenced differently?" The only way in which it can do this is to determine how he ought to be sentenced and then to see to what extent, if at all, that differs from the order made in the court below. If it differs to a significant extent, then the appeal should be allowed to that extent.[6]

(7) Powers of Crown Court on appeal

In the course of hearing an appeal the Crown Court may correct any error or mistake in the order or judgment incorporated in the decision which is the subject of the appeal.[7] This power does not, however, extend to exercising a power which the court below could not exercise, such as amending the information on which the appellant was tried.[8]

On the termination of the hearing of an appeal, whether or not the appeal is against the whole of the decision,[9] the Crown Court may confirm, reverse or vary the decision appealed against,[10] remit the matter with its opinion thereon to the court whose decision is appealed,[11] or make such other order in the matter as it thinks just, and by such order exercise any power which the court below might have exercised.[12] These powers do not, however, authorise the Crown Court to substitute on appeal a conviction for an offence different from that on which the appellant was convicted below.[13]

On determining an appeal, whether against conviction or sentence, the Crown Court may award any punishment, whether more or less severe than that awarded by the magistrates' court whose decision is appealed,[14] if that is a punishment which that magistrates' court might have awarded.[15] The Crown Court has no power to commit an appellant to itself for sentence.[16]

It is the usual practice for the appropriate officer of the Crown Court to send a copy of the record sheet to the clerk of the magistrates' court by which the decision appealed was given, stating the result of the appeal.

(8) Costs in the appeal

Where an appeal is brought to the Crown Court against a conviction by a

---

[6] *Dyson* v. *Ellison*, *supra*, at pp. 153–154, *per* Lord Parker C.J.
[7] Courts Act 1971, s. 9 (1).
[8] See, *e.g. Meek* v. *Powell* [1952] 1 K.B. 164; *Garfield* v. *Maddocks* [1974] Q.B. 7. *Cf. Wright* v. *Nicholson* [1970] 1 W.L.R. 142.
[9] Courts Act 1971, s. 9 (5).
[10] *Ibid.* s. 9 (2) (*a*).
[11] *Ibid.* s. 9 (2) (*b*).
[12] *Ibid.* s. 9 (2) (*c*). In *Killington* v. *Butcher* [1979] Crim. L.R. 458, the Crown Court, on allowing an appeal against a conviction for dangerous driving, directed in accordance with the magistrates' powers under the Road Traffic Act 1972, Sched. 4, Pt. IV, para. 4, that a charge of careless driving, contrary to *ibid.* s. 3 be preferred. In *R.* v. *Inner London Crown Court, ex p. Obajuwana* (1979) 123 S.J. 142, the Divisional Court held that when dismissing an appeal against a recommendation for deportation, the Crown Court has the power of the justices under the Immigration Act 1971, Sched. 3, para. 2 (1), to order the appellant to be detained, or to be released, pending any deportation order being made.
[13] *Lawrence* v. *Same* [1968] 2 Q.B. 93.
[14] The Crown Court is not bound by limitations such as those imposed on the Criminal Division of the Court of Appeal, for which see p. 95, *post*.
[15] Courts Act 1971, s. 9 (4). This power will not be reviewed by order of certiorari, see *R.* v. *Leicester Recorder, ex p. Gabbitas* [1946] 1 All E.R. 615.
[16] *R.* v. *Bullock* [1964] 1 Q.B. 481.

magistrates' court of an indictable offence, or against the sentence[17] imposed on such a conviction, the Crown Court may order the payment out of central funds[18] of the costs of the prosecution and, if the appeal is against conviction, and the conviction is set aside in consequence of the decision on the appeal, may order the payment out of central funds of the costs of the defence.[19] The costs so payable out of central funds are such sums as appear to the Crown Court reasonably[20] sufficient (a) to compensate the prosecutor or the appellant, as the case may be, for the expenses properly incurred by him in carrying on the proceedings,[21] and (b) to compensate any witness[22] for the prosecution or the defence, for the expense, trouble or loss of time properly incurred in, or incidental to, his attendance.[23]

The amount of costs ordered to be paid under these provisions is ascertained as soon as practicable by the appropriate officer of the Crown Court.[24]

The Crown Court may also make such orders as to costs payable between parties as it thinks just[25] save that no order is to be made by the Crown Court on the abandonment of an appeal from a magistrates' court, where abandonment is effected by giving notice under Rule 9 of the Magistrates' Courts Rules.[26] Where an appeal is brought to the Crown Court from the decision of a magistrates' court, and the appeal is successful, the court may make any order as to the costs of the proceedings in the magistrates' court which that court had power to make.[27]

The Crown Court may make an order for costs on dismissing an appeal

---

[17] "Sentence" includes any order made by the court when dealing with the offender, including a hospital order under Part V of the Mental Health Act 1959, and a recommendation for deportation: Costs in Criminal Cases Act 1973, s. 3 (7).

[18] See *ibid.* s. 13. References in the Act to costs paid, or ordered to be paid out of central funds are construed as including references to any sums so paid or ordered to be paid as compensation to, or expenses of, a witness or other person, or as counsel's or a solicitor's fees: *ibid.* s. 20 (2).

[19] *Ibid.* s. 3 (2).

[20] See *Practice Note* [1977] 1 All E.R. 540, at p. 542, for the disallowance of costs improperly incurred, and for work unreasonably done.

[21] These may include the costs of carrying on the defence in the magistrates' court: Costs in Criminal Cases Act 1973, s. 3 (9).

[22] The expression "witness" means a person properly attending to give evidence, whether or not he gives evidence. A person who, at the instance of the court, is called or properly attends to give evidence, may be made the subject of an order whether or not he is a witness for the defence: *ibid.* s. 3 (8).

Reference to a "witness" in these provisions includes any person who is a witness to character only and in respect of whom the court certifies that the interests of justice required his attendance, but no sums will be payable to, or in respect of, a witness to character only, if no such certificate is given: *ibid.* s. 3. (5).

[23] Costs in Criminal Cases Act 1973, s. 3 (3).

[24] *Ibid.* s. 3 (6). A special avenue of appeal against the award of costs payable out of central funds is provided by the Costs in Criminal Cases (Central Funds) (Appeals) Regulations 1977 (S.I. 1977, No. 248), copy of which is to be found in Appendix H, *post.*

[25] Crown Court Rules 1971, r. 10 (2).

[26] *Ibid.* r. 10 (4). See *ante*, p. 17 as to the power of the magistrates' court to award costs in such circumstances.

[27] Crown Court Rules 1971, r. 11. Section 41 (2) and para. 16 of Part 2 of Sched. 9 to the Administration of Justice Act 1970 provide for the enforcement of such an order summarily as a civil debt. The Crown Court has no power, when allowing an appeal, to order payment of such costs to the magistrates' court, and proceedings for enforcement must be instituted thereafter by the appellant if payment is not made: see Crown Court Business Circular No. 10/77 dated July 22, 1977, and annexed to the judgment in *R.* v. *Bunce* (1978) 66 Cr. App. R. 109.

where the appellant has failed to proceed with the appeal or on the abandonment of an appeal, not being one to which Rule 9 applies.[28]

Where, on an appeal against sentence, the police appear merely to state the facts of the case and give evidence of antecedents, costs should not be awarded against them if the appeal against sentence succeeds.[29]

(9) Enforcement proceedings

After the determination of an appeal from a magistrates' court, the decision appealed, as confirmed or varied by the Crown Court, or any decision substituted by the Crown Court for the decision appealed, may[30] be enforced. It is enforced either by the court whose decision was appealed issuing any process that it could have issued had it decided the case as the Crown Court decided it, or, so far as the nature of any process already issued to enforce the original decision permits, by that process.[31]

If, on the determination of the appeal, any sum of money is payable by the appellant, whether by virtue of an order of the Crown Court or by virtue of the conviction or order of the magistrates' court against whose decision the appeal was brought, then if that person is before it, the Crown Court may order him to be searched.[32] Any money found on him in such a search may be applied, unless the court otherwise directs, towards payment of the fine or other sum payable by him, the balance, if any, being returned to him.[33]

---

[28] *Ibid.* r. 10 (5). As to the provisions of Rule 9, see *ante*, pp. 16–17.
[29] *David* v. *Metropolitan Police Commissioner* [1962] 2 Q.B. 135.
[30] Without prejudice to the powers of the Crown Court, as a court of record, to enforce its own decision.
[31] Magistrates' Courts Act 1952, s. 86; Courts Act 1971, s. 56 (1), Sched. 8, para. 34 (1). The decision of the Crown Court has effect as if it had been made by the magistrates' court against whose decision the appeal was brought: *ibid.*
[32] Powers of Criminal Courts Act 1973, s. 34A (1); Criminal Law Act 1977, s. 49.
[33] *Ibid.* s. 34A (2).

PART II

APPEALS TO THE HIGH COURT BY WAY OF CASE STATED

APPEAL lies to the High Court by way of case stated in a criminal case: (a) from a magistrates' court under the provisions of the Magistrates' Courts Act 1952, and; (b) from the Crown Court under the provisions of section 10 of the Courts Act 1971, in the exercise of its appellate jurisdiction.

An appeal by way of case stated is a form of consultation with the High Court to obtain an answer on a point of law; it is not a rehearing of the case.[1] The duty of the High Court is to answer the question or questions submitted to it by the court below. The High Court will not generally hear argument on a point not raised before the justices and set out in the case.[2] The result of the appeal will turn essentially on the facts stated in the case submitted to the court. The court will rely upon the justices and take the case as stated unless there is some defect patent upon the face of it.[3]

The High Court will not reduce a sentence or other penalty on an appeal by way of case stated, but may substitute a valid sentence for one that is invalid.[4]

A. APPEAL FROM MAGISTRATES' COURTS

1. GENERAL PROVISIONS

(1) Right of appeal

Any person who is a party to proceedings before a magistrates' court[5] or is aggrieved[6] by the conviction, order, determination or other proceedings of such a court, may question the proceeding on the ground that it is wrong in law or in excess of jurisdiction[7] by applying to the justices comprising the court to state a case for the opinion of the High Court on any question of law or jurisdiction involved.[8]

The words "party to the proceedings" are apt to include an unsuccessful prosecutor.[9]

---

[1] *Harris, Simon & Co.* v. *Manchester City Council* [1975] 1 W.L.R. 100, at p. 105 *per* Lord Widgery C.J. The Divisional Court has no power to hear witnesses: see p. 36, *post*.
[2] See p. 36, *post*.
[3] See p. 36, *post*.
[4] See p. 37, *post*.
[5] But see p. 26, *post*.
[6] Including an informant whose success was incomplete, *i.e.* under the Obscene Publications Act 1959, s. 3 (8) and a third party under, *e.g.* the Food and Drugs Act 1955, s. 113. See *Oxo Ltd.* v. *Chappell* [1966] 2 Q.B. 228. In *Moss* v. *Hancock* [1899] 2 Q.B. 111 a person adversely affected by an order for the restitution of stolen goods was permitted to state a case even though he was not a party to the proceedings.
[7] See below.
[8] Magistrates' Courts Act 1952, s. 87 (1). Where it is sought to challenge an interlocutory decision, the proper course is to continue the proceedings until they are concluded and then apply for a case to be stated: *Piggot* v. *Sims* [1973] R.T.R. 15.
[9] It matters not that the case is a criminal one and the "party" is the prosecutor who has failed: *R.* v. *Newport (Salop) JJ., ex p. Wright* [1929] 2 K.B. 416.

(2) "Wrong in law; excess of jurisdiction"

The words "wrong in law or in excess of jurisdiction" give the key to this type of procedure. The High Court does not sit as a general court of appeal against magistrates' decisions in the same way as the Crown Court does. The High Court, on an appeal by way of case stated, sits only to review magistrates' decisions on points of law, being bound by the facts which they have found, provided always that there is evidence on which they could have come to the conclusions of fact at which they arrived.[10]

A proceeding may be "wrong in law" where there is no evidence to support a relevant finding of fact, or where the decision of the magistrates' court is one to which no reasonable bench of justices, applying their mind to proper considerations and giving themselves proper directions, could come. If justices come to a decision to which no reasonable bench could come, the High Court may interfere, because the position is the same as if the magistrates had come to a decision without evidence to support that decision.[11] The High Court has jurisdiction to reverse the findings of justices where it is apparent that those findings are perverse.[12]

Where the matter in issue depends upon the exercise of the justices' discretion, it cannot be said that they are "wrong in law" in the manner in which they exercise it.[13]

In questions arising from an excess of jurisdiction, appeal lies by way of case stated only where the magistrates' court has actually heard and determined the case, and has, for example, dismissed the prosecution for want of jurisdiction.[14] Appeal by way of case stated is not appropriate where the magistrates have declined to hear the case at all on the basis that they have no jurisdiction[15]; in such a case the remedy is to apply for an order of mandamus.[16]

In cases where a denial of justice is alleged, as where the defence is given no opportunity to answer the charge, the remedy is not by way of case stated.[17] Although a radical departure from the well-known principles of natural justice and procedure may make a decision given after such departure "wrong in law" within the meaning of section 87 of the Magistrates' Courts Act 1952[18] such a complaint is generally the subject of an order of certiorari.[19]

---

[10] *Bracegirdle* v. *Oxley* [1947] K.B. 349 (a decision of five judges) *per* Lord Goddard C.J. at p. 353. The Crown Court may, it is true, hear appeals on questions of law, but that court primarily exists in its appellate jurisdiction, to deal with disputed questions of fact: *R.* v. *Wandsworth JJ., ex p. Read* [1942] 1 K.B. 281, *per* Humphries J. at 285.
[11] *Ibid.* at p. 353. See also *Afford* v. *Pettit* (1949) 113 J.P. 433.
[12] *Bracegirdle* v. *Oxley, supra*, at p. 353 *per* Lord Goddard C.J.
[13] *Diss Urban Sanitary Authority* v. *Aldrich* (1877) 2 Q.B.D. 179. See also *R.* v. *Tottenham Magistrates' Court, ex p. Riccardi* (1977) 66 Cr. App. R. 150.
[14] *Ex p. McLeod* (1861) 3 L.T. 700; *Muir* v. *Hore* (1877) 47 L.J.M.C. 17; *R.* v. *Wisbech Justices* (1890) 54 J.P. 743.
[15] *Wakefield Local Board* v. *West Riding Rail Co.* (1866) 30 J.P. 628 followed in *Pratt* v. *A. A. Sites Ltd.* [1938] 2 K.B. 459.
[16] See, *e.g. R.* v. *Leicester Licensing Committee, ex p. Lyner* (1968) 66 L.G.R. 736.
[17] See the observations of Viscount Caldecote in *R.* v. *Wandsworth JJ., ex p. Read* [1942] 1 K.B. 281, at p. 284.
[18] *R.* v. *Wandsworth JJ., ex p. Read, supra.*
[19] *Ibid.* See also *Rigby* v. *Woodward* [1957] 1 W.L.R. 250.

Certain matters are expressly excluded from appeal to the High Court by way of case stated.[20]

(3) "Conviction, order, determination or other proceeding"

An appeal by way of case stated lies from the decision of a "magistrates' court" as defined in section 124 of the Magistrates' Courts Act 1952.[21] It has been held[22] that section 87 of the Act is to be construed as being confined to final proceedings and therefore, since committal proceedings do not lead to any final proceedings, examining justices have no power to state a case for the opinion of the High Court.[23]

(4) Loss of right of appeal to Crown Court

On the making of an application to state a case in respect of a decision, any right of the applicant to appeal to the Crown Court against the decision ceases.[24] It seems, however, that if the High Court remits the case to the magistrates' court which then convicts, a right of appeal to the Crown Court against conviction is still open.[25] Where a case stated in respect of conviction is dismissed, it has been said[26] that the right of appeal to the Crown Court against sentence still obtains.

2. STATING THE CASE; BAIL; LEGAL AID

(1) Applying to the justices

An appeal to the High Court by way of case stated under section 87 of the Magistrates' Courts Act 1952 is initiated by applying to the justices comprising the court whose decision it is sought to question, to state a case for the opinion of the High Court on the question of law or jurisdiction involved.[27] Where a party seeks to appeal in a number of cases heard together by the same justices and involving the same point or points of law, one application may be made in respect of all those cases.[28]

---

[20] See, in relation to the general provisions of the Act, Magistrates Courts Act 1952, s. 87 (1), proviso.

[21] i.e. "any justice or justices of the peace acting under any enactment or by virtue of his or their commission or under the common law."

[22] See Card v. Salmon [1953] 1 Q.B. 392; Atkinson v. United States Government [1971] A.C. 197. (A magistrate at Bow Street exercising jurisdiction under the Extradition Act 1870 has no wider powers in this regard than he has in domestic proceedings.)

[23] Where an indictable offence not dealt with summarily was dismissed, and the examining justices ordered the prosecutor to pay the costs of the defence of the ground that the charge was not made in good faith (for the modern provisions in this respect, see the Costs in Criminal Cases Act 1973, s. 2 (4)) it was held that the prosecutor was entitled to apply to the justices to state a case: R. v. Allen, ex p. Hardman [1912] 1 K.B. 356.

[24] Magistrates' Courts Act 1952, s. 87 (4). See Kirk v. Civil Aviation Authority [1978] C.L.Y. 1895. As to the rights of appeal to the Crown Court, see ante, pp. 1–5.

[25] See the Irish case of R. v. Waterford Justices [1900] 2 I.R. 307.

[26] Sivalingham v. Director of Public Prosecutions [1975] C.L.Y. 2037. Judge Box said that the "decision" in section 87 (4) being the decision in respect of which he applied to the justices to state a case, i.e. the decision to convict, it did not include the decision to fine him.

[27] Magistrates' Courts Act 1952, s. 87 (2); Criminal Law Act 1977, Sched. 12.

[28] Director of Public Prosecutions v. Lamb [1941] 2 K.B. 89.

An application must be made within 21 days[29] after the day on which the decision was made,[30] but where the justices have adjourned the trial of an information after conviction, the day on which the decision is made is the day on which they sentence or otherwise deal with the offender.[31] There are no provisions for extending the time within which an application may be made, and where the application is not made within time, the High Court will not compel the magistrates to state a case.[32]

No special form of application is prescribed,[33] but the application must be in writing,[34] must be signed by or on behalf of the applicant, and must identify the question or questions of law or jurisdiction on which the opinion of the High Court is sought.[35] Where one of the questions on which the High Court's opinion is sought is whether there was evidence on which the magistrates' court could come to its decision, the particular finding of fact made by the court, which it is claimed cannot be supported by the evidence, must be specified in the application.[36]

The application must be sent to the clerk of the magistrates' court whose decision is questioned.[37]

(2) Obligation to state case

A case cannot be stated merely by consent of the parties, but once an application is made within the prescribed time, and the applicant has entered into the recognisances required by the Act,[38] the justices have no choice but to proceed to state the case unless they are of opinion that, as a matter of law, no appeal lies,[39] or they have not been informed of the point of law to be raised,[40] or they are of opinion that the application is frivolous.

If the justices are of opinion that an application is frivolous, they may refuse to state a case, and if the applicant so requires[41] must give him a certificate stating that the application has been refused.[42]

[29] See *ante*, p. 8, n. 76.
[30] Magistrates' Courts Act 1952, s. 87 (2); Criminal Law Act 1977, Sched. 12.
[31] *Ibid.* s. 87 (3).
[32] *R.* v. *Stoke-on-Trent Justices* [1926] 2 K.B. 461; *Michael* v. *Gowland* [1977] 1 W.L.R. 296.
[33] See *Director of Public Prosecutions* v. *Lamb* [1941] 2 K.B. 89; *R.* v. *Oxford (Bullingdon) JJ., ex p. Bird* [1948] 1 K.B. 100. A form of precedent is suggested in Stones' Justices' Manual, No. 194.
[34] See *ante*, p. 8, n. 78.
[35] Magistrates' Courts Rules 1968, r. 65 (1).
[36] Magistrates' Courts Rules 1968, r. 65 (2).
[37] *Ibid.* As to service, see *ibid.* r. 67A.
[38] *Ibid.* s. 90, and see p. 30, *post*. These may be entered into at any time before the case is finally stated or delivered (*Stanhope* v. *Thorsby* (1866) L.R. 1 C.P. 423), but not afterwards (*Walker* v. *Delacombe* (1894) 63 L.J.M.C. 73).
[39] The justices will not be ordered to state a case on the ground that the decision is erroneous in point of law if they are bound by a previous decision of the Queens Bench Division from which there is no right of appeal (*R.* v. *Shiel* (1900) 82 L.T. 587), but a magistrates' court may not refuse to state a case on such a ground if the previous decision was that of a court which is not a final court of appeal (*R.* v. *Watson, ex p. Bretherton* [1945] K.B. 96.
[40] *R.* v. *Middlesex Area JJ., ex p. Goff*, February 9, 1972 (unreported).
[41] A form of application is suggested at 5 Court Forms No. 193.
[42] Magistrates' Courts Act 1952, s. 87 (5). The certificate should state merely that the justices consider the application frivolous. A form of refusal is suggested in Stones' Justices Manual, precedent No. 195, also in 5 Court Forms No. 194.
An application by the Attorney-General cannot be refused: Magistrates' Courts Act 1952, s. 87 (5) proviso.

Apart from these considerations, the justices cannot refuse, since they have no discretion in the matter. Where justices refuse to state a case, the High Court may, on the application of the person who applied for the case to be stated, make an order of mandamus requiring them to state a case.[43]

(3) Consideration of draft case

The clerk to the magistrates' court whose decision is questioned must, within 21 days after[44] receipt of an application to state a case, unless the justices refuse to state a case,[45] or after the date on which an order of mandamus[46] is made, send a draft case, in which are stated: (a) the facts found by justices; and (b) the question or questions of law or jurisdiction on which the opinion of the High Court is sought,[47] to the applicant or his solicitor, and he must send a copy to the respondent or his solicitor.[48] If he is unable to do this within the 21 days prescribed he must do so as soon as practicable thereafter, attaching to the draft case[49] a statement of the delay and the reasons for it.[50]

Unless one of the questions on which the opinion of the High Court is sought is whether there was evidence on which the court could come to its decision, the case ought not to contain a statement of the evidence.[51] Where the question, or one of the questions, is whether there was such evidence, the particular finding of fact which it is claimed cannot be supported by the evidence must be specified in the case.[52]

It is better practice in a case where the justices agree to state a case, if they state it themselves or cause their clerk to draft it.[53] Exceptionally, in a case of any complication, it should be left to the parties themselves to draft the case and submit it to the justices for their consideration.[54] Even in the exceptional

---

[43] Magistrates' Courts Act 1952, s. 87 (6). The court will not, however, issue mandamus unless the application to state a case was made in time: see *R.* v. *Stoke Justices* [1926] 2 K.B. 461.
    As to the right of the justices to show cause by means of affidavits under the Review of Justices' Decisions Act 1872, see p. 36, *post*, and *R.* v. *Daejan Properties, ex p. Merton London Borough Council, The Times,* April 25, 1978, D.C.
[44] See *ante*, p. 8, note 76.
[45] Under the Magistrates' Courts Act 1952, s. 87 (5) on the ground that the application is frivolous, see *ante*, p. 27.
[46] Under the Magistrates' Courts Act 1952, s. 87 (6).
[47] It is usual to include also a statement of the contentions of the parties and the opinions or decision of the court.
[48] Magistrates Courts Rules 1968, rr. 65A (1), 68 as amended. In "third party" cases such as those under the Food and Drugs Act 1955, s. 113 (1) the "third party" ought to be made a party to the appeal, as it may result in a rehearing, and the rights of the defendant to bring in the "third party" on the rehearing ought to be preserved: see *Elkington* v. *Kelsey* [1948] 2 K.B. 256.
[49] And to the final case when it is sent to the appellant or his solicitor, see p. 30, *post*.
[50] Magistrates' Courts Rules 1968, as amended, r. 67 (1). As to service, etc., of documents, *ibid.* r. 67A.
[51] Magistrates' Courts Rules 1968, as amended, r. 68 (3) and see *Practice Direction* [1972] 1 W.L.R. 3. The High Court will send back a case in which the evidence is set out instead of the facts found: see *Star Tea Co.* v. *Neale* 73 J.P. 511.
[52] Magistrates' Courts Rules 1968, as amended, r. 68 (2).
[53] *Cowlishaw* v. *Chalkley* (Practice Note) [1955] 1 W.L.R. 101, per Lord Goddard C.J.
[54] *Ibid.* It should not be necessary in a simple case where the appellant was professionally represented at the hearing in the magistrates' court, to obtain a copy of the clerk's notes before drafting the case: *Practice Direction* [1972] 1 W.L.R. 3.

case the justices' clerk is under a duty to send the draft case to both parties within the 21 days prescribed.[55]

The parties have 21 days after[56] the receipt of the draft case in which to make representations on it. These representations must be in writing,[57] must be signed by, or on behalf of, the party making them, and sent to the clerk to the justices.[58]

If the clerk receives an application in writing[59] for, or on behalf of, one of the parties for an extension of time within which to make representations, together with reasons in writing for that application, he may, by giving notice in writing to that party, extend the time and, if he does so, he must attach to the final case, when it is set out, a statement of the extension and the reasons for it.[60]

(4) Preparation and submission of final case

After considering any representations the justices whose decision is questioned must make such adjustments to the draft case as they think fit, and must state and sign the case within 21 days after[61] the latest day on which representations might be made.[62] The case may be stated on behalf of the justices whose decision is questioned by any two or more of them.[63] It is the decision of the bench as a whole which comes before the High Court and it matters not whether it is a majority or a unanimous decision, indeed no mention of any majority decision ought to appear in the case.[64] There is no requirement that the justices who state and sign the case should have been in agreement with the majority decision.

It is important to ensure that the case contains all the points which it is desired to raise on appeal, since the High Court will not generally hear argument on a point not raised before the justices and set out in the case[65] unless the point is one of jurisdiction, when it may be raised subject to sanctions in the form of costs.[66]

If the justices so direct, the case may be signed by their clerk on their behalf.[67]

[55] Magistrates' Courts Rules 1968, as amended, r. 65A (1).
[56] See *ante*, p. 8, n. 76.
[57] See *ante*, p. 8, n. 78.
[58] Magistrates' Courts Rules 1968, as amended, r. 65A (2).
[59] See *ante*, p. 8, n. 78.
[60] *Ibid.* r. 67 (2).
[61] See *ante*, p. 8, n. 76.
[62] Magistrates' Courts Rules 1968, as amended, r. 66 (1).
[63] *Ibid.* r. 66 (2).
[64] *More O'Ferrell Ltd.* v. *Harrow U.D.C.* [1947] 1 K.B. 66, at p. 70, *per* Lord Goddard C.J.
[65] See *Purkis* v. *Huxtable* (1859) 1 E. & E. 780; *Mottram* v. *Eastern Counties Rail Co.* (1859) 7 C.B.N.S. 58; *Marshall* v. *Smith* (1873) L.R. 8 C.P. 416; *Yorkshire Tyre and Axle Co.* v. *Rotherham Local Board of Health* (1858) 4 C.B.N.S. 362; *Crowther* v. *Boult* (1884) 13 Q.B.D. 680; *Kates* v. *Jefferey* [1914] 3 K.B. 160; *London County Council* v. *Farren* [1956] 1 W.L.R. 1297.
[66] *London, Edinburgh & Glasgow Assurance Co. Ltd.* v. *Partington* (1903) 67 J.P. 255.
[67] Magistrates' Courts Rules 1968, as amended, r. 66 (2). As to the form of the case, see Magistrates' Courts (Forms) Rules 1968, as amended, Form 148, suggested forms at 5 Court Forms, Nos. 195–198; *Practice Note* [1954] 2 All E.R. 349; *Practice Direction* [1972] 1 W.L.R. 3; and Appendix D, *post*.
The signing of the case is a ministerial act and a case can be signed by a justice no longer in office: *Grocock* v. *Grocock* [1920] 1 K.B., at p. 4.

It seems probable that the periods of time stated in the Rules are directory only and if, through no fault of the appellant, a case is not stated within time the High Court may, in its discretion, extend the time or hear the appeal out of time.[68] Where, on the other hand, there has been a complete disregard of the rules, an application for an extension of time is unlikely to be granted.[69]

After the case has been stated and signed, the clerk must send it forthwith to the applicant or his solicitors, together with a statement of any delay.[70]

(5) Amendment; restatement

The High Court has power[71] to send the case back to the justices for amendment. If one of the parties considers that relevant facts found by the justices have been omitted from the case as finally drafted his remedy is to apply[72] to the High Court for a restatement, setting out by means of a supporting affidavit[73] the finding or findings of fact which, in his opinion have been omitted. The High Court will consider the matter and may, if it sees fit, send the case back to the justices for restatement.[74] By consent of the parties, the Court may on the motion give leave to make an amendment to the case without remitting it to the justices where there is a mere slip or ambiguity corrected by a letter or affidavit from the court below, but usually the Court will not amend the case even by consent.

(6) Recognisances

Justices to whom an application has been made to state a case for the opinion of the High Court on any proceedings of a magistrates' court, are not required to state the case until the applicant has entered into a recognisance, with or without sureties, before the magistrates' court, conditioned to prosecute the appeal without delay and to submit to the judgment of the High Court, and to pay any costs that the court may award.[75]

(7) Lodging the case; entry of appeal

Where a case has been stated by a magistrates' court, the appellant must, within 10 days after receiving the final case, lodge it in the Crown Office, and within four days after lodging the case, must serve on the respondent[76] a notice

---

[68] *Moore* v. *Hewitt* [1947] K.B. 831.
[69] *Rippington* v. *Hicks & Sons (Oxford) Ltd.* [1949] 1 All E.R. 239; *Roberts* v. *Evans* (1949) 113 J.P. 137.
[70] *i.e.* under the Magistrates' Courts Rules 1968, r. 67, see *ante*, p. 28.
[71] Under the Summary Jurisdiction Act 1857, s. 7.
[72] Application is by two-day motion supported by an affidavit; the application should be made without delay. A form of application is suggested in 5 Court Forms No. 200.
[73] *Practice Note* [1953] 1 W.L.R. 334.
[74] The justices may be compelled by mandamus to act upon the restatement (see *R.* v. *Corsen*, 8 T.L.R. 563) and may be ordered to pay the costs of the restatement (see *Edge* v. *Edwards* 48 T.L.R. 449). If a case, so remitted, is later abandoned, the applicant may be ordered to pay the respondent's costs: see *Crowther* v. *Boult* 13 Q.B.D. 680. See also *Spicer* v. *Warbey* [1953] 1 All E.R. 284; *Cowlishaw* v. *Chalkley* [1955] 1 W.L.R. 101.
[75] Magistrates' Courts Act 1952, s. 90. A form of recognisance is suggested in 5 Court Forms, No. 192.
[76] See *ante*, p. 28, n. 48.

of the entry of the appeal together with a copy of the case.[77] Eight clear days must then elapse between the service of the notice and the hearing of the appeal unless the High Court otherwise orders.[78]

(8) Bail on case stated

Where a person applies to the justices to state a case for the opinion of the High Court, the justices may[79] grant him bail[80] unless the applicant has been committed to the Crown Court for sentence under sections 28 or 29 of the Magistrates' Courts Act 1952.[81]

The High Court[82] has power, if bail is witheld by a magistrates' court, or is granted on unacceptable conditions, to grant bail or to vary the conditions on which bail is granted.[83]

(9) Legal aid

A legal aid order made for the purpose of proceedings before a magistrates' court is authority for the solicitor assigned by that court to give advice on the question whether there appear to be reasonable grounds of appeal from any determination in those proceedings and assistance by him in making an application for a case to be stated, being an application made within the ordinary time for doing so.[84] Thereafter, an application for legal aid for the purpose of the proceedings must be made under Part I of the Legal Aid Act 1974, to the appropriate Area Committee of the Law Society.

(10) Abandonment

There are no statutory or other provisions for the abandonment of an appeal by way of case stated, but in practice, abandonment is effected by

---

[77] R.S.C., O. 56, r. 6 (1). A form of Notice is suggested at 5 Court Forms, No. 192.

Lodgment within time is a condition precedent to the High Court hearing, and where compliance has become impossible the case will be struck out: *Williams* v. *Watkins* (1933) 49 T.L.R. 315. An application to extend the time (under O. 3, r. 4) may be made by notice of motion to the Divisional Court supported by affidavit (see 5 Court Forms No. 199).

Service on the respondent of a copy of the application to the justices and a copy of the case was held sufficient in *Dickson & Co.* v. *Mayes* [1910] 1 K.B. 45. *Cf. Rust* v. *Churchwardens, etc., of St. Botolph's Bishopsgate* (1906) 94 L.T. 575 (service of case only).

[78] R.S.C., O. 56, r. 6 (2). As to entry in the "expedited list," see p. 35, *post.*

[79] There is no general right to bail in respect of proceedings on or after a person's conviction, see Bail Act 1976, s. 4 (1), (2) and *ante*, p. 8.

[80] Magistrates' Courts Act 1952, s. 89 (1), (1A); Bail Act 1976, Sched. 2. Section 37 (6) of the Criminal Justice Act 1948, which provides that the time spent on bail pending appeal shall not count towards any term of imprisonment, applies in such a case: Magistrates' Courts Act 1952, s. 89 (3); Bail Act 1976, Sched. 2.

A form of application is suggested at 5 Court Forms No. 191.

Where bail is granted, the time and place at which that person is to appear (except in the event of the justices' determination being reversed by the High Court) will be at the magistrates' court, at such time within 10 days after the judgment of the High Court has been given as may be specified by the justices, and any recognisance taken from him (in a non-criminal case) or from any surety for him, will be conditioned accordingly: Magistrates' Courts Act 1952, s. 89 (1A).

[81] *Ibid.*, s. 89 (2).

[82] As to the power of the High Court to grant bail, and the manner in which an application is made, see pp. 54–57, *post.*

[83] Criminal Justice Act 1967, s. 22 (1); Bail Act 1976, s. 12, Sched. 2.

[84] Legal Aid Act 1974, s. 30 (5).

lodging in the Crown Office the other party's consent[85] and an application to withdraw the case.[86]

Where an appellant fails to prosecute his appeal the respondent may apply to the High Court to have the appeal dismissed.[87]

B. APPEAL FROM THE CROWN COURT

1. GENERAL PROVISIONS

(1) Right of appeal

There are no statutory provisions providing for any appeal as such[88] from a decision of the Crown Court in the exercise of its appellate jurisdiction, but proceedings on appeal to the Crown Court may be questioned by any party to them[89] on the ground that the decision is wrong in law[90] or in excess of jurisdiction.[91] A party who is dissatisfied with the determination of the Crown Court in such circumstances may apply to that court to state a case for the opinion of the High Court on the point of law or jurisdiction.[92]

An appeal by way of case stated is a form of consultation with the High Court to obtain an answer on a point of law; it is not a rehearing of the case. In this respect an appeal by way of case stated from the Crown Court is analagous to an appeal by way of case stated from a magistrates' court.[93]

(2) Applying to the court

An application to the Crown Court to state a case for the opinion of the High Court must be made in writing[94] to the appropriate officer of the court within 14 days after[95] the date of the decision in respect of which the application is made.[96] The time for making the application may be extended,[97] either before or after it expires, by the Crown Court.[98]

---

[85] A form of consent is suggested at 5 Court Forms, No. 202.

[86] See 5 Court Forms at p. 100.

[87] See *Crowther* v. *Boult* (1884) 13 Q.B.D. 680.

[88] There is no appeal from the appellate jurisdiction of the Crown Court to the Criminal Division of the Court of Appeal, see p. 58, *post*.

[89] The expression "party to the proceedings" is discussed *ante*, p. 24.

[90] The concept "wrong in law" is discussed *ante*, pp. 25–26.

[91] Courts Act 1971, s. 10 (1), (2).

[92] *Ibid.* s. 10 (1), (3). There is no power to state a case in relation to the jurisdiction of the Crown Court on indictment: *ibid.* s. 10 (1).

[93] *Harris, Simon & Co.* v. *Manchester City Council* [1975] 1 W.L.R. 100, at p. 105, *per* Lord Widgery C.J.

[94] See *ante*, p. 8, note 78. A form of application is suggested at 5 Court Forms, No. 204.

[95] See *ante*, p. 8, note 76.

[96] Crown Court Rules 1971, r. 21 (1). In view of the provisions of the Rules, it is submitted that the common law procedure exemplified by such cases as *Chesterton R.D.C.* v. *Ralph Thompson Ltd*. [1944] K.B. 447 and *R.* v. *Northumberland Quarter Sessions Justices, ex p. Williamson* [1965] 1 W.L.R. 700 is to be treated as obsolete. See also *ante*, p. 17.

[97] Which is not the case on an appeal from a magistrates' court by way of case stated, see *ante*, p. 27.
    A form of application is suggested in 5 Court Forms, No. 206.

[98] Crown Court Rules 1971, r. 21 (2).

The Crown Court may, in the same way as a magistrates' court,[99] refuse to state a case if it considers the application to be frivolous, and in that event, if the applicant requires it, must cause a certificate stating the reasons for its refusal[1] to be given to him.[2]

Before the case is stated and delivered to the applicant, the Crown Court may order that he enter into a recognisance before an officer of the court, with or without sureties, and in such sum as the court thinks proper having regard to his means, conditioned for the prosecution of the appeal without delay.[3]

(3) Form of case

In general, subject to Rules of court[4] the same form and content is required of a case stated by the Crown Court as is already prescribed for a case stated by a magistrates' court.[5] The duty of the Crown Court, like that of the magistrates' court,[6] is to find the facts, state the contentions of the parties, express the opinions of the court, and formulate any questions of law for determination by the High Court.

In the case of the Crown Court, however, where its judgment, order or decision in respect of which the case is to be stated states all the relevant facts found and the questions of law to be determined by the High Court, a copy of that judgment, order or decision, signed by the person who presided at the hearing,[7] is annexed to the case and the facts so found and the questions of law are sufficiently stated in the case by referring to the statement of it in the judgment, order or decision of the court.[8]

There is no limit within which the case must be stated, provided that it is lodged with the Crown Office within six months.[9]

2. BAIL; LEGAL AID; ENTRY OF APPEAL

(1) Bail

The Crown Court[10] or the High Court[11] may grant bail to a person who,

---

[99] See *ante*, p. 27.

[1] It is probably sufficient to state merely that the application is frivolous. See Form 5053 in the Appendix to the Crown Court Manual.

[2] Crown Court Rules 1971, r. 21 (3).

It is doubtful whether mandamus lies to compel the Crown Court to state a case. Before 1925 mandamus did not lie to quarter sessions to state a case: see the historical summary in the judgment of Lord Goddard in *R. v. Somerset JJ., ex p. Ernest J. Cole & Partners* [1950] 1 K.B. 519, at pp. 521–523. The Criminal Justice Act 1925, s. 20 (4) provided for mandamus in a criminal case (see also *R. v. Northumberland Quarter Sessions Justices, ex p. Williamson, supra*), but section 20 of that Act was repealed by the Courts Act 1971, s. 56, Sched. 11, Pt. IV, and the provisions of section 20 (4) do not seem to have been re-enacted.

[3] Crown Court Rules 1971, r. 21 (4). See as to forms, 5 Court Forms, Nos. 207, 208.

[4] Pending amendment of the Rules, the contents of the case should comply with the Magistrates' Courts Rules 1968, s. 68 and the form with Form 148 in the Magistrates' Courts (Forms) Rules 1968: *Practice Direction* (1979) 68 Cr. App. R. 119.

[5] *Practice Direction* (1979 68 Cr. App. R. 119.

[6] See *ante*, p. 28.

[7] See *ante*, p. 18, n. 77.

[8] R.S.C., O. 56, r. 2.

[9] *Ibid*. O. 56, r. 1 (4).

[10] Courts Act 1971, s. 13 (4) (*d*).

[11] Criminal Justice Act 1948, s. 37 (1) (*a*), as amended.

after the decision of his case by the Crown Court, has applied for the statement of a case for the opinion of the High Court on that decision.[12]

(2) Legal aid

Where legal aid was ordered to be given to a person for the purpose of an appeal to the Crown Court,[13] and that court confirms or varies the conviction or sentence, or where, in the case of those appeals peculiar to the Children and Young Persons Act 1969,[14] the court dismisses the appeal or otherwise alters the order to which the appeal relates, the legal aid order in force is authority for counsel or the solicitor assigned to the appellant to give advice on the question whether there appear to be reasonable grounds of appeal from the decision of the Crown Court and, if such grounds appear to exist, assistance in making an application for a case to be stated.[15]

Thereafter, any application for legal aid in relation to further proceedings on the appeal must be made under Part I of the Legal Aid Act 1974 to the appropriate Area Committee of the Law Society.

(3) Entry of appeal

An appeal by way of case stated from the Crown Court will not be entered for hearing unless and until the case, a copy of the judgment, order or decision in respect of which the case has been stated, and a copy of the judgment, order or decision appealed from, have been lodged in the Crown Office.[16]

The applicant, or if the applicant so wishes, an officer of the Crown Court, must lodge three copies of the case, together with three copies of the judgment, order or decision, and three copies of the decision appealed against, in the Crown Office.[16] When these documents have been lodged the case will immediately be entered for hearing.[16] No appeal may be entered for hearing after the expiration of six months from the date of the judgment, order or decision in respect of which the case is stated, unless the delay is accounted for to the satisfaction of the High Court.[17] An application for extension of time in which to enter the appeal must be made by notice of motion[18] and served on the respondent at least two clear days before the day named in the notice for the hearing of the application.[19]

Where an appeal has not been entered for hearing because of default in complying with the Rules, the Crown Court is entitled to proceed as if no case had been stated.[20]

[12] The time during which a person is released on bail does not count as part of any term of imprisonment under his sentence, and any sentence of imprisonment imposed by a magistrates' court or, on appeal, by the Crown Court, after the imposition of which a person is released on bail, is deemed to begin to run, or to be resumed, as from the day on which he is received in prison under the sentence: Criminal Justice Act 1948, s. 37 (6) (the expression "prison" includes a detention centre). See also Courts Act 1971, s. 13 (4) (d) and R.S.C., O. 79, r. 9.
[13] See ante, p. 17.
[14] i.e. under ibid. s. 2 (12), 3 (8), 16 (8), 21 (4) or 31 (6), for which see ante, p. 3.
[15] Legal Aid Act 1974, s. 30 (6).
[16] R.S.C., O. 56, r. 1 (3).
[17] R.S.C., O. 56, r. 1 (4). See Collyer v. Dring [1952] W.N. 505.
[18] R.S.C., O. 56, r. 1 (4). A form of notice is suggested at 5 Court Forms, No. 212.
[19] R.S.C., O. 56, r. 1 (4).
[20] R.S.C., O. 56, r. 1 (5).

Where the appeal is entered for hearing, the appellant must serve notice on the respondent within four days.[21]

(4) "Expedited hearing list"

A list of selected cases pending in the Divisional Court, called the "expedited hearing list" is maintained in the Crown Office.[22] The main purpose of this list is to secure the early disposal of simple cases, particularly those which involve sentences of imprisonment, disqualification from driving or possession of property.[23]

As soon as a case stated is lodged in the Crown Office and a notice and a copy of the case have been served,[24] any party may apply to the head clerk to enter the case in the "expedited hearing list" and may do so either informally where the consent of the other parties has been obtained, or by obtaining an appointment with the head clerk and giving notice in writing of the appointment to the other parties.[25] The court may also, of its own motion, enter any case in the list, and give notice to the parties. If any party objects to such a course, the objection should be made in writing to the head clerk of the Crown Office.[26] A party who is dissatisfied with a decision of the head clerk,[27] may make an application in respect thereof to the court on a two-day motion.[28]

3. THE HEARING BEFORE THE HIGH COURT

(1) Hearing before Divisional Court

An appeal by way of case stated in a criminal cause or matter, whether from the magistrates' court[29] or from the Crown Court,[30] is heard before a Divisional Court of the Queen's Bench Division.[31]

A right of appeal is a strictly personal right and, in general, dies with the appellant. If the sentence imposed on the appellant was a custodial one, the High Court will not allow an appeal to be continued after the appellant's death.[32] Where the penalty is of a financial nature, the personal representatives of the deceased may, in some circumstances, be permitted to continue the appeal after his death.[33]

---

[21] R.S.C., O. 56, r. 4. A form of notice is suggested at 5 Court Forms, No. 211.
[22] See *Practice Direction (Expedited Hearing List)* [1974] 1 W.L.R. 1219.
[23] *Ibid*. The purpose is that cases which will occupy the court for a short period but urgently require hearing because disqualification or the like attaches to them, will be picked up from the list and will be dealt with within two to three weeks of the matter coming to the cognisance of the court: *ibid*. para. 6.
[24] In accordance with R.S.C., O. 53, r. 3 (2).
[25] Forms of notice are obtainable from the Crown Office.
[26] *Practice Direction (Expedited Hearing List), supra*, para. 4.
[27] Or an application for the expedited hearing of a case to which para. 4 of the *Practice Direction* does not or has not been applied.
[28] *Practice Direction, supra*, para. 6. At the time when a case is entered in the list, the week in which it will be heard will be nominated by reference to the date of the Monday in that week. *Ibid*. para. 5.
[29] Under R.S.C., O. 56, r. 5 (1).
[30] Under *ibid*. O. 56, r. 1 (1).
[31] See also pp. 36–38, *post*.
[32] *R.* v. *Rowe* [1955] 1 Q.B. 573, and see p. 79, *post*.
[33] *Hodgson* v. *Lakeman* [1943] K.B. 15.

(2) Representation of justices

Upon an appeal by way of case stated from a magistrates' court, as upon an application for judicial review,[34] any one or more of the justices whose decision is questioned may make and file an affidavit setting forth the grounds of the decision brought under review and any facts which that justice considers to have a material bearing upon the question at issue, such affidavit being forwarded to one of the Masters of the Court for the purpose of being filed.[35] An affidavit should be filed in this manner rather than appearance be made by counsel, unless an allegation of misconduct is made against the justices,[36] because if the justices choose to appear, they make themselves parties to the *lis* and take the risk of being ordered to pay costs.[37]

Where justices file affidavits in this manner, the High Court is bound to take them into consideration, notwithstanding that no counsel appears on their behalf.[38]

(3) The hearing

At the hearing of an appeal by way of case stated it is the function of the Divisional Court to answer the questions of law raised on the case.[39] The result of the appeal will turn essentially upon the facts stated in the case submitted to the court, and as a general rule the court will not be prepared to go outside the four corners of the case and, for example, look at the notes of evidence. The court will rely upon the justices or the lower court and will take the case as stated unless there is some defect patent upon the face of it, notwithstanding that one of the parties to the appeal disputes by affidavit the facts found, and avers that they raise a different question.[40]

The appellant must show, in order to succeed, that the decision of the court below was wrong, and this is so even where the respondent does not appear.[41] Where neither party to the appeal appears the court will decline to give a decision.[42] The court has no power to hear witnesses.[43]

On an appeal relating to a criminal charge, the court is prepared to hear and determine any point of law which, if sound, might afford a defence, despite the fact that the point was first appreciated after conviction and was, therefore,

---

[34] See p. 51, *post*.
[35] Review of Justices' Decisions Act 1872, s. 2. No fee is payable in respect of filing the affidavit.
[36] See *R.* v. *Camborne JJ., ex p. Pearce* as reported in [1952] 2 All E.R. 850, at p. 856; *R.* v. *Llanidloes Licensing Justices, ex p. Davies* [1957] 1 W.L.R. 809n; *R.* v. *Marlow (Bucks) JJ., ex p. Schiller* as reported in [1957] 2 All E.R. 783, at p. 784.
[37] *R.* v. *Llanidloes Licensing Justices, ex p. Davies, supra*; also *R.* v. *Kingston-upon-Hull Rent Tribunal* [1949] 1 All E.R. 260.
[38] Review of Justices' Decisions Act 1872, s. 3. A justice who dissented from the decision of the court has neither the right to appear nor the right to make and file an affidavit: *R.* v. *Waddingham, etc., (Gloucestershire) JJ. & Tustin* (1896) 60 J.P. 372.
[39] *Buckmaster* v. *Reynolds* (1862) 13 C.B.N.S. 62.
[40] *Musther* v. *Musther* 58 J.P.J. 53; but see *Edge* v. *Edwards* (1932) 48 T.L.R. 449. As to amendment and restatement, see *ante*, p. 30.
[41] *Watkins* v. *Fenwick* (1858) 23 J.P. 516.
[42] *Walters* v. *Williams* (1860) 9 C.B.N.S. 179.
[43] *Stroud* v. *Bradbury* (1952) March 4 (unreported).

not taken before the court below,[44] and will consider any point of law arising on the facts as stated in the case. It will not, however, in general, be prepared to infer any fact which the court below has not considered or found.[45] Where a point was not taken below and would depend upon further findings of fact, the court will not allow it to be raised.[46] The findings of fact of the court below cannot be questioned except on the ground that there is no evidence to support them, or that they were findings to which no reasonable bench could have come.[47]

(4) Powers of court

The court will hear and determine the question or questions of law in the case, and may reverse, affirm or amend the decision appealed against, or may send it back for amendment, or may remit the matter to the court below with its opinion thereon,[48] or make such other order in relation to the matter as it thinks fit.[49]

The court has no power to vary the sentence on an appeal by way of case stated,[50] although it may substitute a valid for an invalid sentence.[51]

(5) Costs

Costs as between parties on an appeal by way of case stated are in the discretion of the court.[52] The court may make such order as to costs as may seem fit, provided that no justice or justices who stated a case in pursuance of section 87 of the Magistrates' Courts Act 1952, are liable to any costs in respect of, or by reason of, such appeal.[53]

A Divisional Court may also order the payment out of central funds of the costs of any party to proceedings before it in a criminal cause or matter[54] being such sums as appear reasonably sufficient to compensate the party concerned

---

[44] *Whitehead* v. *Haines* [1965] 1 Q.B. 200. In particular it "appears to be essential for the due performance of justice that the court should not uphold a conviction for an offence non-existent in law": *ibid*. at p. 209, *per* Winn J.

[45] *Cf. Northern Theatres Co.* v. *Shillito* [1925] 2 K.B. 100; and *Chivers & Sons Ltd.* v. *Cambridge County Council* [1957] Q.B. 68, at p. 76.

[46] *Ross* v. *Ross* [1965] 2 Q.B. 396, at p. 407, *per* Lord Parker C.J.

[47] *Bracegirdle* v. *Oxley* [1947] K.B. 349. See also *ante*, p. 25.

[48] The court can only order that the proceedings be resumed, it cannot order a retrial: *Rigby* v. *Woodward* [1957] 1 W.L.R. 250. It follows that a case remitted is not to be heard by a different bench: *Cotterell* v. *Morgan* (1948) June 21 (unreported). A case will not be remitted to justices to deal with a point which arose for the first time on the appeal: *London County Council* v. *Farren* [1956] 1 W.L.R. 1297.

[49] Summary Jurisdiction Act 1857, s. 6 as amended.

[50] *Evans* v. *Hemingway* (1887) 52 J.P. 134.

[51] Administration of Justice Act 1960, s. 16.

[52] Summary Jurisdiction Act 1857, s. 6 as amended. See also R.S.C., O. 62, r. 3 (2).

[53] Supreme Court (Consolidation) Act 1925, s. 25 (2), (3). Where justices are made parties to an appeal, costs may be awarded either in their favour or against them (see *R.* v. *Llanidloes Licensing Justices, ex p. Davies* [1957] 1 W.L.R. 809n), but if they are not made parties, they have no right to appear and costs cannot be awarded against them in respect of, or by reason of, their decision, unless possibly, they state the case incorrectly (*Edge* v. *Edwards* (1932) 48 T.L.R. 449). See also *ante*, p. 36.
Costs of the proceedings before the justices are sometimes given, see *Turner & Son Ltd.* v. *Owen* [1956] 1 Q.B. 48.

[54] Costs in Criminal Cases Act 1973, s. 5 (1).

for any expenses properly incurred by him in the proceedings or in any court below.[55] The amount of costs to be paid is ascertained by the master of the Crown Office.[56]

(6) Enforcement

Any conviction, order, determination or other proceeding of a magistrates' court varied on appeal by case stated, or any judgment or order on such an appeal, may be enforced as if it were a decision of the magistrates' court.[57]

---

[55] *Ibid*. s. 5 (2). See *Cannings* v. *Houghton (No. 2)* (1979) R.T.R. 567.
[56] *Ibid*. s. 5 (3). An appeal against the award of costs out of central funds is provided by the Costs in Criminal Cases (Central Funds) (Appeals) Regulations 1977 (S.I. 1977 No. 248), a copy of which is to be found in Appendix H, *post*.
[57] Magistrates' Courts Act 1952, s. 88.

PART III

JUDICIAL REVIEW: THE PREROGATIVE ORDERS OF
MANDAMUS, CERTIORARI AND PROHIBITION

1. GENERAL PROVISIONS

(1) The nature of prerogative orders

There may be occasions when it is sought to challenge the act or order of an inferior court under circumstances in which no right of appeal as such is conferred, or where the existing rights of appeal do not apply to the specific matter which it is sought to challenge. Interlocutory matters, for instance, such as the refusal of a magistrates' court to issue process, or to withdraw a warrant, or a refusal of jurisdiction by a magistrates' court, or by the Crown Court in the exercise of its appellate jurisdiction, are not matters in respect of which any right of appeal is conferred.

Again, there are matters in respect of which an appeal is expressly excluded,[1] or in respect of which an appeal has been held not to lie.[2] In these circumstances it may be possible, by means of one of the prerogative orders, to challenge the actions of the inferior court. In a case where it can be shown that the court has failed to exercise its proper jurisdiction, or has acted in excess of its proper jurisdiction, or is threatening to assume a jurisdiction which it does not have, the proper remedy may be to apply for judicial review.

(2) Limitations on prerogative orders

An application for judicial review is not, strictly, an avenue of appeal; the prerogative orders "are the great residual jurisdiction whereby ... [the High Court] controls the activities of subordinate tribunals, and it controls them in three main categories (i) against excesses of jurisdiction; (ii) against errors of law on the face of their judgments; and (iii) against a denial of natural justice."[3] The prerogative orders provide a speedy and effective remedy in a proper case, but the ambit of judicial review is limited. The High Court will not, for instance, attempt to solve direct conflicts of evidence on material facts[4]; the issue of the prerogative orders is reserved for simple and straightforward cases.[5] Nor will the High Court seek to substitute its views for those of the lower court; it may compel the lower court to act but will not direct the manner in which it should carry out that duty. It is clear that in the case of

---

[1] *i.e.* under the Magistrates' Courts Act 1952, s. 83 (3).
[2] There is no appeal by way of case stated from examining justices, see *ante*, p. 26.
[3] *R.* v. *West Sussex Quarter Sessions, ex p. Johnson (Albert and Maud) Trust* [1973] Q.B. 188, *per* Lord Widgery C.J. at p. 194.
[4] See, *e.g. R.* v. *McLean, ex p. Aikens and Others* (1975) 139 J.P. 261, at p. 264; also *R.* v. *Abingdon (County) Magistrates' Court, ex p. Clifford* [1978] Crim. L.R. 165.
[5] See *R.* v. *McLean, etc., supra.*

certiorari at any rate, the order will not issue until the proceedings in the court below are complete.[6]

The particular order which will be appropriate will depend upon the stage which the proceedings in the court below have reached.

(3) The Crown Court as an "inferior court"

The High Court has the same jurisdiction to make orders of mandamus, prohibition and certiorari in relation to the jurisdiction of the Crown Court[7] as it possesses in relation to the jurisdiction of inferior courts,[8] save that the prerogative orders do not lie to the Crown Court[9] in relation to its jurisdiction in matters relating to trials on indictment.[10] The High Court has thus no jurisdiction to issue certiorari to quash an order as to costs,[11] or the making of a legal aid contribution order,[12] following a trial on indictment; nor is the order of the Crown Court that a solicitor pay the costs of proceedings personally liable to be quashed by certiorari.[13]

Where the High Court does have power to issue the prerogative orders to the Crown Court, that power is not limited to questions of jurisdiction, but extends to other situations in which an order of certiorari is commonly issued.[14]

(4) The order of mandamus

Mandamus lies to an inferior court to compel it to exercise its proper jurisdiction. It is a command from the High Court ordering the inferior court to carry out a duty imposed on it by law.[15] Its principal purpose is to supply defects of justice and it will lie where there is a specific right, yet no appropriate remedy, or where although a remedy exists, it is less effective, less convenient or less beneficial than the order of mandamus.[16] Its issue is discretionary,[17] and the High Court will generally refuse to issue mandamus where there is an adequate alternative remedy available, such as an appeal.[18]

Mandamus lies to an inferior court to compel it to exercise a jurisdiction

---

[6] See *R.* v. *Carden* (1879) 5 Q.B.D. 1; *R.* v. *Rochford JJ., ex p. Buck* (1979) 68 Cr. App. R. 114; *R.* v. *Wells Street Stipendiary Magistrate, ex p. Seillon* [1978] 3 All E.R. 257.

[7] The Crown Court is a superior court of record; it is part of the Supreme Court: Courts Act 1971, s. 1.

[8] *Ibid.* s. 10 (5). See, *e.g. R.* v. *Middlesex Crown Court, ex p. Riddle* [1975] Crim. L.R. 731; *R.* v. *Knightsbridge Crown Court, ex p. Martin* [1976] Crim. L.R. 463; *R.* v. *Carlisle Crown Court, ex p. Armstrong* [1979] Crim. L.R. 253.

[9] As they did to the courts of quarter session.

[10] Courts Act 1971, s. 10 (5).

[11] *Ex p. Meredith* [1973] 1 W.L.R. 435; see also *ex p. Marlowe* [1973] Crim. L.R. 294.

[12] *R.* v. *Cardiff Crown Court, ex p. Jones* [1974] 2 W.L.R. 495.

[13] *R.* v. *Smith (Martin)* [1974] 2 W.L.R. 495.

[14] *R.* v. *Exeter Crown Court, ex p. Beattie* [1974] 1 W.L.R. 429; *R.* v. *Leeds Crown Court, ex p. Bradford Chief Constable* [1975] Q.B. 314.

[15] See the Administration of Justice (Miscellaneous Provisions) Act 1938, s. 8.

[16] *R.* v. *Thomas* [1892] 1 Q.B. 426.

[17] There is ample authority to the effect that certiorari, and by parity of reasoning, mandamus, will not go where there has been an unequivocal and accepted plea of guilty to a valid charge in summary proceedings: see *R.* v. *Guest, ex p. Anthony* [1964] 1 W.L.R. 1273 (overruled on another point in *S (An infant)* v. *Manchester City Recorder* [1971] A.C. 481) and see p. 45, *post*. *Cf. R.* v. *Eastbourne JJ., ex p. Barsoum* [1979] 2 C.L. 41.

[18] *R.* v. *Thomas* [1892] 1 Q.B. 426, at p. 429, *per* Hawkins J. See also *R.* v. *Smith* L.R. 8 Q.B. 140; *R.* v. *Denbighshire Justices* (1841) 9 Dowl. 509.

which it has declined to exercise.[19] It lies to an inferior court for refusal to issue process for reasons which are extraneous or inappropriate.[20] It has been issued to justices who refused to withdraw a warrant even though, on the admitted facts, the person sought had committed no offence.[21] The order has ben issued to justices who dismissed an information on a point of jurisdiction[22] and to both justices and quarter sessions who declined jurisdiction to hear an application.[23] It has issued to a court which heard one party to an appeal but declined to hear the other.[24]

Mandamus lies to an inferior court which has rejected evidence to such an extent as to amount to a refusal of jurisdiction[25]; also to justices who fail to pass sentence on an offender, thus failing to dispose of a case finally.[26]

Mandamus does not lie to a court which *has* exercised its jurisdiction[27] whether its decision be right or wrong,[28] and even where its decision is one of law.[29]

Mandamus will issue in that class of case where the inferior court purports to set up rules or principles which it will follow, rather than considering each particular case on its merits. This has been the case where justices made a general rule that they "would not allow costs to prosecutors,"[30] or that they would only allow a fixed sum in respect of costs, irrespective of the actual circumstances.[31] A similar situation arises where a court acts upon general considerations (even though those general considerations may be similar from one case to another) rather than upon the considerations peculiar to the case in question,[32] or where the court fails to consider the issues sufficiently.[33]

[19] For a modern example, see *R. v. Tottenham JJ., ex p. Rubens* [1970] 1 W.L.R. 800; also *R. v. Lancashire JJ., ex p. Tyrer* [1925] 1 K.B. 200.
[20] *R. v. Adamson* (1875) 1 Q.B.D. 201. In *R. v. Derby JJ., ex p. Kooner* the justices refusal to grant legal aid on extraneous grounds was the subject of an order of mandamus. See also *R. v. Guildford JJ., ex p. Scott* [1975] Crim. L.R. 286; *R. v. Guildhall JJ., ex p. Marshall* [1976] 1 W.L.R. 335; *R. v. Highgate JJ., ex p. Lewis* [1977] Crim. L.R. 611; *R. v. Solihull JJ. (unreported)*, March 16, 1976, D.C.
  In *R. v. Fairford JJ., ex p. Brewer* [1975] 3 W.L.R. 59, Lord Widgery C.J. expressed the opinion that there must be power in the Divisional Court to control excesses in relation to the issue of process (in this case delay), as there is in most other similar features of proceedings. And "I do not for one moment think the courts are powerless in this regard."
[21] *Ex p. Chetwynd* (1908) L.T. 760.
[22] *R. v. Brown* (1857) 26 L.J.M.C. 183; see also *R. v. Ogden, ex p. Long Ashton R.D.C.* [1963] 1 W.L.R. 274.
[23] Modern examples are to be found in *R. v. Tottenham JJ., ex p. Rubens* [1970] 1 W.L.R. 800 and *R. v. Mutford and Lothingland JJ., ex p. Harber* [1971] 2 Q.B. 281. See also *R. v. Lewes Crown Court, ex p. Rogers* [1974] 1 W.L.R. 196.
[24] *R. v. Caernarvon Justices* (1826) 4 B. & Ald. 86.
[25] See *R. v. Marsham* [1892] 1 Q.B. 371. But *cf. R. v. Wells Street Stipendiary Magistrate, ex p. Seillon* [1978] 3 All E.R. 257, at p. 261.
[26] *R. v. Norfolk JJ., ex p. Director of Public Prosecutions* [1950] 2 K.B. 558 (a decision of five judges).
[27] *R. v. Worcestershire Justices* (1854) 3 E. & B. 447; *R. v. Middlesex Justices* (1877) 2 Q.B.D. 516.
[28] *R. v. Caernarvon Justices* (1820) 4 B. & Ald. 86; *R. v. West Riding of Yorkshire Justices* (1834) 5 B. & Ald. 1003; *R. v. Dayman* (1857) 22 J.P. 39.
[29] *Re Pratt* (1837) 7 Ad. & El. 27.
[30] See *R. v. Oldham Justices* (1909) 101 L.T. 430; *R. v. Ely JJ., ex p. Mann* (1928) 93 J.P. 45; see also *R. v. Nuneaton JJ., ex p. Parker* [1954] 1 W.L.R. 1318.
[31] *R. v. Glamorgan Justices* (1850) 19 L.J.M.C. 172.
[32] *R. v. Evans* (1890) 62 L.T. 570; *R. v. Surrey Justices* (1875) 10 L.J.M.C. 171; *R. v. Merioneth Justices* (1908) 99 L.T. 89.
[33] *R. v. Ogden, ex p. Long Ashton R.D.C.* [1963] 1 W.L.R. 274, and the cases cited there.

The High Court will consider whether, by its actions, the inferior court has wrongly refused jurisdiction in a particular aspect of the case. Refusal of jurisdiction may be manifested by a complete refusal to hear the matter[34] or by the court permitting itself to be influenced by some wholly extraneous consideration which ought not to have been allowed to influence its deliberations.[35] It has been held that a court declines jurisdiction where it wholly disregards the law, even though it be on the ground that it considers the law unjust,[36] or where it acts on manifestly wrong principles.[36]

Mandamus lies to compel an inferior court to exercise its jursidiction but it does not lie to dictate the particular manner in which that jurisdiction is to be exercised, nor does it lie to direct what evidence the court should accept and what it should reject[37] unless the duty is to act ministerially rather than judicially.[38] In particular, a magistrate is not to be controlled by mandamus in the conduct of a case, nor can the High Court in that way prescribe what evidence he shall receive and what evidence he shall reject[39]; nor, where proceedings are being heard, will the High Court exercise jurisdiction to issue a prerogative order to control or direct the manner in which the proceedings are to be heard.[40]

Where a magistrates' court declines to state a case for the opinion of the High Court, mandamus will lie at the instance of the person who applied for the case, requiring it to do so.[41] In the case of the Crown Court refusing to state a case, however, the position is not so clear[42]; it may be that mandamus will only lie where the Crown Court originally agreed to state a case, but subsequently declines to do so.[43]

The High Court will not review a discretion exercised by the lower court, provided that the discretion was exercised in good faith[44] upon a proper consideration of the relevant principles,[45] and this appears to be so even though the court exercised its discretion wrongly.[46]

(5) The order of certiorari

Certiorari lies to bring up and quash a decision of an inferior court which has purported to exercise jurisdiction which it does not have, thus ensuring that

[34] *R.* v. *Marsham* [1892] 1 Q.B. 371.
[35] *R.* v. *Adamson* (1875) 1 Q.B.D. 201; *R.* v. *Essex Justices* (1877) 36 L.T. 534.
[36] *R.* v. *Boteler* (1864) 33 L.J.M.C. 101.
[37] *R.* v. *Carden* (1879) 5 Q.B.D. 1. *R.* v. *Rochford JJ., ex p. Buck* (1979) 68 Cr. App. R. 114, at p. 118, *per* Lord Widgery C.J.
[38] *R.* v. *Kingston JJ., ex p. Davey* (1902) 66 J.P. 547.
[39] *R.* v. *Carden, supra.*
[40] *e.g.* where a magistrate refuses to permit a particular line of cross-examination by defence counsel in the course of committal proceedings, the court will not issue mandamus directing the magistrate to allow that cross-examination: *R.* v. *Wells Street Stipendiary Magistrate, ex p. Seillon* [1978] 3 All E.R. 257. See also *R.* v. *Rochford JJ., ex p. Buck, supra.*
[41] Magistrates' Courts Act 1952, s. 87 (6).
[42] See *ante*, p. 33, n. 2.
[43] See Halsbury's *Laws of England* (4th ed.), Vol. 11, para. 1524. Also *R.* v. *Somerset JJ., ex p. Ernest Cole & Partners* [1950] 1 K.B. 519, *per* Lord Goddard C.J. at p. 521; also *R.* v. *Hallett, ex p. Smith* [1939] 2 K.B. 276.
[44] *R.* v. *Lewis* (1888) 21 Q.B.D. 191.
[45] *R.* v. *Wisbech Justices* (1890) 54 J.P. 743.
[46] *R.* v. *MacMahon* (1883) 48 J.P. 70; *Ex p. Reed* (1885) 49 J.P. 600; but see *R.* v. *Nuneaton JJ., ex p. Parker* [1954] 1 W.L.R. 1318.

inferior courts act within the limits of their jurisdiction. Certiorari lies in an appropriate case to a magistrates' court, or to the Crown Court in the exercise of its appellate jurisdiction, in respect of any decision, judgment or order made without, or in excess of, jurisdiction.[47] An order of certiorari requires the order of the magistrates' court, or the record of the Crown Court, as the case may be, to be brought up and enquired into in the High Court and, if necessary, quashed.[47]

Certiorari lies most frequently in respect of errors of procedure in the magistrates' court. It has been issued to quash the order of a magistrates' court where the charge stated in the information did not constitute an offence triable by such a court, and where the charge did not amount in law to the offence of which the defendant was convicted.[48] Certiorari will lie where an order is made which is not authorised by law,[49] or where the sentence is not authorised by law.[50]

Certiorari lies to quash a witness summons issued under section 77 of the Magistrates' Courts Act 1952[51]; also to quash an invalid committal for sentence under section 29 of that Act.[52] Bias is a matter of a jurisdiction, in respect of which certiorari will lie.[53]

---

[47] But see R. v. Northumberland Compensation Appeal Tribunal, ex p. Shaw [1951] 1 K.B. 711, at pp. 714–716, per Lord Goddard, C.J.

[48] R. v. Bolton [1841] 1 Q.B. 66.

[49] See, e.g. R. v. Highgate JJ., ex p. Petrou [1954] 1 W.L.R. 485; R. v. Arundel JJ., ex p. Jackson [1959] 2 Q.B. 89.

[50] R. v. Willesden JJ., ex p. Utley [1948] 1 K.B. 397 (fine exceeding maximum for the offence); R. v. East Grinstead JJ., ex p. Doeve [1969] 1 Q.B. 136. (justices purporting to exercise power under the Aliens Order, requiring foreign national to leave the country within a specified time); R. v. Birmingham JJ., ex p. Wyatt [1976] 1 W.L.R. 260 (sentence of imprisonment imposed in breach of s. 21 of the Powers of Criminal Courts Act 1973).

The High Court now has power, under the Administration of Justice Act 1960, to substitute a valid for an invalid sentence, so that the refinements argued in R. v. Arundel JJ., ex p. Jackson, supra, need not arise.

[51] R. v. Hove JJ., ex p. Donne (1967) 131 J.P. 460; R. v. Cheltenham JJ., ex p. Secretary of State for Trade [1977] 1 W.L.R. 95. A special procedure applies in relation to a witness summons issued under the Criminal Procedure (Attendance of Witnesses) Act 1965, s. 2, as to which see ibid. s. 3, and R. v. Lewes JJ., ex p. Gaming Board of Great Britain [1972] 1 Q.B. 232; on appeal sub nom. Gaming Board for Great Britain v. Rogers [1973] A.C. 388 H.L.

[52] See, e.g. the line of cases R. v. Kings Lynn JJ., ex p. Carter [1969] 1 Q.B. 488; R. v. Tower Bridge Magistrate, ex p. Osman [1971] 1 W.L.R. 1109; R. v. Lymm JJ., ex p. Browne [1973] 1 W.L.R. 1039; R. v. Hartlepool JJ., ex p. King [1973] Crim. L.R. 637; R. v. Rugby JJ., ex p. Prince [1974] 1 W.L.R. 736; R. v. Harlow JJ., ex p. Galway [1975] Crim. L.R. 288.

A committal for sentence of this nature cannot be challenged on appeal to the Crown Court, see ante, p. 7 or on appeal to the Criminal Division of the Court of Appeal, see p. 93, post, note 72.

[53] Any direct pecuniary or proprietary interest in the subject matter of the proceedings, however small, operates automatically to disqualify from membership of the bench. Apart from such circumstances, however, there must be a real likelihood of bias and not merely a suspicion of it, before certiorari will lie to quash the proceedings: see R. v. Rand (1866) L.R. 1 Q.B. 230; R. v. Hertfordshire JJ. [1911] 1 K.B. 512; R. v. Camborne JJ., ex p. Pearce [1955] 1 Q.B. 41; R. v. Pwllhelli JJ., ex p. Soane [1948] 2 All E.R. 815; R. v. Grimsby Recorder, ex p. Fuller [1956] 1 Q.B. 36; R. v. Altrincham JJ., ex p. Pennington [1975] Q.B. 549. Cf. R. v. McLean, ex p. Aikens (1974) 139 J.P. 261.

See generally Metropolitan Properties Ltd. v. Lannon [1969] 1 Q.B. 577, per Lord Denning, M.R. at pp. 598–600.

A judge or magistrate who has heard one case against a litigant cannot, without more, be said to be likely to be biased one way or the other in a subsequent case concerning the same litigant: see Re B. (T.A.) (An Infant) [1971] Ch. 270, per Megarry J., at pp. 277–278. This is particularly apposite in relation to stipendiary magistrates, see e.g. R. v. McElligott, ex p. Gallagher & Seal [1972] Crim. L.R. 332.

Analagous to a case of jurisdiction is a case involving the denial of natural justice,[54] which is more suitably challenged by an application for judicial review than by an appeal by way of case stated.[55] In general, the cases have turned upon the denial of justice by the court, but in the recent case of *R.* v. *Leyland Justices, ex p. Hawthorn*,[56] certiorari went to quash the decision of the magistrates' court, where the fault lay with the prosecutor.

Certiorari will lie to justices who purport to alter an adjudication once they are *functus officio*[57] or where the judgment of the Crown Court has been obtained by fraud[58] or on perjured evidence.[59] It will not lie on the ground that the inferior court was wrong in law, nor will it lie because the court has wrongly admitted or rejected evidence, or has misdirected itself as to the weight of the evidence,[60] nor apparently, even where there is no evidence to support the conviction.[61] Certiorari will not lie to quash a decision on the ground that the inferior court was wrong on matters of fact unless, possibly, where the facts are set out on the face of the record.[62] Certiorari does not lie to quash the decision of an inferior court merely on the ground that fresh evidence has come to light since the date of the hearing, which might affect the result.[63]

Certiorari to quash depends upon the fact of conviction[64]; it does not lie in respect of an acquittal[65]; nor does it lie to remove an order of examining justices refusing to commit for trial on indictment.[66]

---

[54] *R.* v. *Wandsworth JJ., ex p. Read* [1942] 1 K.B. 281.

   Most of the reported cases have turned on a situation where evidence, or possibly advice (see *R.* v. *Birmingham City JJ., ex p. Chris Foreign Foods (Wholesalers) Ltd.* [1970] 1 W.L.R. 1428) has been tendered to the court in the absence of one or both the parties: see, *e.g. R.* v. *Bucks JJ.* (1922) 86 J.P.N. 636; *R.* v. *Bodmin JJ., ex p. McEwen* [1947] (witness interviewed in justices' private room); *R.* v. *East Kerrier JJ., ex p. Mundy* [1952] 2 Q.B. 719 (police officer handing document to court clerk who then retired with the justices). See also *Hill* v. *Tothill* [1936] W.N. 126; *Davies* v. *Griffiths* [1937] 2 All E.R. 671; *R.* v. *Stafford JJ., ex p. Ross* [1962] 1 W.L.R. 456; *R.* v. *Aberdare JJ., ex p. Hones* [1973] Crim. L.R. 45 (justices interviewing social worker in their room).

   Other cases have turned on the retirement of the clerk with the justices. It is now settled law that the justices' clerk should not retire with the bench as a matter of course (*R.* v. *Consett JJ., ex p. Postal Bingo Ltd.* [1967] 2 Q.B. 9) but should remain in court unless the justices return to court, or send for him (*R.* v. *Barry (Glamorgan) Justices, ex p. Nagi Kashim* [1953] 1 W.L.R. 1320). It is, of course, otherwise where the justices really require his advice on a question of law (*R.* v. *Welshpool JJ., ex p. Holley* [1953] 2 Q.B. 403; *Ex p. How* [1953] 1 W.L.R. 480). It is, however, improper for the clerk to hand up a note setting out the arguments on the facts before the justices retire (*R.* v. *Stafford JJ., ex p. Ross, supra*).

   As to the unreasonable refusal of an adjournment, see *R.* v. *Thames Magistrates' Court, ex p. Polemis* [1974] 1 W.L.R. 1371.

[55] See *ante*, p. 25.

[56] [1979] 2 W.L.R. 28.

[57] *R.* v. *Essex JJ., ex p. Final* [1963] 2 Q.B. 816, and the cases considered there. The cases must, however, be read in the light of the provisions of s. 41 of the Criminal Justice Act 1972, as amended by the Criminal Law Act 1977, s. 65, Sched. 12.

[58] *R.* v. *Gillyard* (1848) 12 Q.B.D. 527.

[59] *R.* v. *Recorder of Leicester, ex p. Wood* [1947] K.B. 726. *Cf. R.* v. *Ashford JJ., ex p. Richley (No. 2)* [1956] 1 Q.B. 167.

[60] *R.* v. *Nat Bell Liquors* [1922] A.C. 128 P.C.; also *R.* v. *Northumberland Compensation Appeal Tribunal, ex p. Shaw* [1952] 1 K.B. 338; *Davies* v. *Price* [1958] 1 W.L.R. 434.

[61] See, however, as to challenging such an issue by way of case stated, *ante*, p. 25.

[62] *R.* v. *Birmingham Compensation Appeal Tribunal* [1952] 2 All E.R. 100.

[63] *R.* v. *West Sussex Quarter Sessions, ex p. Johnson (Albert & Maud) Trust* [1974] Q.B. 188.

[64] *R.* v. *Campbell, ex p. Nomikos* [1956] 1 W.L.R. 622.

[65] *R.* v. *Simpson* [1914] 1 K.B. 66.

[66] See the Irish cases of *R.* v. *Roscommon Justices* (1894) 2 I.R. 158; *R.* v. *Galway County Justices* (1904) 43 I.L.T. 185.

Certiorari on the ground of lack of jurisdiction will be refused where the applicant has appealed against his conviction, since the act of appealing implies an acceptance of that jurisdiction.[67] Where a defendant is convicted in a magistrates' court and that conviction is quashed by the Crown Court on appeal, certiorari will lie, in a proper case, to remove the appeal decision.[68]

Certiorari, being a discretionary remedy, will not ordinarily lie where there has been an unequivocal and accepted plea of guilty to a valid charge in summary proceedings.[69] Where the High Court quashes an order, however, other convictions based on that order may be quashed in the exercise of ancillary relief, even though the defendant pleaded guilty.[70]

There is no comparable rule to that in the case of mandamus,[71] that certiorari will not lie unless there is no other effective remedy.[72] Where the requisite grounds for its issue exist, it will lie, even though a right of appeal be conferred by statute.[73]

(6) Order of prohibition

Prohibition lies to restrain an inferior court from assuming a jurisdiction which it does not have; it lies to a magistrates' court and to the Crown Court in the exercise of its appellate jurisdiction, to prohibit the court from proceeding further in excess of its jurisdiction.

Prohibition lies, not only where there is an excess of jurisdiction[74] but also where there is a radical departure from the well known principles of natural justice.[75] It will therefore lie where the judge of an inferior court is biased, or interested in the subject matter of the proceedings[76] or where the court unlawfully purports to alter its adjudication.[77]

The fact that justices have power to state a case on an issue relating to jurisdiction does not prevent prohibition issuing.[78]

An order of prohibition will lie as soon as the inferior court purports to apply a wrong principle of law in deciding upon its jurisdiction.

---

[67] R. v. Pereira, ex p. Khotoo Basawab [1949] W.N. 96.
[68] See Halsbury's Laws of England (4th ed.), Vol. 11, para. 1529, text to note 10.
[69] R. v. Guest, ex p. Anthony [1964] 1 W.L.R. 1273 (overruled on another point in S (an Infant) v. Manchester Recorder [1971] A.C. 481. See also R. v. Sheridan [1937] 1 K.B. 223; R. v. Stafford JJ., ex p. Stafford Corporation [1940] 2 K.B. 33; R. v. Campbell, ex p. Nomikos [1956] 1 W.L.R. 622; R. v. Essex JJ., ex p. Final [1963] 2 Q.B. 816; R. v. Burnham (Bucks) JJ. [1959] 1 W.L.R. 1043. But see R. v. Eastbourne JJ., ex p. Barsoum [1979] 2 C.L. 41.
[70] R. v. Middleton, Bromley and Bexley JJ., ex p. Collins [1970] 1 Q.B. 216: also McVitie v. Marsden [1917] 2 K.B. 878.
[71] See ante, p. 40.
[72] See R. v. Middleton, Bromley and Bexley JJ., ex p. Collins [1970] 1 Q.B. 216; R. v. Brighton JJ., ex p. Robinson [1973] 1 W.L.R. 69.
[73] See R. v. Patents Appeal Tribunal, ex p. Geigy S.A. [1963] 2 Q.B. 728; also R. v. Hove JJ., ex p. Donne [1967] 2 All E.R. 1253n.
[74] R. v. Swansea Income Tax Commissioners, ex p. English Crown Smelter Co. [1925] 2 K.B. 250.
[75] R. v. North, ex p. Oakey [1927] 1 K.B. 491.
[76] See ante, p. 43, for bias.
[77] R. v. Wilson, ex p. Neil, The Times, April 18, 1953, D.C.
[78] R. v. Wimbledon JJ., ex p. Derwent [1953] 1 Q.B. 380.

2. THE APPLICATION FOR LEAVE

(1) General

An application for an order of mandamus, certiorari or prohibition is made by way of an application for judicial review.[79]

The application is made in two stages. It is first necessary to obtain the leave of the court, and only if, and to the extent that such leave is granted, will the High Court hear the substantive application for judicial review.

(2) Application for leave

No application for judicial review may be made unless leave is granted.[80] An application for leave is made *ex parte* to a Divisional Court of the Queen's Bench Division of the High Court, except in vacation when it may be made to a judge in chambers.[81] The application must be supported by a statement setting out the name and description of the applicant, the relief sought, and the grounds on which it is sought, and must be supported by affidavits, to be filed before the application is made, verifying the facts relied on.[82]

The applicant must give notice of the application to the Crown Office not later than the day before the application is made and must, at the same time, lodge in the Crown Office copies of the statement and any affidavit in support.[83]

On an application for judicial review, any relief, whether an order of mandamus, certiorari or prohibition may be claimed as an alternative, or in addition, to any other relief claimed, if it arises on, or relates to, or is connected with, the same matter.[84]

The court will not grant leave unless it considers that the applicant has a sufficient interest in the matters to which the application relates.[85]

Where leave is sought to apply for an order of certiorari to remove, for the purpose of being quashed, any judgment, order or conviction, or other proceeding which is subject to an appeal, and a time is limited for the bringing

---

[79] The new O. 53 of the R.S.C. (as substituted by S.I. 1977 No. 1955) creates an entirely new procedure. In a single application, called an application for judicial review, an applicant may apply for any of the prerogative orders, whether single or in the alternative, without having to select the particular order appropriate to his case.

[80] Administration of Justice (Miscellaneous Provisions) Act 1938, s. 10; R.S.C., O. 53, r. 3 (1). In *R.* v. *Newcastle-under-Lyme JJ., ex p. Whitehouse* [1952] 2 All E.R. 531n, the court made a peremptory order on the application for leave, the irregularities in the conviction under review having been admitted on affidavit.

[81] R.S.C., O. 53, r. 3 (2).

[82] R.S.C., O. 53, r. 3 (2). For suggested form of statement, see 14 Court Forms (2nd. Ed.) 66, Form 14; 70, Form 22; 74, Form 28. For suggested forms of supporting affidavit, see *ibid*. 76–80, Forms 31–37. The facts should be stated in the affidavit: see *R.* v. *Wandsworth JJ., ex p. Read* [1942] 1 K.B. 281; also *R.* v. *Pratt, ex p. Rigau* [1954] Crim. L.R. 551. The statement should contain no more than the rule requires; but it is not enough to lodge a statement of all the facts verified by an affidavit: *Practice Note* [1948] W.N. 267.

The statement may be amended with leave on the hearing of the application, whether by specifying different or additional grounds of relief, or otherwise, as the court thinks fit: R.S.C., O. 53, r. 3 (4).

[83] O. 53, r. 3 (3).

[84] O. 53, r. 2.

[85] O. 53, r. 3 (5).

of the appeal, the court may adjourn the application for leave to apply for judicial review until the appeal is determined, or the time for appealing has expired.[86]

If the High Court grants leave, it may impose such terms as to costs and as to giving security, as it thinks fit.[87] The court or judge may also order short, simple and urgent cases to be entered in the "expedited hearing list."[88]

(3) "Expedited hearing list"

Where leave is given to move for a prerogative order, the court may direct that the motion be entered in the "expedited hearing list."[89]

If such a direction is given, the court will nominate the week, usually two clear weeks ahead, in which the motion will be heard. The applicant should at once inform the respondent of the court's directions, should supply him with copies of the papers used in the application for leave and agree, where possible, the date or dates convenient to all parties, being a date or dates in the nominated week.[90]

The notice of motion should be entered for hearing in the Crown Office as soon as practicable[91] and the return date shown in the notice should be the actual date fixed for the hearing, or if that date is not yet known, the Monday in the week nominated by the court for the hearing.[92]

(4) Delay in applying for relief

Where in any case[93] the High Court considers that there has been undue delay in making an application for judicial review, it may refuse to grant leave for the making of an application, or any relief sought on the application if, in its opinion, the granting of the relief sought would be likely to cause substantial hardship to, or substantially prejudice the rights of, any person or would be detrimental to sound administration.[94] In the case of certiorari it will be regarded as unreasonable delay if the application is made three months after the date of the proceedings.[95]

In general, no specific time limit is fixed within which an application for leave must be made in respect of an order of mandamus, but except in those cases where the delay is accounted for, it will not be granted unless applied for

---

[86] O. 53, r. 3 (6).
[87] O. 53, r. 3 (7).
[88] See below.
[89] *Practice Direction (Expedited Hearing List)* [1974] 1 W.L.R. 1219, para. 31. See also *ante*, p. 35
[90] If informed of a convenient date the Head Clerk of the Crown Office will take it into account in fixing the date of the hearing.
[91] See O. 53, r. 3 (2).
[92] *Practice Direction (Expedited Hearing List) supra*, para. (3). As to an application by a person dissatisfied with such a decision, see *ibid*. para. (6) and *ante*, p. 35.
[93] Without prejudice to any statutory provisions which have the effect of limiting the time within which an application may be made.
[94] O. 53, r. 4 (1). See *R. v. Inner London Crown Court, ex p. London Borough of Greenwich* [1975] 2 W.L.R. 310 at pp. 314, 315; also *R. v. Aston University Senate, ex p. Roffey* [1969] 2 Q.B. 538; *R. v. Herrod, ex p. Leeds City Council* [1976] Q.B. 540.
[95] O. 53, r. 4 (2).

within a reasonable time.[96] There is, of course, no time limit for applying for an order of prohibition provided that there is still something left to prohibit.

(5) Stay of proceedings

Where leave to apply for judicial review is granted, and the relief sought is an order of prohibition, or an order of certiorari, and the court so directs, the grant of leave will operate as a stay of the proceedings to which the application relates until the determination of the application or until the court otherwise directs.[97]

(6) Refusal of leave

Where an application for leave to apply for judicial review is refused by a judge in chambers the applicant may make a fresh application to a Divisional Court.[98] Such an application must be made within 10 days after the judge's refusal or, if a Divisional Court does not sit within that period, on the first day on which it sits after that.[99]

3. BAIL; LEGAL AID

(1) Bail

The High Court may grant bail to a person who has been convicted or sentenced by a magistrates' court and has applied for an order of certiorari to remove the proceedings into the High Court, or who has applied for leave to make such an application.[1] Justices have no power to grant bail to a convicted person pending a review of their conviction by certiorari.[2]

The High Court may also grant bail to a person who has applied to the High Court for an order of certiorari to remove proceedings from the Crown Court in his case into the High Court, or has applied for leave to make such an application.[3]

Where the High Court grants bail, the time at which the appellant is to appear in the event of the conviction being quashed, is such time within 10 days after the judgment of the High Court has been given, as may be specified by the High Court,[4] and the place at which he must appear in that event is a magistrates' court acting for the same petty sessions area as the court which convicted or sentenced him.[4]

---

[96] O. 53,r. 4 (1).
[97] O. 53, r. 3 (10).
[98] O. 53, r. 3 (8).
[99] O. 53, r. 3 (9). An appeal from a decision of a Divisional Court in a criminal cause or matter lies to the House of Lords under the Administration of Justice Act 1960, s. 1 (for which see pp. 102–116, *post*) and not to the Court of Appeal.
[1] Criminal Justice Act 1948, s. 37 (1) (*d*) as substituted by the Bail Act 1976, s. 12 Sched. 2, para. 11 (3).
[2] *Ex p. Blyth* [1944] 1 All E.R. 587. See also *Practice Note* [1946] W.N. 103.
[3] Criminal Justice Act 1948, s. 37 (1) (*b*); Bail Act 1976, s. 12, Sched. 2, para. 11 (2).
[4] Criminal Justice Act 1948, s. 37 (1A) as inserted by the Bail Act 1976, s. 12, Sched. 2, para. 11 (4).

The time during which such a person is released on bail does not count as part of any term of imprisonment under his sentence, and any sentence of imprisonment imposed by a magistrates' court, or on appeal, by the Crown Court, after the imposition of which a person is thus released on bail, is deemed to begin to run or to be resumed as from the day on which he is received in prison under the sentence; for this purpose "prison" is deemed to include a detention centre.[5]

(2) Legal aid

There are no provisions in Part II of the Legal Aid Act 1974, in relation to applications for judicial review similar to those authorising solicitor or counsel assigned to a defendant in a magistrates' court or the Crown Court, to give advice and assistance on whether there appear to be reasonable grounds of appeal, and for giving notice of appeal.[6]

An application for legal aid in connection with an application for judicial review must be made under the provisions of Part I of the Legal Aid Act 1974, to the appropriate Area Committee of the Law Society.

4. LEAVE GRANTED; APPLYING FOR THE ORDER

(1) Making the application

Once leave has been granted to make an application for judicial review, the application is made by originating motion to a Divisional Court of the Queen's Bench Division, except in vacation when it may be made by originating summons to a judge in chambers.[7]

Where leave was granted by the Divisional Court and that court so directs, the application for the order may be made by motion to a single judge sitting in open court,[8] or, if so directed[9] by originating summons to a judge in chambers.[10]

(2) Service of motion or summons

A notice of motion or summons[11] must be served on all persons directly affected, and where it relates to any proceedings in or before a court, and the object of the application is either to compel an officer of the court to do any act in relation to the proceedings, or to quash them or any order made in them, the notice or summons must also be served on the clerk of the court, and where an objection is made to the conduct of the judge, on the judge also.[12]

---

[5] Criminal Justice Act 1948, s. 37 (6).
[6] See *ante*, pp. 13, 31.
[7] O. 53, r. 5 (1). Suggested forms of notice are to be found at 14 Court Forms (2nd. Ed.) Forms 48–52.
[8] See, *e.g. R.* v. *Secretary of State for the Environment, ex p. Stewart, The Times*, April 21, 1978.
[9] Without prejudice to O. 22, r. 13.
[10] O. 53, r. 5 (2).
[11] Copies of the statement supporting the application must be served with the notice: O. 53, r. 6 (1).
[12] O. 53, r. 5 (3).

Unless the court granting leave directed otherwise, there must be at least 10 days between the service of the notice of motion or summons and the day named in it for the hearing.[13] The motion must be entered for hearing within 14 days after the grant of leave.[14]

An affidavit giving the names and addresses of, and the places and dates of service on, all persons who have been served with the notice of motion or summons must be filed before the motion or summons is entered for hearing. If any person who ought to have been served has not been served, the affidavit must state the fact and the reasons for it, and the affidavit will be before the court on the hearing of the motion or summons.[15]

If, on the hearing of the motion or summons, the court is of opinion that a person who ought to have been served[16] has not been served, it may adjourn the hearing on such terms, if any, as it it may direct in order that the notice or summons may be served on that person.[17]

(3) Claim for damages

On an application for judicial review the High Court may award damages to the applicant provided that (a) he has included in the statement in support of his application a claim for damages arising from any matter to which the application relates and (b) the court is satisfied that, if the claim had been made in an action begun by the applicant at the time of making his application, he would have been awarded damages.[18]

(4) Statements and affidavits

Copies of the statement in support of the application must be served with the notice of motion or summons and, subject to the court allowing any amendment,[19] no grounds may be relied upon or any relief sought at the hearing except the grounds and relief set out in the statement.[20] The court may, at the hearing, allow the applicant to amend his statement, whether by specifying different or additional grounds of relief or otherwise, on such terms, if any, as it thinks fit, and may allow further affidavits to be used if they deal with new matters arising out of an affidavit of any other party to the application.[21] Where the applicant intends to ask to be allowed to amend his statement or affidavit or to use further affidavits, he must give notice of his intention and of any proposed amendment to any other party.[22]

Each party to the application must supply to every other party, on demand, and on payment of the proper charges, copies of every affidavit which he

---

[13] O. 53, r. 5 (4).
[14] O. 53, r. 5 (5).
[15] O. 53, r. 5 (6).
[16] Whether under O. 53, r. 5 or otherwise.
[17] O. 53, r. 5 (7).
[18] O. 53, r. 7. O. 18, r. 12 applies to a statement of claim for damages as it applies to a pleading.
[19] See below.
[20] O. 53, r. 6 (1).
[21] O. 53, r. 6 (2).
[22] O. 53, r. 6 (3).

proposes to use at the hearing, including in the case of the applicant, the affidavit in support of his application for leave.[23]

(5) Lodging of order, etc., in case of certiorari

Where the relief sought is, or includes, an order of certiorari to remove proceedings for the purpose of quashing them, the applicant may not question the validity of any order, warrant, commitment, conviction or record unless, before the hearing of the motion or summons, he has lodged in the Crown Office a copy of it, verified by affidavit, or accounts for his failure to do so to the satisfaction of the court hearing the motion or summons.[24]

(6) Discovery; interrogatories; cross-examination

The making of interlocutory applications such as those for discovery of documents[25] and interrogatories,[26] and orders for the deponent of an affidavit to attend for cross-examination[27] are now introduced into applications for judicial review. An application of this nature may, unless the High Court otherwise directs, be made to a judge or a Master of the Queen's Bench Division, notwithstanding that the application for judicial review was made by motion and is to be heard by a Divisional Court.[28]

5. REPRESENTATION OF JUSTICES

Whenever the decision of justices is called in question in any superior court of common law by a rule to show cause or by other process issued upon an *ex parte* application, it is lawful for any such justice[29] to make and file an affidavit in such court[30] setting forth the grounds of the decision so brought under review and any fact which he considers to have a material bearing upon the question at issue.[31]

Whenever such an affidavit has been filed, the Divisional Court, before determining the matter so as to overrule or set aside the order or decision of the justices, must take into consideration the matters set forth in the affidavit or affidavits, notwithstanding that no counsel appears on behalf of the justices.[32]

---

[23] O. 53, r. 6 (4).
[24] O. 53, r. 9 (2). See also *Practice Note* (1948) W.N. 207; and *R.* v. *Newington Licensing Justices* [1948] 1 K.B. 6811
[25] R.S.C., O. 24.
[26] *Ibid*. O. 26.
[27] *Ibid*. O. 38, r. 2 (3).
[28] O. 53, r. 8. An "interlocutory application" includes an application under Orders 24.26, or O. 38, r. 2 (3) for an order dismissing the proceedings by consent of the parties.
[29] The affidavit must be made by one of the justices, not by the clerk: *R.* v. *Sperling* (1873) 37 J.P.N. 87. Justices who dissented from the majority decision have no right to make affidavits or to appear: *R.* v. *Waddingham (Gloucestershire) JJ. and Tastin* (1896) 60 J.P.N. 372.
[30] The clerk to the justices should send it to "C.O. & A." Department of the High Court.
[31] Review of Justices Decisions Act 1872, s. 2. See *R.* v. *Daejan Properties, ex p. Merton London Borough Council, The Times,* April 25, 1978, D.C. No fee is payable for filing.
[32] *Ibid*. s. 3.

Cross-examination on such an affidavit is allowed[33] but it has always been treated as exceptional.[34]

Unless some attack is made on the justices, as that they have acted improperly by showing bias, or have misconducted themselves, they should not appear by counsel on an application for judicial review. They should take advantage of the provisions of the Review of Justices' Decisions Act 1872; if they do more they will not get their costs.[35] If they avail themselves of the provisions of the Act they do not make themselves liable for costs; if they choose to appear they make themselves parties to the *lis* and take the risk of being ordered to pay costs, although they are, of course, entitled to receive costs if they succeed in defeating the application.[36]

6. HEARING BEFORE THE DIVISIONAL COURT

(1) The hearing

The hearing in the Divisional Court follows the usual pattern for such hearings.[37] It is the practice for cases involving the issue of the prerogative orders to be moved by counsel,[38] but from time to time the court permits an application to be made by a litigant in person.[39] It is the practice to hear one counsel only on either side; counsel in support of the application begins and has a right of reply.[40] Any person who desires to be heard in opposition to the motion and who appears to be a proper person to be heard, must be heard notwithstanding that he has not been served with notice of it.[41]

(2) Evidence

The practice has always been for the application to be decided on affidavit evidence[42]; it remains to be seen whether the new Order 53 will result in witnesses actually being called at the hearing.

Where certiorari is sought on the ground of error of law on the face of the record the court will not admit any extraneous evidence; the error must be apparent from the record itself.[43] Where certiorari is sought on the ground of absence or excess of jurisdiction, bias by interest, fraud or breach of natural

---

[33] R.S.C., O. 59, r. 47.
[34] See *R.* v. *Kent JJ., ex p. Smith* (1928) W.N. 137, at p. 138; also *R.* v. *Stokesley (Yorkshire) JJ., ex p. Bartram* [1956] 1 W.L.R. 254, *per* Lord Goddard C.J.
[35] *R.* v. *Camborne JJ., ex p. Pearce* [1955] 1 Q.B. 41, *per* Lord Goddard C.J.; *R.* v. *Marlow (Bucks) JJ., ex p. Schiller* as reported in [1957] 2 All E.R. 783, at p. 784, *per* Lord Goddard C.J.
[36] *R.* v. *Llanidloes Licensing JJ., ex p. Davies* [1957] 2 All E.R. 610; also *R.* v. *Kingston upon Hull Rent Tribunal, ex p. Black* [1949] 1 All E.R. 260.
[37] See *ante*, pp. 35–38.
[38] *Ex p. Wallace* [1902] 2 K.B. 488.
[39] *Practice Note* (1947) W.N. 218.
[40] *R.* v. *Bunne, ex p. Sinnate* [1943] K.B. 516.
[41] O. 53, r. 9 (1).
[42] And see *ante*, p. 36.
[43] *R.* v. *Nat Bell Liquors* [1922] A.C. 128, at p. 155, 156; *R.* v. *Northumberland Compensation Appeal Tribunal, ex p. Shaw* [1952] 1 K.B. 338 at pp. 342, 343; *R.* v. *Agricultural Land Tribunal*

justice, clearly these are matters which require to be dealt with by extraneous evidence,[44] if such matters are not apparent from the record.

Where mandamus or prohibition are sought, affidavit evidence will be required to bring out the facts constituting the ground of the application.[45] Again, where mandamus is sought, affidavit evidence will be admitted to show that the inferior court has refused to exercise its jurisdiction, or has been influenced by extraneous matters, or has failed to consider relevant matters.[46]

(3) Powers of the court

In general it may be said that the powers of the court extend to either issuing the appropriate prerogative order or refusing to issue it. The circumstances in which a particular order will or will not issue are dealt with under the particular order concerned.[47]

Where an order of certiorari is issued, the order will ordinarily direct that the proceedings of the court below be quashed forthwith on their removal into the Queen's Bench Division.[48] Where a conviction is quashed in respect of which a sentence of imprisonment was imposed and the applicant is still serving the sentence, the order of the court will direct that he be discharged forthwith from custody in respect of that sentence.[49]

Where the relief sought is an order of certiorari and the court is satisfied that there are grounds for quashing the decision to which the application relates, it has power in addition to quashing the decision, to remit the matter to the court concerned with a direction to reconsider it and reach a decision in accordance with the findings of the Divisional Court.[50]

Where a person who has been sentenced for an offence by a magistrates' court or, on appeal against conviction or sentence, by the Crown Court, applies for an order of certiorari, and the High Court determines that the lower court had no power to pass the sentence, the High Court may, instead of quashing the conviction, amend it by substituting for the sentence passed any sentence which the magistrates' court had power to impose.[51]

---

for South Eastern Area, ex p. Bracey [1960] 1 W.L.R. 911. See also *R. v. Southampton JJ., ex p. Green* [1975] 3 W.L.R. 277; *R. v. Southampton JJ., ex p. Corker* (1976), *The Times*, February 12, D.C.

[44] *R. v. Northumberland Compensation Appeal Tribunal, supra.*

[45] See *R. v. Fulham, Hammersmith and Kensington Rent Tribunal ex p. Hierowski* [1953] 2 Q.B. 1471

[46] *Ibid.* but *cf. R. v. Agricultural Land Tribunal for South Eastern Area, ex p. Bracey, supra.*

[47] See *ante*, pp. 40–45.

[48] O. 53, r. 9 (3).

[49] Notification of the order is given forthwith to the Under-Secretary of State, Home Office, by the "C.O. and A" department. (Direction of Lord Goddard C.J., February 5, 1947).

[50] O. 53, r. 9 (4). See the observations of Denning L.J. in *R. v. Northumberland Compensation Appeal Tribunal* [1952] 1 K.B. 338 at p. 347.

[51] Administration of Justice Act 1960, as amended, s. 16 (1). See, *e.g. R. v. Billericay Justices, ex p. Rumsey* [1978] Crim. L.R. 305.

Such a sentence begins to run, unless the High Court otherwise directs, from the time when it would have begun to run in the proceedings of the court below; any time during which the offender was at large after being released on bail, being disregarded: Administration of Justice Act 1960, s. 16 (2). As to the award of costs out of central funds to any party to proceedings before the Divisional Court, see *ante*, pp. 37, 38.

PART IV

APPLICATIONS TO THE HIGH COURT FOR BAIL

(1) General

While no appeal as such lies from any decision of a court in relation to bail in criminal proceedings, where a magistrates' court withholds bail in such proceedings, or imposes conditions in granting bail, the High Court is empowered to grant bail or vary the conditions.[1] Where the High Court grants bail in these circumstances, it may direct him to appear at a time and place which the magistrates' court could have directed, and the recognisance of a surety will be conditioned accordingly.[2]

The High Court may also grant bail to a person who, after the decision of his case by the Crown Court sitting in its appellate jurisdiction, has applied for the statement of a case for the opinion of the High Court on that decision,[3] or to a person who has been convicted or sentenced by a magistrates' court and applies for an order of certiorari to remove those proceedings into the High Court[4] or a person who applies for an order of certiorari to remove proceedings from the Crown Court into the High Court.[5]

An application for bail pending the determination of an appeal to the Criminal Division of the Court of Appeal is made to that court and not to a judge of the High Court.[6]

(2) Making the application

An application to the High Court in respect of bail in criminal proceedings is made, where the defendant is in custody, by summons[7] before a judge in chambers, to show cause why he should not be granted bail, or where he has already been granted bail, by summons[8] to show cause why some variation in the arrangements for bail proposed by the defendant should not be made.[9] Every such application must be accompanied by an affidavit.

[1] Criminal Justice Act 1967, s. 22 as amended.
[2] *Ibid.* s. 22 (2). The ancillary provisions contained in the Criminal Justice Act 1948, s. 37 (4) and (6) (for which see *ante*, p. 48) apply in relation to bail granted under these provisions: Criminal Justice Act 1967, s. 22 (3). Again, where a person appeals to the Crown Court under the Magistrates' Courts (Appeals from the Binding Over Orders) Act 1956 (see *ante*, p. 2), in relation to a person in custody for failure to comply with an order, so much of s. 37 of the Criminal Justice Act 1948 as relates to the release of a *convicted* person pending his appeal, applies as if the appeal were an appeal against conviction: Magistrates' Courts (Appeals from Binding Over Orders) Act 1956, s. 1 (2) (*b*).
from Binding Over Orders) Act 1956, s. 1 (2) (*b*).
[3] Criminal Justice Act 1948, s. 37 (1) (*a*) as amended, see *ante*, p. 32.
[4] Criminal Justice Act 1948, s. 37 (1) (*d*) as substituted by the Bail Act 1976, s. 12, Sched. 2, para. 11 (3), see *ante*, p. 48.
[5] Criminal Justice Act 1948, s. 37 (1) (*b*); Bail Act 1976, s. 12, Sched. 2, para. 11 (2).
[6] See p. 71, *post.*
[7] The summons must be in Form 97, set out in the Sched. to R.S.C., O. 79, and in Appendix E, *post*, No. 1.
[8] The summons must be in Form 97A, set out in the Sched. to R.S.C., O. 79, and Appendix E, *post*, No. 2.
[9] R.S.C., O. 79, r. 9 (1) as amended by S.I. 1967 No. 1809; S.I. 1971 No. 1955; S.I. 1978 No. 251.

(3) Assignment of Official Solicitor

Where a defendant in custody who desires to apply for bail is unable, through lack of means, to instruct a solicitor, he may give notice to the judge in chambers stating his desire to apply for bail and requesting that the Official Solicitor act for him in the application, and the judge, may, if he thinks fit, assign the Official Solicitor to act for him accordingly.[10] Where the Official Solicitor has been assigned, the judge may, if he thinks fit, dispense with the requirements for a summons, notice and affidavit[11] and may deal with the application in a summary manner.[12]

(4) Service of summons

The summons[13] must, at least 24 hours before the day named in it for the hearing, be served, where the application is made by the defendant, on the prosecutor and on the Director of Public Prosecutions if the prosecution is being carried on by him, or where the application is made by the prosecutor or by a constable,[14] on the defendant.[15]

(5) Grant of application

Where the judge in chambers, before whom an application for bail in criminal proceedings is heard, grants the defendant bail, a copy of the order[16] will be transmitted forthwith, where the defendant has been committed to the Crown Court for trial, or for sentence or to be otherwise dealt with, to the appropriate officer of the Crown Court, and, in any other case, to the clerk of the court which committed the defendant.[17]

A copy of any order made by a judge in chambers varying the arrangements under which a defendant has been granted bail[18] will be sent to the same persons, in the same manner.[19]

(6) Recognisances and other requirements

The recognisances of any surety required as a condition of bail granted, may, where the defendant is in prison or some other place of detention, be entered into before the governor or keeper of the prison, as well as before any of those person specified in the Bail Act 1976.[20]

Where the judge in chambers imposes[21] any requirement to be complied with before a person's release on bail, he may give directions as to the manner

---

[10] R.S.C., O. 79, r. 9 (4).
[11] *i.e.* the requirements of *ibid*. O. 79, r. 9 (1)–(3).
[12] R.S.C., O. 79, r. 9 (5). *Cf.* the provisions for the assignment of the Official Solicitor at the Crown Court, *ante*, p. 11.
[13] In Form 97 or 97A, as appropriate, see Appendix E, *post*, Nos. 1 and 2.
[14] *i.e.* under the Bail Act 1976, s. 3 (8).
[15] R.S.C., O. 79, r. 9 (2).
[16] In Form 98 set out in Appendix A to O. 79, and Appendix E, *post*, No. 3.
[17] R.S.C., O. 79, r. 9 (6).
[18] Set out in Form 98A as contained in Sched. A to O. 79, and the Appendix E, *post*, No. 4.
[19] R.S.C., O. 79, r. 9 (10).
[20] *i.e.* in section 8 (4) of the Bail Act 1976: R.S.C., O. 79, r. 9 (6) (*a*).
[21] Under the Bail Act 1976, s. 3 (5) or (6).

in which, and the person or persons before whom, the requirement is to be complied with.[22]

A person who, in pursuance of an order for the grant of bail made by a judge in chambers, proposes to enter into a recognisance, or give security[23] must, unless the judge otherwise directs, give notice[24] to the prosecutor at least 24 hours before he enters into the recognisance or complies with the requirement.[25]

Where a recognisance is entered into, or a requirement complied with, before any person, it is the duty of that person to cause the recognisance, or as the case may be, a statement of the requirement complied with, to be transmitted forthwith, where the defendant has been committed to the Crown Court for trial, or to be sentenced or otherwise dealt with, to the appropriate officer of the Crown Court, or in any other case, to the clerk of the court which committed him, and a copy of the recognisance or statement, must, at the same time, be sent to the governor or keeper of the prison or other place of detention in which the defendant is detained, unless the recognisance was entered into or the requirement complied with before such person.[26]

(7) Refusal of bail

An appellant who is refused bail in criminal proceedings by the judge in chambers has no right to make a fresh application to any other judge or to a Divisional Court.[27]

(8) Record of bail

The record required to be made[28] by the High Court is made by including in the file relating to the case in question a copy of the relevant order of the court[29] which will contain the particulars set out in the particular form, whichever is applicable, except that in the case of a decision to withhold bail, the record is made by including a statement of the decision in the court's copy of the relevant summons and including it in the file relating to the case in question.[30]

(9) Enforcement proceedings

Where, in pursuance of an order of a judge in chambers or the Crown Court, a person is released on bail in criminal proceedings, pending the determination of an appeal to the High Court or the House of Lords, or an application for an order of certiorari, then, upon the abandonment of the appeal or application, or upon the decision of the High Court or the House of

---

[22] R.S.C., O. 79, r. 9 (6B).
[23] In accordance with section 3 (5) of the Bail Act 1976.
[24] In form 100 contained in Appendix A to O. 79, and in Appendix E, *post*, No. 5.
[25] R.S.C., O. 79, r. 9 (7).
[26] *Ibid*. O. 79, r. 9 (8).
[27] R.S.C., O. 79, r. 9 (12).
[28] By s. 5 of the Bail Act 1976.
[29] *i.e.* Form 98 or 98A contained in Appendix A to O. 79, and Appendix E, *post*, Nos. 3 and 4.
[30] R.S.C., O. 79, r. 9 (13).

Lords being given, any justice acting for the same petty sessions as the magistrates' court by which the person was convicted or sentenced, may issue process for enforcing the decision in respect of which the appeal or application was brought, or as the case may be, enforcing the decision of the High Court or the House of Lords.[31]

---

[31] *Ibid*. O. 79, r. 9 (11).

PART V

APPEALS FROM THE CROWN COURT TO THE CRIMINAL DIVISION OF THE COURT OF APPEAL

1. GENERAL PROVISIONS

(1) General

The jurisdiction of the Criminal Division of the Court of Appeal is wholly statutory[1] and the court has no powers other than those conferred by statute.[2]

Appeal lies to the Criminal Division only from the Crown Court; it does not lie from a conviction in a magistrates' court[3] or against a sentence imposed in a magistrates' court. Appeal does not lie to the Criminal Division from a decision of the Crown Court in its appellate jurisdiction.[4]

Appeal to the Criminal Division is by way of argument. It does not take the form of a rehearing, and evidence is heard only in the most exceptional circumstances.[5] The court regards itself as bound by its own previous decisions unless previous decisions conflict, or are in conflict with a decision of the House of Lords, or, applying the *ratio* of *Young* v. *Bristol Aeroplane Co.*,[5a] appear to have been given *per incuriam*. In *R.* v. *Gould*[6] the court departed from a previous decision on the basis that the law had previously been misapplied or misunderstood.

Because of the need for certainty in the criminal law, it is the practice for only one judgment to be given unless the question is one of law and the presiding judge is of opinion that separate judgments would be convenient.[7]

(2) Rights of appeal

Appeal lies to the Criminal Division of the Court of Appeal: (a) by a person convicted on indictment in the Crown Court,[8] against his conviction[9]; (b) by a

---

[1] See the Criminal Appeal Acts 1964, 1966 and 1968 and the Rules of Court made under the Supreme Court of Judicature (Consolidation) Act 1925, s. 99, the Criminal Appeal Act 1964, s. 2 (5), and the Criminal Appeal Act 1968, s. 46.
[2] *R.* v. *Jefferies* [1969] 1 Q.B. 120.
[3] The conviction of an incorrigible rogue committed to the Crown Court under the Vagrancy Act 1824 is a conviction in the magistrates' court and no appeal lies to the Criminal Division against it: *R.* v. *Johnson* [1909] 1 K.B. 439, but see p. 93, *post*.
[4] As to case stated see *ante*, pp. 32–35.
[5] See pp. 89 *et seq*.
[5a] [1944] K.B. 718.
[6] [1968] 2 Q.B. 65.
[7] An example is *R.* v. *Head* (1958) 41 Cr. App. R. 249.
[8] All proceedings on indictment in England and Wales are brought before the Crown Court: Courts Act 1971, s. 6. The jurisdiction of the Crown Court being limited to England and Wales, the jurisdiction of the Criminal Division extends no further: see Criminal Appeal Act 1968, s. 55 (3).
[9] Criminal Appeal Act 1968, s. 1 (1). Where a person is convicted before the Crown Court of a "schedule offence" to which the Criminal Law Act 1977, s. 23 applies, it is not open to him to appeal to the Criminal Division against that conviction on the ground that the decision of the court which committed him for trial as to the value involved was mistaken: *ibid*. s. 23 (8).

58

person convicted on indictment at the Crown Court, against his sentence, not being a sentence fixed by law[10]; (c) by a person sentenced at the Crown Court, having been committed for sentence or to be dealt with after conviction in the magistrates' court, in certain circumstances against his sentence[11]; (d) by a person in whose case there was returned a verdict of not guilty by reason of insanity,[12] against that verdict[13]; (e) by a person in whose case there has been a determination of the question of his fitness to be tried,[14] against the jury's finding[15] that he was under disability.[16]

Where, upon conviction in the Crown Court, judgment is respited and the defendant is bound over to be of good behaviour and to come up for judgment when called upon, and is subsequently sentenced for breach of those recognisances, appeal lies to the Criminal Division against the sentence imposed, and the court may enquire into the sufficiency of the facts on which that sentence was based.[17]

Where the Crown Court makes an order requiring the parent or guardian of a child or young person to pay a fine, costs or compensation in respect of an offence committed by that child or young person the parent or guardian may appeal to the Criminal Division as if he or she had been convicted on indictment and the order or sentence was passed upon that conviction.[18]

The Criminal Division has no jurisdiction to hear appeals against interlocutory matters,[19] nor will matters within the particular discretion of the judge of the court of trial, such as the power to grant bail during the trial,[19] the power to order separate trials,[20] or the power to discharge the jury,[21] generally found an appeal to the court.

No appeal lies against an acquittal on indictment.[22]

(3) The need for leave

Appeal lies against conviction, against a verdict of not guilty by reason of insanity or against a finding of disability, without the leave of the Criminal

[10] Criminal Appeal Act 1968, s. 9. As to sentence appeals, see pp. 91 *et seq., post.*
   The jurisdiction of the Court of Appeal under the Administration of Justice Act 1960, s. 13, to hear and determine an appeal from a decision of the Crown Court dealing with an offence under the Bail Act 1976, s. 6 as if it were a contempt of court, is exercised by the Criminal Division: R.S.C. O. 59, r. 20 (7) as amended by S.I. 1978 No. 251: see also *R.* v. *Harbax Singh* [1979] 2 W.L.R. 100.
[11] Criminal Appeal Act 1968, s. 10, and see pp. 93 *et seq., post.*
[12] Criminal Appeal Act 1968, s. 12, and see pp. 86 *et seq., post.*
[13] But not against any order made in consequence of the verdict.
[14] Under the provisions of the Criminal Procedure (Insanity) Act 1964, s. 4.
[15] But not against any order made in consequence of the finding.
[16] Criminal Appeal Act 1968, s. 15, and see p. 87, *post.* The court may also entertain an appeal against conviction on the ground that the hearing of the preliminary issue with regard to fitness to plead was open to an objection of error in law so that the defendant ought not to have been tried on the indictment: see *R.* v. *Podola* [1960] 1 Q.B. 325.
[17] *R.* v. *Smith* [1925] 1 K.B. 603; also *R.* v. *Pine* (1932) 24 Cr. App. R. 10; *R.* v. *David* [1939] 1 All E.R. 782. The same principle applies in the case of a sentence imposed on the breach of a conditional discharge or a probation order: see *R.* v. *Green* [1959] 2 Q.B. 127.
[18] Children and Young Persons Act 1933, s. 55 (5) (b); Courts Act 1971, s. 56 (1), (2), Sched. 8, para. 22 (b), Sched. 9.
[19] *R.* v. *Collins* [1970] 1 Q.B. 710.
[20] *R.* v. *Gronkowski* [1946] K.B. 369.
[21] *R.* v. *Graham* (1975) 61 Cr. App. R. 292.
[22] But see as to a reference by the Attorney-General, p. 97, *post.*

Division, only: (a) on a ground which involves a question of law alone[23]; (b) on the certificate of the trial judge that the case is fit for appeal[24] on a question of fact or of mixed law and fact; or (c) where a case is referred to the court by the Home Secretary.[25] The only circumstances in which an appeal against sentence lies without leave is where the case is referred to the court by the Home Secretary.[25]

In all other cases the leave of the Criminal Division[26] to appeal is required.

Where a ground is put forward as being a question of law, it must be one which in the opinion of the Criminal Division is a question of law. A right of appeal without leave is not established merely by asserting that such a question exists.[27] Again, a person who is entitled to appeal without leave on a question of law does not thereby acquire a right of appeal on other grounds not involving questions of law merely by including such grounds in his notice of appeal.[28]

(4) Certificate of trial judge

While a judge of the Crown Court has no power to give leave to any person to appeal, the judge of the court of trial[29] may grant a certificate that a case is fit for appeal on a question of fact or a question of mixed law and fact.[30] Nothing empowers him, however, to grant a certificate that a case is fit for appeal on a question of law or on a matter relating to the sentence; a purported grant on such an issue is a nullity.[31]

The effects of the grant of a certificate are these: (a) the appeal lies without the necessity for the leave of the Criminal Division; (b) the appellant becomes entitled to be present at the hearing of his appeal against conviction[32]; and (c) the Criminal Division will have no power to give a direction for "loss of time."[33] Since, therefore, the grant of a certificate is tantamount to a grant of leave to appeal, it follows that it should not be granted lightly, nor indeed unless the case is clearly within the ambit of the Criminal Appeal Act.[34] In the absence of clear and cogent grounds it is better that the matter be left to the

---

[23] Criminal Appeal Act 1968, ss. 1 (2), 12, 15 (2).
[24] See below.
[25] See p. 88, *post*.
[26] Leave to appeal may be granted by a single judge of the court, see p. 69, *post*.
[27] *R.* v. *Hinds* (1962) 46 Cr. App. R. 327.
[28] *R.* v. *Robinson* [1953] 1 W.L.R. 872.
[29] The "judge of the court of trial" means, where the Crown Court consists of justices, the judge presiding: Criminal Appeal Act 1968, s. 51 (1); Courts Act 1971, s. 56 (1), Sched. 8. The "court of trial" means the court from which the appeal lies: *ibid*.
[30] Criminal Appeal Act 1968, ss. 1 (2), 12, 15 (2).
[31] *R.* v. *Bogacki* (1973) 57 Cr. App. R. 593; *R.* v. *Smith* (1974) 58 Cr. App. R. 320; *Director of Public Prosecutions* v. *Withers* (1974) 58 Cr. App. R. 187; *R.* v. *Saunders* (1974) 58 Cr. App. R. 238.
[32] See p. 80, *post*.
[33] See p. 96, *post*.
[34] *R.* v. *Auker-Howlett* [1973] R.T.R. 109. A certificate should not be given merely because counsel asks for it (*R.* v. *Langley* (1923) 17 Cr. App. R. 199), or because the trial judge is uneasy about the verdict (*R.* v. *Perfect* (1917) 12 Cr. App. R. 273). It should be granted only where the judge considers that the point indicated is such that it ought to be investigated by the Criminal Division: *R.* v. *Parkin* (1928) 20 Cr. App. R. 173; *R.* v. *Boseley* (1937) 26 Cr. App. R. 99; *R.* v. *Yindrich (Practice Note)* (1953) 39 Cr. App. R. 118; *R.* v. *Eyles* (1963) 47 Cr. App. R. 260.

Criminal Division to decide, that court, or the single judge, having all the relevant matters before them and being assisted by grounds of appeal formulated by counsel in the light of the transcript.[35]

(5) Conviction after plea of guilty

The term "conviction" is apt to include a conviction upon a defendant's plea of guilty as well as upon the verdict of a jury.[36] Where a plea of guilty is recorded on indictment, the Criminal Division is prepared to entertain an appeal against the consequent conviction in the circumstances summarised by Avory J. in the case of *R. v. Forde*,[37] namely where it appears that the appellant did not appreciate the nature of the charge to which he pleaded,[38] or did not intend to admit that he was guilty of it,[39] or where, upon the admitted facts, the appellant could not in law have been convicted of the offence charged.[40]

(6) Single right of appeal

The Criminal Appeal Act 1968, confers a right of appeal in respect of a particular conviction or sentence, and that right of appeal incorporates the right to apply once, and once only, for leave to appeal.[41] Once an appeal has been effectively determined, as where an appeal or an application for leave is abandoned,[42] or an application for leave has been refused by the single judge and has not been renewed within the time prescribed,[43] or an appeal has been dismissed, or an application for leave referred to the court[44] has been refused,

---

[35] A procedure for applying for the certificate is suggested in *Proceedings in the Criminal Division of the Court of Appeal* by Master Thompson, Peter Morrish and Ian McLean, at pp. 36–39.
   The certificate ought to be in Form 1, contained in the Schedule to the Criminal Appeal Rules 1968, and set out in Appendix F, No. 1, *post*. When issued it should be sent to the Registrar of Criminal Appeals forthwith, a copy being sent to the appellant or his legal representatives: Criminal Appeal Rules 1968, r. 1 (2), (3). It must set out the precise ground or grounds which are being certified for consideration by the Criminal Division: *R. v. McMahon* [1963] Crim. L.R. 103.
   Any notice of appeal submitted in From 2 (N) should indicate that a certificate has been given, see p. 63, *post*, note 69.
[36] The lacuna in s. 2 (1) (*a*) of the Criminal Appeal Act 1968, identified in *Director of Public Prosecutions* v. *Shannon* [1975] A.C. 717, was supplied by the Criminal Law Act 1977, s. 44.
[37] [1923] 2 K.B. 400.
[38] As in *R. v. Forde*, *supra*.
[39] *R. v. Hussey* (1924) 18 Cr. App. R. 121; *R. v. Field* (1943) 29 Cr. App. R. 151; *R. v. Jones* (1948) 33 Cr. App. R. 11.
   A defendant must have complete freedom of choice in deciding whether to plead guilty or not guilty, and the court may be prepared to hear evidence on the question whether he had or not: see the line of cases commencing with *R. v. Hall* [1968] 2 Q.B. 788 and *R. v. Turner* [1970] 2 Q.B. 321.
[40] As in *R. v. Ingleson* [1915] 1 K.B. 512; *R. v. Griffiths* (1932) 23 Cr. App. R. 153; *R. v. Gould* [1968] 2 Q.B. 65; *R. v. Cox* [1968] 1 W.L.R. 88. Where the trial judge accepts a plea of guilty where the indictment does not disclose an offence known to the law, such pleas are wrongly received in law, and the Criminal Division has jurisdiction to entertain an appeal against conviction in respect of them: *R. v. Whitehouse* (1977) 65 Cr. App. R. 33 applying a dictum of Salmon L.J. in *R. v. Rollafson* (1969) 53 Cr. App. R. 389, at p. 390; see also *R. v. Lidiard* (1979) 123 S.J. 743.
[41] *R. v. Grantham* (1969) 53 Cr. App. R. 369, Cts. M.A.C.
[42] See p. 78, *post*.
[43] See p. 70, *post*.
[44] See p. 70, *post*.

the Criminal Division has no jurisdiction to entertain a subsequent appeal, or application for leave, against the same conviction or sentence.[45]

(7) Effect of appealing

In general, the giving of notice of appeal does not suspend the operation of any sentence or order of the court of trial unless a statutory enactment provides to the contrary.[46] Special provisions do, however, apply to restitution and compensation orders, and in relation to criminal bankruptcy orders.

The operation of an order for the restitution of property,[47] and for this purpose that order includes a compensation order,[48] made on conviction on indictment, is suspended until the expiration of 28 days from the date of conviction, and, where notice of appeal, or of application for leave to appeal, is given within that time, until the determination of the appeal, unless the court of trial otherwise directs.[49]

The fact that an appeal is pending[50] against any conviction by virtue of which a criminal bankruptcy order[51] was made, does not[52] preclude the taking of proceedings in consequence of the order,[53] but where a person is adjudged bankrupt in proceedings pursuant to a criminal bankruptcy petition no property may be distributed by his trustee in bankruptcy and no order[54] may be made by the High Court so long as an appeal is pending against his conviction of any offence by virtue of which the criminal bankruptcy order was made.[55]

2. Initiating an Appeal

(1) General

A person seeking to initiate an appeal to the Criminal Division under Part I of the Criminal Appeal Act 1968 must give notice in the manner laid down, by completing the appropriate forms within the time prescribed by the Criminal

[45] There are cases where the court permits an appeal or application for leave to be relisted for further argument if some procedural defect or administrative error appears to have occurred in the original disposal of the case, so that the appeal or application cannot be regarded as having been effectively determined: see *R. v. Grantham, supra; also R. v. Daniel* (1977) 64 Cr. App. R. 50.
[46] See *ante*, p. 7, n. 72 as to the statutory enactments concerned. The provisions relating to capital cases (for which see the Criminal Appeal Act 1968, s. 48, Sched. 4) are hardly relevant at the present time.
[47] An order under the Theft Act 1968, s. 28 is treated as an "order for the restitution of property" for the purposes of the Criminal Appeal Act 1968, ss. 30, 42: Theft Act 1968, s. 28 (5).
[48] Made under the Powers of Criminal Courts Act 1973, s. 36 (1).
[49] Criminal Appeal Act 1968, s. 30 (1); Theft Act 1968, s. 33 (3), Sched. 3. As to the powers of the Criminal Division in dealing with such an order, see p. 97, *post*. As to the position on further appeal to the House of Lords, see p. 115, *post*.
[50] An appeal is "pending" in any case until the expiration of the period of 28 days beginning with the date of conviction. If notice of appeal is given during that period and during that period the appellant notifies the Official Receiver, the appeal is pending until its determination: Powers of Criminal Courts Act 1973, s. 39 (5), Sched. 2, para. 13 (*a*), (*b*). As to the position on further appeal to the House of Lords, see p. 115, *post*.
[51] Made under the Powers of Criminal Courts Act 1973, s. 39.
[52] Subject to the statutory provisions, see Powers of Criminal Courts Act 1973, Sched. 2, para. 13.
[53] *i.e.* by virtue of *ibid*. Sched. 2.
[54] *i.e.* no order under *ibid*. Sched. 2, para. 10 (recovery of assets).
[55] *Ibid*. s. 39 (5), Sched. 2, para. 13 (2). As to the powers of the Criminal Division in relation to a criminal bankruptcy order, see p. 97, *post*. As to the position on further appeal to the House of Lords, see p. 115, *post*.

Appeal Rules 1968.[56] The forms are clearly phrased and self-explanatory,[57] being designed for use, in an appropriate case, by an unrepresented appellant. They may be obtained by an appellant in custody from the authorities at the place in which he is confined, otherwise from the Registrar of Criminal Appeals.

It is important to ensure, in completing the forms, that all items are stated completely and accurately, for in the initial stages of an appeal, or application for leave to appeal, the Registrar has no information other than that contained in the forms and an appellant may be prejudiced if the information given is not complete or is not strictly accurate.[58]

(2) Notice of appeal

Notice of appeal, or of application for leave to appeal,[59] is given by serving notice on the Registrar within 28 days from the date of the conviction,[60] verdict or finding[61] appealed against, or within 28 days from the date on which sentence was passed, or in the case of an order treated as being made on conviction, from the date of the making of that order.[62]

Notice of appeal, or of application for leave to appeal,[63] is given by completing Part 1 of Form 2 (N)[64] and as much of Part 2 of the form as relates to the particular appeal or application[65] and serving it on the Registrar of Criminal Appeals.[66] The notice of appeal must be accompanied by a statement in Form 3 (G)[67] of the grounds of the appeal or the application,[68] and where an appellant has been convicted of more than one offence, Form 3 (G) must specify the particular convictions and sentences in respect of which the appellant is giving notice.[69] Form 3 (G) must also specify any exhibit produced at

---

[56] A step-by-step account of the procedure is given in the pamphlet "Preparation for Proceedings in the Court of Appeal, Criminal Division" issued by the Registrar, with the approval of the court (*Practice Note* [1974] 1 W.L.R. 774). The pamphlet is revised to January 1976. A fuller account of the procedure also appears in Thompson, Morrish and McLean, *op. cit.* under the title "Initial Steps in Procedure."

[57] The relevant forms are set out in Appendix B, *post*.

[58] General advice is given to solicitors in relation to an appeal in "Preparation for Proceedings in the Court of Appeal, Criminal Division" (see note 56, *infra*) at paras. 1, 2.

[59] A person becomes an "appellant" on giving notice of appeal, and an "appellant" includes one who has given notice of application for leave to appeal: Criminal Appeal Act 1968, s. 51 (1); Criminal Appeal Rules 1968, r. 25 (1). Notice of application for leave given by a person who does not require it is treated as notice of appeal; notice of appeal given by a person who requires leave is treated as a *notice of application for leave: ibid.* r. 2 (7).

[60] In *R.* v. *Anderson* [1972] 1 Q.B. 304 (although the case is not reported on this point) the appeal against conviction was determined before the trial judge passed sentence.

[61] For insanity cases, see p. 86, *post*; for disability cases, p. 87, *post*.

[62] Criminal Appeal Act 1968, s. 18 (1), (2). Where a sentence or other order is varied by the Crown Court under the powers conferred by the Courts Act 1971, s. 11, the sentence or order is regarded as having been imposed on the day on which it was varied: *ibid.* s. 11 (5), proviso.

[63] See note 59, *infra*.

[64] The Form is set out in Appendix F, *post* No. 2.

[65] Pt. 2 of Form 2 (N) also relates to an application for extension of time (see p. 91, *post*) and to secondary applications such as those for legal aid, bail, leave to be present and leave to call a witness.

[66] As to service of documents, see p. 66, *post*.

[67] See Appendix F, *post*, No. 3, and No. 4.

[68] Criminal Appeal Rules 1968, r. 2 (2) (*a*).

[69] *Ibid.* r. 2 (2) (*b*). Where the trial judge gives his certificate (see *ante*, pp. 60–61) the notice of appeal in Form 2 (N) should indicate that fact and the grounds in Form 3 (G) should echo the grounds in the certificate. If further grounds are submitted, and the latter are such as to require leave to appeal, the leave of the Criminal Division must be obtained.

the trial which the appellant desires should be kept in the custody of the court for the purpose of an appeal against his conviction.[70] Forms 2 (N) and 3 (G) must be signed by or on behalf of the appellant.[71] If either form is not signed by him, and he is in custody, the Registrar will, as soon as practicable after receiving it, send a copy to him.[72]

(3) Extension of time

A person seeking to initiate an appeal to the Criminal Division who fails to give notice of appeal, or of application for leave to appeal,[73] within the 28 days prescribed, loses his right of appeal unless the court is prepared to grant him an extension of time.[74]

The time for giving notice may be extended by the court either before or after the prescribed time expires[75] but the court has expressed itself as unwilling to grant any considerable extension except for good reason.[76]

Notice of application for an extension of time in which to give notice of appeal, or of application for leave to appeal, is given by completing Part 1 of Form 2 (N) in the usual way, by completing the relevant parts of Part 2 of that form, and specifying in Form 3 (G) the reasons for the delay.[77]

(4) Grounds of appeal: general

Grounds of appeal set out in, or attached to Form 3 (G)[78] are an integral part of a notice of appeal or of application for leave to appeal,[79] and a notice in Form 2 (N) is ineffective unless accompanied by a statement in Form 3 (G) setting out proper grounds of appeal as fully as is practicable at the time of completing the notice.[80] It is not enough, as it is in the Crown Court to put forward as grounds of appeal a formula such as "the sentence is too severe" or the "verdict was unsafe or unsatisfactory," without identifying the matters which should be considered.[81] Grounds of appeal must be sufficient to enable

---

[70] Criminal Appeal Rules 1968, r. 2 (4).

[71] *Ibid.* rr. 2 (5), 25 (1). The Rules do not of themselves, confer on any person authority to sign on behalf of the appellant. Rule 2 (5) merely provides that the signature of an agent is acceptable if otherwise authorised: see *R.* v. *Jones* (1971) 55 Cr. App. R. 321 (agent signing after defendant had absconded). Solicitors have no implied authority from their clients to appeal against any order of a court; they must have express instructions: *R.* v. *McCready and Others* [1978] 1 W.L.R. 1376.

[72] Criminal Appeal Rules 1968, s. 2 (4).

[73] See *ante*, p. 63, note 59.

[74] *R.* v. *Marsh* (1936) 25 Cr. App. R. 49; *R.* v. *Lesser* (1940) 27 Cr. App. R. 69; *R.* v. *Cullum* (1943) 28 Cr. App. R. 150.

[75] Criminal Appeal Act 1968, s. 18 (2).

[76] See *R.* v. *Rhodes* (1910) 5 Cr. App. R. 35; *R.* v. *Moore* (1923) 17 Cr. App. R. 155; *R.* v. *Marsh* (1935) 25 Cr. App. R. 49; *R.* v. *Ramsden* [1972] Crim. L.R. 547.

[77] Criminal Appeal Rules 1968, r. 2 (3) (*a*), (*b*).

[78] Set out in Appendix F, *post*, No. 3, or Form FG, set out in Appendix F, No. 4.

[79] "Preparation for Proceedings in the Court of Appeal, Criminal Division" (see *ante*, p. 63, note 56, para. 3.1.

[80] *R.* v. *Wilson* [1973] Crim. L.R. 572. Where grounds are settled and signed by counsel, the original, and not a copy should be sent to the Registrar with the notice of appeal: "Preparation for Proceedings in the Court of Appeal Criminal Division" (see *ante*, p. 63, note 56), para. 3.2

[81] *Ibid.* 5.1. See also *R.* v. *Nicco* [1972] Crim. L.R. 420. If forms of notice are sent to the Registrar with no grounds, or with a mere formula instead of grounds, the forms will not be effective as a notice of appeal or of application for leave. In such a case the Registrar may return the forms. If the deficiency is not made good within the time limit for giving notice, it will be necessary to apply for an extension of time: "Preparation for Proceedings in the Court of Appeal, Criminal Division," para. 5.2.

the court or a judge of the court to identify the particular matters which should be considered, and to indicate the parts of the transcript which should be obtained, if any.[82]

Where counsel considers that particular parts of the transcript are required, he may specify those parts in the grounds of appeal,[83] and if he considers that a transcript of part of the evidence is required he should give the names of the witnesses concerned and the dates on which those witnesses were called.[84]

(5) Grounds of appeal: counsel's responsibility

In settling grounds of appeal counsel has a duty not only to his client but to the court. His duty to his client does not extend to putting forward grounds of appeal merely because the appellant wishes him to do so. Grounds should be put forward only where they are arguable, and where they afford some real chance of success.[85]

The grounds which are put forward should be settled carefully and accurately,[86] and must be substantial and stated with particularity.[87]

Grounds of appeal set out initially in, or attached to, Form 3 (G) may be varied or amplified within such time as the court may allow.[88]

(6) Grounds of appeal: "initial," "provisional," "perfected"

The term "initial grounds" of appeal is given to grounds which are settled by counsel on the footing that, while they are capable of forming the basis of a substantial oral argument as settled, yet they require "perfection" in the light, for instance, of the transcript, or of any other information which is not to hand at the time the grounds are settled, as they must be within the prescribed 28 day period.[89]

---

[82] *Ibid.* para. 3.3.

[83] The Registrar may nevertheless decline to order the transcript specified if he does not think it justified in all the circumstances. He will, however, if requested, refer the question to a judge: *Ibid.* para. 3.5.

[84] *Ibid.* para. 3.4. To reduce delays, demands for transcript have to be kept to a minimum and must be selective. It is wrong to ask for a transcript of the whole proceedings, without giving thought to the question whether parts of it only would be sufficient: *ibid.* para. 3.6.

[85] See *Practice Direction* (1966) 50 Cr. App. R. 290. See generally on this topic, Thompson, Morrish and McLean *op. cit.* p. 89, also "Settling Grounds of Appeal in the Court of Appeal (Criminal Division) "by Peter Morrish and Ian McLean, (1977) 141 J.P.J. at pp. 78–81.

[86] *R.* v. *Upton, R.* v. *Hendry* [1973] 3 All E.R. 318n. The position must be put fairly and properly, see *R.* v. *Singh* [1973] Crim. L.R. 36 and *R.* v. *Morson* [1976] Crim. L.R. 323.

[87] *Practice Direction* (1970) 54 Cr. App. R. 280. The grounds settled by counsel must be sufficient to enable the Registrar to decide what form the case is going to take in the court, and to enable the court or the single judge to identify the matters of real complaint and to decide whether any, or any further, transcripts are required. See again on this topic, Morrish and McLean (1977) 141 J.P.J. at pp. 78–81.

[88] Criminal Appeal Rules 1968, r. 2 (2) (c). As to "provisional" and "perfected" grounds, see below.

No further grounds will be entertained unless the court's consent is obtained: *Practice Direction* (1973) 57 Cr. App. R. 838; *R.* v. *Haycraft* (1973) 58 Cr. App. R. 122. The court will sometimes permit grounds to be varied at the hearing, but the general rule is that all grounds on which it is intended to rely should be lodged with the Registrar in advance of the hearing: *R.* v. *Brown and Others* [1963] Crim. L.R. 636 and see the strictures of the court in *R.* v. *Grundy, R.* v. *White* [1963] Crim. L.R. 425.

[89] Counsel may indicate in the grounds that he requires a copy of the transcript when it becomes available in order to perfect the grounds, or that he requires other specified information for that purpose: "Preparation for Proceedings in the Court of Appeal (Criminal Division)" (see *ante* p. 63, note 56), para. 3.7.

It is not appropriate for counsel to settle and sign grounds of appeal so long as the grounds he has in mind are provisional only.[90] In these circumstances counsel should give an opinion in writing, together with a draft "Note to the Registrar (Provisional Grounds)" if the Registrar's assistance is required.[91] Such note should indicate as fully as possible what the provisional "grounds" are, and as precisely as possible the information which counsel requires to assess them.[92]

Once counsel receives the transcript or other information which he requires, he should "perfect" his grounds as soon as possible, and in any event before the application for leave to appeal is referred to the single judge or, again, unless the court otherwise directs, before the date of the hearing by the court is fixed.[93]

Where grounds of appeal give no indication that some further action or information is required to enable counsel to perfect them, the Registrar may refer the application for leave to the court or to a judge on the assumption that the grounds are perfected.[94]

(7) Service of documents, etc.

Completed notice of appeal or of application for leave to appeal in Form 2 (N), accompanied by a statement of the grounds of appeal set out in, or attached to, Form 3 (G) or Form FG, and any other documents relating to an appeal or application, may be served on the Registrar of Criminal Appeals, in the case of an appellant in custody by delivering them to the person having custody of him, for onward transmission to the Registrar, or in any case, by delivering them to the Registrar, or by addressing them to him and leaving them at his office in the Royal Courts of Justice,[95] or by posting them to him.[96]

---

[90] Where counsel was present at the trial, there is no reason why initial grounds should not be given without waiting for a sight of the transcript: see *R.* v. *Adler* (1923) 17 Cr. App. R. 105; *R.* v. *Ellson* [1962] 1 W.L.R. 312; *R.* v. *Kooner* [1972] Crim. L.R. 323; *R.* v. *Campbell* (unreported) April 9, 1976 C.C.

See generally "Preparation for Proceedings in the Court of Appeal (Criminal Division)" (*ante*, p. 63, n. 56), para. 6.

[91] *Ibid.* para. 6.2, *e.g.* in obtaining a transcript or to advise as to legal aid fo the purpose of obtaining witness statements. The Registrar is not empowered to act unless notice of appeal or of application for leave to appeal is given: *ibid.* para. 6.3.

[92] *Ibid.* para. 6.4. If a transcript is required it should be described in sufficient detail to enable the Registrar to obtain it and supply a copy. If it is a question of legal aid for obtaining a witness statement, the note should include an outline of what the witness will say and the reason for the witness not being called at the trial: *ibid.* para. 6.4. See also *ibid.* para. 6.5.

Where it is suggested that the transcript when received is inaccurate, the Registrar should be told what is alleged. He will then take up the matter with the shorthand writers and, if necessary, with the trial judge: *Practice Note* (1978) 67 Cr. App. R. 50.

[93] *Ibid.* para. 7.2. A step-by-step procedure for solicitor and counsel dealing with provisional grounds is set out at *ibid.* para. 6.6.; and for "perfecting" initial grounds of appeal, at *ibid.* para. 7.1.

As to the contents and form of "perfected" grounds, see *ibid.* para. 7.3.

If the Registrar considers that further assistance from counsel is required to perfect the grounds, he may return them for that purpose: *ibid.* para. 7.4.

As to the position in relation to a possibility of calling evidence on appeal, see p. 89, *post*.

[94] "Preparation for Proceedings in the Court of Appeal (Criminal Division)" (see *ante*, p. 63, note 56), para. 3.8.

[95] Royal Courts of Justice, Strand, London W.C.2 2LL. General enquiries may be made to (01) 405 7641, Ext. 3014.

[96] Criminal Appeal Rules 1968, r. 25.

3. Preparation of Case for Hearing

(1) Duties of Registrar

The duty of taking all necessary steps for obtaining the hearing of any appeal, or application for leave to appeal,[97] and the task of laying before the Criminal Division in proper form all the documents, exhibits and other things which appear necessary for the proper determination of such an appeal or application[98] is imposed by the Act upon the Registrar of Criminal Appeals.[99] As part of his multitudinous duties, the Registrar will obtain the trial documents from the Crown Court,[1] order any necessary transcripts of the proceedings in the Crown Court and supply them to any interested party,[2] supply, on request, to the appellant or respondent, copies of any documents or other things required for the appeal,[3] and make arrangements, on request, for the appellant or the respondent to inspect any document or other thing required for the appeal.[4]

The Registrar will generally give advice and assistance to either party to an appeal, and having the procedural requirements of the court at his fingertips will generally be able to identify those points of law likely to be of assistance to an appellant which appear from a perusal of the trial documents and the transcript. It is important to emphasise, however, that the Registrar is an officer of the court and it is not part of his duties to give professional advice to the parties. He is not in any way the appellant's solicitor[5]; it is his duty to remain impartial.[6]

(2) The Registrar and legal aid

The power of the Criminal Division to grant legal aid is widely exercised not only by the single judge,[7] but by the Registrar.[8]

---

[97] Of which notice is given to him and which is not referred by him and summarily dismissed by the court under the Criminal Appeal Act 1968, s. 20 (as to which see p. 79, *post.*)

[98] In discharging these functions he may require the Crown Court to furnish the Criminal Division with any assistance it requires for the purpose of exercising its jurisdiction: Criminal Appeal Rules 1968, r. 22 (1).

[99] Criminal Appeal Act 1968, s. 21 (1).

[1] These include: the indictment or memorandum of conviction; the original depositions, or statements under the Criminal Justice Act 1967, s. 2; the exhibit list and any original documentary exhibits kept in custody for the appeal, unless of excessive bulk and unsuitable for transmission; copy exhibit list and copy exhibits; copies of any documents mentioned in sentencing proceedings, including the appellant's statement to the police; the appellant's antecedents; any notice of additional evidence or statement; a list of any offences taken into consideration; any social enquiry or probation report; any note from the jury; any "extended sentence" notice; any admissions made under the Criminal Justice Act 1967, s. 10; any notice of alibi; and the legal aid papers.

[2] See p. 68, *post.*

[3] See p. 68, *post.*

[4] See p. 68, *post.*

[5] As to his functions in relation to legal aid, see p. 110, *post.*

[6] See generally, Thompson, Morrish and McLean *op. cit.* under the title "Initial Steps in Procedure."

[7] See pp. 74–75, *post.*

[8] See pp. 74–75, *post.*

(3) Ordering the transcript

On receiving the trial documents from the Crown Court, the Registrar will be in a position to decide, after considering them together with Forms 2 (N) and 3 (G) what parts if any of the transcript of proceedings in the Crown Court[8a] should be ordered.[9] Counsel for the appellant may also ask the Registrar to order parts of the transcript for the purpose of amplifying or "perfecting" his grounds of appeal.[10]

It is the practice for only a "short transcript" to be ordered initially. This transcript records the arraignment, the summing-up, and proceedings after verdict.[11] No further transcript will be ordered unless authorised by the single judge, except on application to the court, which will need to be satisfied that the additional transcript is really necessary.[12]

(4) Supply of transcripts

The Registrar may, on request, supply to any interested party[13] a transcript of the record of proceedings, or part of it, which is in his possession for the purposes of an appeal, or an application for leave to appeal, and may, in such a case make charges in accordance with the scales and rates fixed by the Treasury.[13] Where the Registrar supplies copies of transcripts and other documents for the purpose of work done under legal aid, he will do so free of charge. He may disallow on taxation under legal aid the cost of a transcript obtained otherwise than through him.[14]

(5) Supply of exhibits and other things

The Registrar will supply on request, to the appellant or the respondent, copies of any documents or other things required for the appeal, and make such charges in accordance with the scales and rates fixed for the time being by the Treasury. On request, he will make arrangements for the appellant or the respondent to inspect any document or thing required for the appeal.[15]

[8a] As to the requirements for recording the proceedings of the Crown Court, see Criminal Appeal Act 1968, s. 32 (1); Criminal Appeal Rules 1968, rr. 18, 20. These provisions seem to be directory only: see, *e.g. R.* v. *Rutter* (1908) 1 Cr. App. R. 174; *R.* v. *Bennett* (1909) 2 Cr. App. R. 152; *R.* v. *Elliott* (1909) 2 Cr. App. R. 171. As to the circumstances in which the insufficiency of the shorthand note may provide a ground of appeal, see *R.* v. *Spillane* (1972) 56 Cr. App. R. 9; *R.* v. *Le Caer* (1972) 56 Cr. App. R. 727. The trial judge has no authority to revise the transcript of his summing-up: *R.* v. *Kluczynski* (1973) 57 Cr. App. R. 836.

[9] See also *ante*, p. 65.

[10] See *ante*, p. 65. Legal aid for advice and assistance on appeal (see p. 74, *post*) includes work done on perfecting the grounds of appeal: "Preparation for Proceedings in the Court of Appeal (Criminal Division)" (see *ante*, p. 63, note 56), para. 7.6.

[11] See *R.* v. *Seillon* (unreported) March 27, 1975, C.A.; also *R.* v. *Passer* [1954] Crim. L.R. 368. Where an application is for leave to appeal against sentence, the "short transcript" will include the plea, the prosecutor's opening address, antecedents, mitigation and sentence: see Thompson, Morrish and McLean, *op. cit.* at p. 161.

[12] See *R.* v. *Lurie* (1951) 35 Cr. App. R. 113.

[13] As to which, see Criminal Appeal Rules, 1968, r. 25 (1).

[14] "Preparation for Proceedings in the Court of Appeal (Criminal Division)" (see *ante*, p. 63, note 56), para. 7.5. As to payment for the transcript as part of the costs awarded against an appellant, see p. 85, note 74.

[15] Criminal Appeal Rules 1968, r. 8. As to the position where the court orders a retrial under the Criminal Appeal Act 1968, s. 7, see Criminal Appeal Rules, r. 7 (3), (4).

(6) Action when papers complete

In general the papers will be complete when the Registrar has obtained the documents relating to the proceedings in the Crown Court,[16] has obtained the transcript, if any is required, and has been supplied with the grounds of appeal "perfected" as necessary.[17]

Where leave to appeal is not required[18] the Registrar will list the appeal for hearing before the court.[19] An application for leave to appeal will normally be referred to the single judge.[20]

4. SINGLE JUDGE PROCEDURE

(1) General

In general an application for leave to appeal, whether against conviction or sentence, where the appellant is seeking legal aid for the purposes of the proceedings[21] will be referred in the first instance to a single judge of the court.[22] The single judge may exercise, in the same manner and subject to the same provisions as they are exercised by the court, the powers of the court to give leave to appeal, extend the time within which notice of appeal or of application for leave to appeal must be given, suspend an appellant's disqualification from driving pending the hearing of the appeal, grant bail, grant legal aid, give leave to be present, issue a witness order, give a direction under the Sexual Offences (Amendment) Act 1976,[23] make an order for costs, give a direction for loss of time,[24] and, on a retrial ordered by the court under section 7 of the Criminal Appeal Act 1968, make ancillary orders under section 8.[25]

(2) Reference to single judge

An application is referred to the single judge by the Registrar.[26] The Registrar puts before the single judge the primary application, whether for leave to appeal or for an extension of time, together with any secondary

---

[16] See *ante*, p. 63, note 1.

[17] "Preparation for Proceedings in the Court of Appeal (Criminal Division)" (see *ante*, p. 63, note 56), para. 11.1.

[18] *i.e.* in the circumstances outlined *ante*, p. 59.

[19] "Preparation for Proceedings in the Court of Appeal (Criminal Division)" (see *ante*, p. 63, note 56), para. 11.4. As to listing, see p. 80, *post.*

[20] "Preparation for Proceedings in the Court of Appeal (Criminal Division)" (see *ante*, p. 63, note 56), para. 11.2. The Registrar may decide to list the application for leave to appeal for hearing before the court, without first referring to a single judge. He may also grant legal aid: *ibid.* para. 11.3.

[21] Where this has not been granted by the Registrar.

[22] References to a "single judge" are references to any judge of the Court of Appeal or of the High Court: Criminal Appeal Act 1968, s. 45 (2); Administration of Justice Act 1970, ss. 9 (3), 54 (3), Sched. 11.

[23] *Ibid.*, s. 4 (4).

[24] See p. 95, *post.*

[25] Criminal Appeal Act 1968, s. 31 (1). As to orders for retrial under s. 7, see p. 99, *post.*

[26] Applications are not to be made to individual judges without going through the Registrar: see *R.* v. *Lambert* [1977] Crim. L.R. 736.

applications, such as those for bail, legal aid, leave to be present, and the like, and all the relevant information in his possession.[27]

In the ordinary way the single judge will deal with both the primary and secondary applications in the light of all the papers including the grounds of appeal, and without hearing oral argument.[28] Exceptionally, as where the appellant makes an urgent application for bail, he may be represented before the judge at an oral hearing.[29] The appellant has no right to be present.[30]

After considering the application on the papers the judge may either grant the application or refuse it; where the judge considers that the primary application for leave to appeal is one which should be heard by the court, he will direct the Registrar to list it accordingly.[31]

Where the single judge refuses the primary application the Registrar will send a notification of that refusal to the applicant who is then informed that he may require the application to be considered by the court.[32]

(3) Renewal after refusal by single judge

Where the single judge refuses the primary application or applications, for leave to appeal or for extension of time, the applicant may either abandon his application or he may renew it before the court.[33] If he fails to renew a primary application within the time prescribed, and does not obtain an extension of time in which to do so, the application is treated as having been refused by the court,[34] and the applicant will be notified accordingly.[35]

Where the primary application is renewed before the court any secondary applications such as those for bail, legal aid, leave to be present and the like, may be renewed at the same time. If the primary application is not renewed, then all secondary applications necessarily lapse.

An appellant seeking to renew his primary application before the court, does so by serving notice on the Registrar in Form 15,[36] signed by him or on his

---

[27] Including the notice of appeal, grounds, any other relevant forms, any transcripts obtained, and the trial documents.
[28] "Preparation for Proceedings in the Court of Appeal (Criminal Division)" (see *ante*, p. 63, note 56), para. 13.3.
[29] See p. 72, *post*. Any party may be represented by counsel or a solicitor in proceedings before the single judge: Criminal Appeal Rules 1968, r. 11 (2).
[30] *Ibid*. r. 22.
[31] "Preparation for Proceedings in the Court of Appeal (Criminal Division)" (see *ante*, p. 63, note 56), para. 13.2. He may also grant further legal aid: *ibid*. Where he considers that further assistance from counsel is required to perfect the grounds, the single judge may direct the Registrar to return them for the purpose: *ibid*. para. 13.1.
  If the single judge grants leave to appeal, he is likely to grant further legal aid: *ibid*. para. 16.1. He may also direct the Registrar to bring some further ground of appeal, or other matter to the notice of solicitor and counsel: *ibid*. para. 16.2.
[32] *Ibid*. para. 14.1. He is also informed that he must send his "renewal" within 14 days: *ibid*. Where notification of refusal is sent to an applicant who is legally aided, the Registrar will send a copy of the notification to the solicitor assigned. This notice includes observations by the single judge: *ibid*. para. 14.2. Advice is given to solicitors on the question of abandoning or renewing the application in *ibid*. para. 14.3.
[33] Criminal Appeal Act 1968, s. 31 (1); Criminal Appeal Rules 1968, r. 12 (1).
[34] *Ibid*. rule 12 (4).
[35] *Ibid*. rule 15 (1).
[36] Which is, in fact, part of the form on which the single judge's refusal is notified.

behalf,[37] within 14 days, or such longer period as a judge of the court may fix, from the date on which notice of the single judge's refusal was served on him.[37]

The power to extend the time in which to renew an application refused by the single judge is exercised only in exceptional circumstances and the court or judge[38] who deals with the matter will require a good and reasonable excuse for the appellant's failure to renew within time. Reasons for the delay should be set out in Form O,[39] and sent with the application.[40]

5. APPLICATIONS IN RELATION TO BAIL

(1) General

The power to grant bail to a person pending the determination of his appeal is vested in the Criminal Division,[41] and that court may also grant bail (a) where it orders an appellant to be retried under section 7 of the Criminal Appeal Act 1968,[42] (b) where an appeal against a finding of disability is allowed, pending the appellant's retrial,[43] (c) where the court orders a *venire de novo*, pending the appellant's trial in the Crown Court,[44] and (d) pending the determination of an appeal to the House of Lords.[45]

(2) Principles governing grant of bail

The power to grant bail pending the determination of an appeal is seldom exercised[46]; while the discretion of the court is unfettered, nevertheless, as a general rule, an application is unlikely to be successful unless supported by strong grounds of appeal.[47]

---

[37] Criminal Appeal Rules 1968, r. 12 (3). If it is not, and the appellant is in custody, the Registrar will send him a copy as soon as practicable after receiving it: *ibid*.

[38] The power to extend the time in such circumstances is vested in "any judge of court": *R. v. Gaston* (1970) 55 Cr. App. R. 88; *R. v. Ward* (1971) 55 Cr. App. R. 509.

[39] See Appendix F, *post*, No. 10.

[40] See *R. v. Hatfield* [1971] Crim. L.R. 700; *R. v. Doherty* (1971) 55 Cr. App. R. 548; *R. v. Sullivan* (1972) 56 Cr. App. R. 541; *R. v. Gallagher* [1978] Crim. L.R. 216; *R. v. Marshall* [1978] Crim. L.R. 424. *Cf. R. v. Cody* [1978] Crim. L.R. 550.

[41] Criminal Appeal Act 1968, ss. 19, 51 (1). The Crown Court has no power to grant bail pending proceedings in the Criminal Division: "Preparation for Proceedings in the Court of Appeal (Criminal Division)" (see *ante*, p. 63, note 56), para. 12.1. The power of the Criminal Division may be exercised by a single judge: *ibid*. para. 12.2, also *ante*, p. 69. An application to a judge in chambers is not appropriate (see *ante*, p. 54).
An application made to a single judge must be made through the Registrar in the proper manner (see p. 69, *post*) and not to an individual judge locally who happens to come within the definition of "single judge": see *R. v. Lambert* [1977] Crim. L.R. 736.

[42] See p. 99, *post*.

[43] Criminal Appeal Act 1968, s. 16 (3); Bail Act 1976, Sched. 2. See also p. 87, *post*.

[44] *R. v. Rowan* (1910) 5 Cr. App. R. 279. Bail may also be granted in these circumstances by the Crown Court.

[45] See p. 107, *post*.

[46] The provisions of the Bail Act 1976, s. 4 and Sched. 1 do not apply to proceedings on or after a person's conviction. The position is of course otherwise where a retrial or a *venire de novo* is ordered.

[47] "Preparation for Proceedings in the Court of Appeal (Criminal Division)" (see *ante*, p. 63, note 56), para. 12.4.
In *R. v. Rowe, The Times*, November 21, 1968, C.A. it was said that there must be exceptional circumstances before bail will be granted. See also *R. v. Walton* [1979] Crim. L.R. 246. The court will not normally grant bail where there is no prospect of the appeal succeeding: see *R. v. Wise* (1922) 17 Cr. App. R.17. There is, however, no absolute rule that bail will not be granted unless leave to appeal is granted. Bail is, after all, a matter for the discretion of the court or judge and there may be special circumstances which ought to be considered: "Preparation for Proceedings in the Court of Appeal (Criminal Division)" (see *ante*, p. 63, note 56), para. 12.4.

There is no general principle that an appellant released on bail pending his appeal will not be returned to prison if his appeal fails; each case may be said to depend upon its own facts.[48]

Time spent on bail pending the determination of an appeal does not count towards the term of any sentence to which the appellant is for the time being subject.[49]

(3) Making an application

An appellant[50] seeking to make an application in relation to bail pending the determination of his appeal must give notice by completing so much of Part 2 of Form 2 (N) as relates to his application, and serving it on the Registrar[51] accompanied by the reasons for the application set out in Form 4 (B).[52] Notice in writing of intention to make such an application must, unless the court or a judge of the court otherwise directs, be served, at least 24 hours before it is made, on the prosecutor and on the Director of Public Prosecutions if the prosecution was carried on by him.[53]

In certain circumstances an application for bail may be made orally to the Criminal Division. This may be appropriate, for example, where the hearing of an appeal or application is adjourned by the court, or immediately following a determination of the court ordering a retrial under section 7 of the Criminal Appeal Act 1968, or making an order of *venire de novo*, or where the court grants leave to appeal to the House of Lords.

(4) Consideration by the single judge

There may be cases in which an application in relation to bail is placed before the court, but as a general rule, any application for bail will be considered by the single judge at the time he considers the primary application for leave to appeal or for extension of time, and will be dealt with on the papers.[54] In an exceptional case, the judge may permit an oral hearing at the express request of the appellant's solicitors.[55] On such an occasion the appel-

---

[48] See *R.* v. *Cullis & Nash* (1969) 53 Cr. App. R. 162; *R.* v. *Page* (1971) 55 Cr. App. R. 184; *R.* v. *Gruffyd* (1972) 56 Cr. App. R. 585, at p. 590; *R.* v. *Lancastle* [1978] Crim. L.R. 367.
[49] Criminal Appeal Act 1968, s. 29 (3).
[50] An application in relation to bail may be made otherwise than by an appellant, see Bail Act 1976, s. 3 (8).
[51] As to service, see *ante*, p. 66. An application for bail will not normally be entertained unless notice of appeal and proper grounds have been served. See the definition of "appellant" *ante*, p. 63, note 59.
[52] Criminal Appeal Rules 1968, r. 3 (1) (a); Criminal Appeal (Amendment) Rules 1978, r. 2A. A revised Form 4 (B) is set out in the Schedule to the 1978 Rules, and at Appendix F, *post*, No. 5.
       The grounds to be set out in Form 4 (B) are those which may affect the decision whether to grant bail or not, the grounds of the appeal or application for leave, already set out in Form 3 (G) should not be repeated: see Thompson, Morrish and McLean, *op. cit.* p. 25.
[53] Criminal Appeal Rules 1968, r. 3 (3); Criminal Appeal (Amendment) Rules 1978, r. 2 (c). If an application is to be made by the prosecutor or a constable under the Bail Act 1976, s. 3 (8), notice must be served on the appellant.
[54] See *ante*, pp. 69–71.
[55] Where the matter is very urgent the Registrar or his staff may be consulted without formality. (See *ante*, p. 66 for the address and telephone number.)
       Section 30 (7) of the Legal Aid Act 1974, does not provide for an application in relation to bail, but the Registrar will consider whether he should grant further legal aid for such an application: "Preparation for Proceedings in the Court of Appeal (Criminal Division)" (see *ante*, p. 63, note 56), para. 12.3.

lant, though not entitled himself to be present,[56] may be represented by counsel or a solicitor.[57]

Notice of such a hearing must be given to the prosecution, and unless the prosecution are represented, the judge will need to be satisfied that they do not intend to be, and that they do not oppose the application.[58]

Where the judge declines to grant bail, the applicant is entitled to renew his application before the court[59] provided, of course, that the primary application is also renewed.[60]

(5) Position where bail granted

Any record required by section 5 of the Bail Act 1976, will be made by including in the file relating to the case in question, where bail is granted, a copy of Form 11[61] and a statement of the day on which, and the time and place at which, the appellant is notified to surrender to custody.[62]

The court, or the single judge, as the case may be, will determine whether, and if so, what conditions should be imposed in respect of the grant of bail.[63] Where the court, or judge, imposes a requirement[64] to be complied with before the appellant's release on bail, it may give directions as to the manner in which, and the person or persons before whom, the requirement is to be complied with.[65]

(6) Taking the recognisances; complying with requirements

Where bail is granted to an appellant, the recognisances of any surety required as a condition of bail may be entered into before the Registrar of Criminal Appeals, or, where the appellant is in a prison or other place of detention, before the governor or keeper of the prison or place, as well as before those persons specified in section 8 (4) of the Bail Act 1976.[66]

[56] See p. 80, *post*.
[57] Criminal Appeal Rules 1968, r. 11 (2).
[58] See Thompson, Morrish and McLean, *op. cit.* p. 28.
[59] See *ante*, p. 70.
[60] If the primary application for leave to appeal or extension of time is refused and is not renewed, all secondary applications lapse.
[61] See note 65, *infra*.
[62] Criminal Appeal Rules 1968, r. 4 (1) substituted by the Criminal Appeal (Amendment) Rules 1978, r. 3. In any other case a copy of the notice of determination served under Rule 15 is sufficient record: *ibid*.
  Where bail is granted pending a retrial under s. 7 of the Act or on *a venire de novo* a copy of the record will be forwarded to the appropriate officer of the Crown Court: *ibid*. r. 4 (9).
[63] Bail Act 1976, s. 3.
[64] *i.e.* under the Bail Act 1976, s. 3 (5) or 3 (6).
[65] Criminal Appeal Rules 1968, r. 4; substituted by the Criminal Appeal (Amendment) Rules 1978, r. 3.
  Where the court has fixed the amount in which a surety is to be bound by recognisance, or under s. 3 (5) or 3 (6) of the Bail Act 1976, has imposed a requirement to be complied with before the appellant's release on bail, the Registrar will issue a certificate in Form 11 showing the amount and conditions, if any, of the recognisance, or as the case may be, containing a statement of the requirement, and a person authorised to take the recognisance or do anything in relation to the compliance with such requirement is not required to take or do it without production of the certificate: Criminal Appeal Rules 1968, r. 4, as substituted by Criminal Appeal (Amendment) Rules 1978, r. 3.
  The new Form 11 is set out in the Schedule to the 1978 Rules and also at Appendix F, *post*, No. 6.
[66] Criminal Appeal Rules 1968, r. 4 (1); Criminal Appeal (Amendment) Rules 1978, r. 3.

A person proposing to enter into a recognisance as a surety or to give security must, unless the court or a judge otherwise directs, give notice to the prosecutor at least 24 hours before he enters into the recognisance or gives security.[67]

The governor or keeper of the prison or place of detention in which the appellant is detained will release the appellant on receipt of the certificate in Form 11[68] stating that the recognisances of all sureties required have been taken and that all requirements have been complied with, or on being otherwise satisfied of these matters.[69]

(7) Forfeiture of recognisances

Where a recognisance has been entered into in respect of an appellant, and it appears that a default has been made in performing the conditions of that recognisance, the Criminal Division[70] may order the recognisance to be forfeited.[71] The order may allow time for payment of the amount due under the recognisance, or direct payment by instalments of such amounts and on such dates respectively as may be specified, or discharge the recognisance or reduce the amount due thereunder.[71]

Where the court is to consider making such an order, the Registrar must give notice to the person by whom the recognisance was entered into, indicating the time and place at which the matter will be considered. No order may be made until the expiry of seven days after the notice has been given.[72]

Any recognisance forfeited by the court on an appeal from the Crown Court is treated for the purposes of collection, enforcement and remission, as if it had been forfeited by the Crown Court.[73]

6. LEGAL AID

(1) Facilities for legal aid

It is the policy of the Criminal Division that no one should be without reasonable facilities for advice on appeal, and for the preparation of grounds

---

[67] *Ibid.* r. 4 (4). The recognisance of a surety will be in Form 8 set out in the Schedule to the Criminal Appeal Rules 1968, except in the case of an appellant granted bail pending a retrial under s. 7 of the Act or on a *venire de novo* when it will be in Form 10; Criminal Appeal Rules 1968, r. 4 (2); Criminal Appeal (Amendment) Rules 1978, rr. 3, 7 (*a*).

It is the duty of the person before whom a recognisance is entered into or a requirement complied with, to cause a copy of the recognisance or a statement that the requirement has been complied with, to be transmitted forthwith to the Registrar: Criminal Appeal Rules 1968, r. 4 (6); Criminal Appeal (Amendment) Rules 1978, r. 3. A copy or a statement must also be sent to the governor or keeper of the prison, etc., in which the appellant is detained, unless the latter is the person before whom the recognisance was entered into or the requirement complied with: *ibid.* A copy of a recognisance must be given to the person entering into it: *ibid.* r. 4 (7).

[68] See *ante*, p. 73, note 65.

[69] Criminal Appeal Rules 1968, r. 4 (8); Criminal Appeal (Amendment) Rules 1978, r. 3.

Where the court has granted bail on ordering a retrial under s. 7 of the Act or on a *venire de novo* the Registrar will forward any recognisances or statements sent to him to the appropriate officer of the Crown Court: *ibid.* r. 4 (9).

[70] The single judge has no power to order a recognisance to be forfeited.

[71] Criminal Appeal Rules 1968, r. 6 (1); Criminal Appeal (Amendment) Rules 1978, r. 5.

[72] *Ibid.* r. 6. (2).

[73] Powers of Criminal Courts Act 1973, s. 32 (3).

of appeal, if there are any. Such facilities are included in the first instance in the legal aid order in force at the trial,[74] but if these fail, facilities will be available through supplementary arrangements for legal aid.[75] The provisions are for "reasonable" facilities, and where in any particular case there is difficulty as to what should be regarded as "reasonable" the Registrar should be consulted.[76]

(2) Extent of facilities

The facilities for legal aid extend beyond the giving of notice of appeal, or of application for leave to appeal, and include preparation of the application itself; they extend up to, but do not include, the moment the application is presented to a judge or to the court. So included are the preparation of "initial" grounds[77] and their perfection, as well as provisional "grounds"[78] and their translation into grounds of appeal properly so called, which process includes the exploration of a reasonable possibility of calling fresh evidence.[79]

Further legal aid is required for oral argument on the grounds of appeal and, in general, such an order will not be made unless the grounds are arguable.[80]

(3) The Crown Court order

A person who was represented at the Crown Court under a legal aid order and was convicted and sentenced there, is entitled to receive from the solicitor and counsel assigned under that order advice on the question whether there appear to be reasonable grounds of appeal, and (a) if such grounds appear to exist, assistance in the preparation of an application for leave to appeal, or in the giving of notice of appeal, and (b) while that question is being considered, assistance in the making of a provisional application, or the giving of a provisional notice.[81]

If notice of appeal, or of application for leave to appeal, is given as a result of such advice, the facilities under the order extend up to, but not beyond, the moment when the application for leave is put before the court or the single judge; beyond this point legal aid for "argument" is required.[82]

(4) Legal aid in the Criminal Division

Legal aid granted by the Criminal Division is either supplementary legal aid for advice and assistance, or legal aid "for argument."

---

[74] See Legal Aid Act 1974, s. 30 (7) and p. 14, *post.* For an account of the practice relating to legal aid in the Criminal Division, see "Practice in the Court of Appeal (Criminal Division)—2" by Peter Morrish and Ian McLean (1977) 141 J.P.J. 78, 123.
[75] See pp. 75–78, *post.*
[76] "Preparation for Proceedings in the Court of Appeal (Criminal Division)" (see *ante*, p. 63, note 56), Introduction.
[77] See *ante*, p. 65.
[78] See *ante*, p. 66.
[79] "Preparation for Proceedings in the Court of Appeal (Criminal Division)" Introduction.
[80] *Ibid.* and see p. 76, *post.*
[81] Legal Aid Act 1974, s. 30 (7).
[82] See *ante*, p. 14.

If there was no legal aid order in force at the Crown Court,[83] or advice and assistance on the question of an appeal is not available under the order,[84] or the arrangements for receiving such advice and assistance have broken down[85] the Registrar may be asked to help.[86]

The Registrar, however, has no power to act unless notice of application for leave to appeal is given[87] and such notice should be given if the Registrar's assistance is required. The notice should contain, or be accompanied by, an explanation of the circumstances and an account of the matters put forward as possible grounds of appeal.[88] Where such notice is given by a solicitor, legal aid may be granted, in a proper case retrospectively, for the work done.[89]

The Registrar may grant legal aid limited in the first instance to advice by counsel or a solicitor on the question whether there appear to be reasonable grounds of appeal and assistance if there are such grounds, in perfecting them.[90]

Legal aid for oral argument before the court or the single judge, may be granted by the Criminal Division, by a judge, or by the Registrar.[91] Notice of application for such further legal aid may be included in Form 2 (N).[92] In general it will not be granted unless the grounds are arguable.[93] The order may be restricted to "counsel only" if it appears from the notice of appeal that counsel requires no instructions beyond those contained in the papers. If, however, there is good reason to assign a solicitor, as where it appears that

---

[83] Where no legal aid order was made for the proceedings in the Crown Court, a person convicted or sentenced in that court is not entitled to receive advice or assistance on appeal under legal aid. That person may have been unrepresented, or may have exhausted his funds in representation at private expense: "Preparation for Proceedings in the Court of Appeal (Criminal Division)" (see *ante*, p. 63, note 56, para. 9.1).

[84] A person who appeals against a finding of disability, or a verdict of not guilty by reason of insanity is not entitled to such advice and assistance as he was not "convicted and sentenced" at the Crown Court.

[85] Where a person is entitled to advice and assistance on appeal but does not receive it, the staff of the place where he is in custody will help him by supplying Form 1481. This is a form of letter addressed to the solicitor who should give the advice or assistance. The letter requests him to do so. If this fails, the Registrar may be asked to help: "Preparation for Proceedings in the Court of Appeal (Criminal Division)" (see *ante*, p. 63, note 56), para. 9.2. See also Thompson, Morrish and McLean, *op cit.* pp. 133 *et seq.*

[86] See *ante*, p. 74. A person who would have been entitled to advice and assistance on appeal but has withdrawn his instructions from his solicitor, may wish to obtain advice or assistance from another solicitor, as may a person who has received advice but has rejected it. It is not appropriate to assign another solicitor by amending the legal aid order made for the proceedings in the Crown Court once those proceedings are concluded. However, the Registrar may be asked to help. He will require good reasons, fully stated, for a change of solicitor or counsel, or both: "Preparation for Proceedings in the Court of Appeal (Criminal Division)" (see *ante*, p. 63, note 56), para. 9.3.
   Where a person was represented by "counsel only" in the Crown Court, he may ask the Registrar to assign a solicitor and counsel, for the purposes of advice or assistance on appeal: *ibid.* para. 9.4. Where a solicitor appeared as advocate in the Crown Court, he may ask the Registrar to provide for the services of counsel for the purposes of advice or assistance on appeal: *ibid.* para. 9.5.

[87] See the definition of "appellant," *ante*, p. 63, note 59.

[88] "Preparation for Proceedings in the Court of Appeal (Criminal Division) (see *ante*, p. 63, note 56), para. 9.6. The notice should be accompanied by a statement of means unless the applicant has already submitted one to the Crown Court: *ibid*.

[89] *Ibid.* para. 9.7.

[90] *Ibid.* para. 9.8.

[91] *Ibid.* para. 10.1.

[92] *Ibid.* para. 10.2.

[93] *Ibid.* para. 10.3.

reports, witness statements or other new material are or may be required, the court will order "full legal aid" either of its own motion or at the request of counsel assigned to the appellant.[94]

(5) Making the application

An application for legal aid for oral argument may be made: (a) by completing so much of Part 2 of Form 2 (N) as relates to the application when giving notice of appeal or of application for leave to appeal, or (b) subsequently, by serving notice on the Registrar, or (c) in an appropriate case, orally to the court, the single judge or the Registrar.[95]

(6) Consideration of application

In the great majority of cases an application for legal aid will be considered by the Registrar in the light of the grounds of appeal and any other papers in the case, without any oral representations being made.[96]

An application may be considered by the single judge when dealing with the primary application for leave to appeal or extension of time.[97] If the single judge grants the primary application he will invariably grant legal aid, if appropriate; where he refuses the primary application, all secondary applications lapse. A similar position obtains if the primary application is renewed before the court.

(7) Statement of means; down payment; contribution

As a general rule it may be asserted that the same administrative provisions apply in relation to legal aid in the Criminal Division as in any other court.[98] Since the majority of appellants are in custody serving a sentence and have, therefore, no earning capacity, and also the fact that if the appellant was represented in the Crown Court under legal aid, that fact is at least prima facie evidence of lack of means, the rules as to statements of means and payments on account do not play such a significant part in the procedure.[99]

For the same reasons, although the Criminal Division like any other criminal court has power to make a contribution order when determining an

[94] *Practice Note* (1974) 59 Cr. App. R. 158. The cases of two or more legally assisted co-appellants may be "consolidated" on a single solicitor or counsel unless the interests of justice require their separate representation: Legal Aid in Criminal Proceedings (General) Regulations 1968, reg. 14.

[95] Legal Aid in Criminal Proceedings (General) Regulations 1968, reg. 3 (1), (2). An application made orally to the court may be referred to a judge for determination; an application made orally to a judge may be referred to the Registrar for determination; *ibid.* reg. 3 (5).

[96] The Registrar may grant the application, or may refuse it unless a down payment on account is first made, or he may refer the application to the single judge. He may not, of course, grant an application already refused by the single judge, unless it was refused pending a down payment and that payment has been made: *ibid.* reg. 3 (6), (9).

[97] *Ibid.* reg. 3 (8). As to the extent of legal aid, see Thompson, Morrish and McLean, *op. cit.* under title "Legal Aid."

[98] The Widgery Committee was of opinion that the principle that legal aid should not be granted if the defendant's means were sufficient to pay his own costs was as valid in appellate courts as in courts of first instance: see Cmnd. 2934, para. 245.

[99] But see Legal Aid Act 1974, s. 29; Criminal Law Act 1977, Sched. 12; Legal Aid in Criminal Proceedings (General) Regulations 1968, regs. 3 (3) (*b*), (7), (8), 4 (3).

appeal,[1] the power is seldom used unless the appellant is at liberty, or though in custody has substantial assets.[2]

(8) Amendment and revocation

A legal aid order made in the Criminal Division may be amended or revoked in an appropriate case. It may be amended on the application of the appellant or otherwise, to substitute for the solicitors and counsel assigned other solicitors or counsel, to provide for the services of a solicitor where only counsel was assigned, and *vice versa*, or to provide for the services of two counsel.[3]

An order may be revoked on the application of the appellant, or where the legal representatives, or all those for the time being assigned, withdraw, and it appears that, because of the appellant's conduct, it is not desirable to amend the order.[4]

7. ABANDONMENT; LAPSE; SUMMARY DISMISSAL

An appeal or application for leave to appeal may be abandoned before the hearing by serving notice on the Registrar.[5] If not abandoned before the hearing, an application for leave to appeal may be abandoned at any time during the hearing; an appeal, once it is part heard, may be abandoned only with the leave of the court.[6]

An appeal which is abandoned is treated as having been dismissed; an application for leave which is abandoned is treated as having been refused by the court.[7]

A person seeking to abandon an appeal, or an application for leave to appeal, does so by serving notice on the Registrar in Form 14 (A).[8] The Registrar will send copies of that form to the appellant, the Home Secretary, the proper officer of the Crown Court and to any person having custody of the appellant.[9] Once an appellant has abandoned his appeal or application the Registrar may put the matter before the court, or a judge of the court, for the purpose of any ancillary orders as to costs, loss of time, legal aid contribution, etc., being made.

Once an appeal or application for leave to appeal has been abandoned, an appellant who seeks to pursue his case further is left with the choice of petitioning the Home Secretary for the exercise of the Royal Prerogative or for a reference to the court,[10] or of persuading the Criminal Division that his purported "abandonment" should be treated as a nullity.

---

[1] Legal Aid Act 1974, s. 32.
[2] Payment is made to the "collecting court," *i.e.* the magistrates' court named in the order: *ibid.* s. 32 (5).
[3] *Ibid.* s. 31 (1).
[4] *Ibid.* s. 31 (2).
[5] Criminal Appeal Rules 1968, r. 10.
[6] *R.* v. *Gibbon* (1946) 31 Cr. App. R. 143; *R.* v. *de Courcey* (1964) Cr. App. R. 323.
[7] Criminal Appeal Rules 1968, r. 10 (4).
[8] *Ibid.* r. 10 (1), r. 24, Sched. 1. Form 14 (A) is set out in Appendix F, *post.* No. 7.
[9] Criminal Appeal Rules 1968, r. 10 (3), 15.
[10] Under section 17 (1) (*a*) of the Act, see, *e.g. R.* v. *Graves* [1978] Crim. L.R. 216.

An appellant seeking to revive an appeal on this basis must write to the Registrar giving the reasons for his application. The Criminal Division reviewed the circumstances in which it may be prepared to treat a purported "abandonment" as a nullity, in the case of *R. v. Medway*.[11] The court said that it would be prepared in very exceptional circumstances to regard a purported notice of "abandonment" as a nullity and so without effect, and in such circumstances the appeal or application would be allowed to proceed. The court would have to be satisfied, however, that the notice of "abandonment" was not the result of a deliberate and informed decision, in other words that the mind of the appellant did not go with the act of abandonment.[12]

The right of appeal is a strictly personal right and in general dies with the convicted person.[13]

The Registrar is empowered, where it appears to him that a notice of appeal purporting to be on a ground involving a question of law alone, does not show any substantial ground of appeal,[14] to refer the appeal to the Criminal Division for summary dismissal, and if the court considers that the appeal is frivolous or vexatious and can be determined without adjourning it for a full hearing, it may dismiss it summarily, without calling on any person to attend the hearing or to appear for the prosecutor.[15]

8. The Hearing

(1) Constitution

The Criminal Division of the Court of Appeal sits in the Royal Courts of Justice in the Strand, London. The judges of the court are the Lord Chief Justice of England, the Lords Justices and any High Court judge requested to attend as a member. No judge may sit as a member of the court on the hearing of, or the determination of any application in proceedings preliminary or incidental to, an appeal against conviction before him, or before a court of which he was a member, or a sentence passed by him or such a court.[16]

(2) Two- and three-judge courts

Appeals are heard by a court consisting of an uneven number of judges, the number being not less than three, and presided over by the Lord Chief Justice

---

[11] (1976) 62 Cr. App. R. 85.
[12] The cases which may still be regarded as valid authority in the light of *R. v. Medway* may be said to be: *R. v. Noble* (1971) 55 Cr. App. R. 329; *R. v. La Plante*, May 19, 1972, C.A. (unreported); *R. v. Siddique*, November 4, 1974, C.A. (unreported); *R. v. Mills*, January 13, 1974, C.A. (unreported); *R. v. Simpson*, January 27, 1976, C.A. (unreported); *R. v. Hewitt*, July 29, 1976, C.A. (unreported).
[13] *R. v. Jefferies* [1969] 1 Q.B. 120; *R. v. Rowe* [1955] 1 Q.B. 573.
[14] See *R. v. Majewski*, (1976) 63 Cr. App. R. 5, at p. 8, for the construction to be put upon this provision.
[15] Criminal Appeal Act 1968, s. 20. It is the practice for appeals to be referred in this manner only on the authority of the Registrar personally and not on the authority of one of his staff: See Thompson, Morrish and McLean, *op. cit.* p. 229; and *R. v. Majewski, supra*.
[16] Criminal Appeal Act 1968, s. 2 (3) (*a*).

or a Lord Justice.[17] Any of the powers of the Criminal Division may be exercised by such a court.[17] A court consisting of two judges only may not[18]:

    (a) refuse an application for leave to appeal, save upon renewal after refusal by the single judge;

    (b) determine an appeal;

    (c) determine an application for leave to appeal from the Criminal Division to the House of Lords.

(3) The appeal papers

Copies of all papers required for the hearing are supplied to the judges by the Registrar.

The Registrar will also, on request, supply to either party to the appeal copies of any documents or other things required for the appeal.[19]

(4) Date of hearing

The Registrar will give as long notice as is reasonably possible of the date on which the court will hear an appeal, or application for leave,[20] to the appellant and to any person having custody of him.[21]

Particulars of cases to be heard are published in a list for each day's sittings and that list is circulated to prisons and other establishments and is also sent to individual appellants if not in custody. The list is displayed in the Royal Courts of Justice daily.

(5) Presence of appellant

An appellant who is not in custody is at liberty to attend the hearing of his appeal, or of any other proceedings preliminary to, or incidental, it, which are heard in open court.[22] An appellant who is in custody is entitled to be present at the hearing of his appeal, if it is against sentence,[23] or if it is against conviction (a) on the trial judge's certificate, or (b) on a reference by the Home Secretary under s. 17 (1) (a) of the Criminal Appeal Act 1968,[24] or (c) if he is given leave to appeal. He is not entitled to be present, where his appeal is against conviction on a question of law alone, or if his appeal is against a verdict of not guilty by reason of insanity or against a finding of disability.[25] The court will require special reasons before giving him leave to be present in such cases.

---

[17] Administration of Justice Act 1970, s. 9 (1).

[18] *Ibid*. s. 9 (2).

[19] Criminal Appeal Rules 1968, rr. 8 (1), 19 (2). He may charge at the official rate or, in his discretion, he may make no charge. No charge is made where papers are supplied to the legal representatives acting under a legal aid order: see *ante*, p. 68.

[20] No notice will be given of the date of a hearing before the single judge.

[21] Criminal Appeal Rules 1968, r. 22 (2).

[22] Proceedings before the single judge are not normally in open court. As to the costs of his appearance, see p. 85, *post*.

[23] The power of the court to pass sentence (under ss. 3, 4, 5, 11 or 13 of the Criminal Appeal Act 1968), may be exercised even though, for any reason, the appellant is not present: *ibid*. s. 22 (3).

[24] A reference under s. 17 (1) (b) is in no way an appeal as such and no formal hearing takes place.

[25] Criminal Appeal Act 1968, s. 22 (1).

An appellant not otherwise entitled, but desiring to be present at the hearing of his appeal, must apply for leave by completing so much of Part 2 of Form 2 (N) as relates to the application, and serving it together with those reasons[26] set out in Form 5 (P) on the Registrar.[27]

(6) Absent appellant

An appellant who is not in custody has a right but no duty to attend the hearing of his appeal. Where the correct steps have been taken to give him notice of the hearing and he chooses not to attend, the court will proceed to determine his appeal in his absence.[28]

Where an appellant absconds from custody and is for that reason not present when his appeal is called on, the court will either dismiss the appeal or adjourn the hearing according to the justice of the case.[29]

(7) Grant of leave to appeal

Where an application for leave to appeal is heard before a court of three judges and is not refused, the court may either grant leave and proceed to the hearing of the appeal without adjourning the matter, or may adjourn the hearing of the appeal to a later date. Even where the appellant would be entitled to be present at the hearing of the appeal, and is not present when leave is given, the court may nevertheless proceed with the hearing if the appellant is represented and his counsel consents to such a course, or his counsel indicates that the appellant does not wish to be present, or on an appeal against sentence, on the basis that if the appellant wishes he may have the appeal restored to the list at a later date when he will be present.

The court may direct that the Director of Public Prosecutions appear on an appeal to the Criminal Division.[30]

The hearing of an appeal will be adjourned to a later date where an unrepresented appellant is granted legal aid to enable him to have the appeal argued by counsel, where the prosecutor is not represented on the application but is to be represented on the appeal, or where further information or reports are required.

(8) Determination of appeal or application

At the conclusion of the hearing of an appeal, or of an application for leave to appeal which is refused, the court may give its decision and the reasons for that decision forthwith, or it may give its decision then and there, reserving its reasons to a later date, or it may reserve both its decisions and the reasons therefore to a later date.

---

[26] The nature of his appeal may require his presence to assist in the presentation of his case; this is especially so where evidence is to be called on appeal.
[27] Criminal Appeal Rules 1968, r. 3 (1) (b), Sched. A specimen Form 5 (P) is set out in Appendix F, *post*, No. 7.
[28] *R.* v. *Field* (1975) October 13, C.A. (unreported).
[29] *R.* v. *Flower* (1965) 50 Cr. App. R. 22.
[30] See the Prosecution of Offences Act 1979, s. 3 (1) (b). There are corresponding provisions relating to an appeal from the Criminal Division to the House of Lords.

Judgment is ordinarily pronounced by the presiding judge, or, if he so directs, by another member of the court. Separate judgments are not pronounced unless the question is one of law and the presiding judge is of opinion that separate judgments would be convenient.[31] An appeal is determined according to the opinion of the majority of the members of the court; an application for leave to appeal, however, is usually granted even where one member only is for granting it.

As soon as practicable the Registrar will give notice of the court's determination to the appellant to any person having custody of the appellant,[32] to the Home Secretary and to the proper officer of the Crown Court.[33]

The court has jurisdiction to alter any order or decision made by it at any time up to the moment when, on receipt of notice of the court's decision from the Registrar, the proper officer of the Crown Court enters that decision in the record of the court of trial.[34]

9. Determination of Appeals against Conviction

(1) General

As a general rule an appeal to the Criminal Division will either be allowed or it will be dismissed. The court must allow an appeal against conviction if it considers that: (a) the conviction should be set aside on the ground that in all the circumstances of the case it is unsafe or unsatisfactory[35]; or (b) the judgment of the court of trial should be set aside on the ground of a wrong decision of any question of law[36]; or (c) there was a material irregularity in the course of the trial.[37]

In any other case, an appeal must be dismissed, subject to the proviso that, notwithstanding that the court is of opinion that the point raised in the appeal might be decided in favour of the appellant, it may dismiss the appeal if it considers that no miscarriage of justice has actually occurred.[38]

(2) "Unsafe or unsatisfactory"

In order to establish that a conviction is "unsafe or unsatisfactory" it will not generally be sufficient to show that the case against the appellant was a weak one[39] or that the verdict was against the weight of the evidence[40] or that the

---

[31] The power is seldom exercised, but see *R.* v. *Head* (1958) 41 Cr. App. R. 249.

[32] In the case of an appellant detained under the provisions of Pt. V of the Mental Health Act 1959, notice is also given to the "responsible authority": Criminal Appeal Rules 1968, r. 15 (3).

[33] *Ibid.* r. 15.

[34] *R.* v. *Cross* [1973] 2 W.L.R. 1049. *Cf. R.* v. *Majewski* [1975] 3 All E.R. 621; *R.* v. *Daniel* [1977] 1 All E.R. 621.

[35] Criminal Appeal Act 1968, s. 2 (1) (*a*); Criminal Law Act 1977, s. 44.

[36] Criminal Appeal Act 1968, s. 2 (1) (*b*). The ambit of the subsection is not limited to the confines of a formal trial and extends to a ruling given before arraignment on a point of law: *R.* v. *Vickers* [1975] 1 W.L.R. 81.

[37] Criminal Appeal Act 1968, s. 2 (1) (*c*).

[38] Criminal Appeal Act 1968, s. 2 (1), proviso (see below).

[39] *R.* v. *McNair* (1909) 2 Cr. App. R. 2.

[40] *Aladesuru* v. *The Queen* [1956] A.C. 49 P.C.

trial judge was dissatisfied with the verdict.[41] In the end, the court will ask itself the subjective question whether it is prepared to let the matter stand as it is, or whether there is not some "lurking doubt" in the mind which makes it wonder whether an injustice has been done.[42]

(3) Application of the proviso

The decision whether or not to apply the proviso[43] depends upon the whole of the circumstances of a particular case, rather than upon the type of irregularity or wrong decision.[44]

A miscarriage of justice within the meaning of the Act[45] may be said to occur where, by reason of some mistake, omission or irregularity in the trial, the appellant has lost a chance of acquittal which was fairly open to him.[46] No chance of acquittal can be said to be open to a defendant if a reasonable jury, properly directed, could have come to no other verdict than one of guilty.[47]

If, in the absence of the mistake, omission or irregularity, the only proper verdict would have been one of guilty, the court will apply the proviso.

(4) Effect of allowing appeal

Where the court allows an appeal against conviction,[48] it must quash that conviction.[49] Unless the court orders a retrial under the provisions of section 7 of the Criminal Appeal Act 1968,[50] such an order operates as a direction to the Crown Court to enter judgment and verdict of acquittal instead of the record of conviction.[51]

(5) Other principal powers on appeal

Apart from the general power to dismiss or to allow an appeal, the Criminal Division has other powers to meet special circumstances,[52] the most pertinent

---

[41] R. v. Hopkins-Husson (1949) 34 Cr. App. R. 47; R. v. Chalk [1961] Crim. L.R. 326.
[42] This is a reaction which may not be based strictly on the evidence; it is a reaction which is produced by the general feel of the case as the court experiences it: R. v. Cooper [1969] 1 Q.B. 267. See also R. v. Savin [1973] Crim. L.R. 289; R. v. Pattinson (1973) 58 Cr. App. R. 4170. There is no specific test to be applied: R. v. Stafford & Luvaglio [1974] A.C. 878, but see R. v. Wallace; R. v. Short (1979) 68 Cr. App. R. 291.
[43] i.e. the proviso to s. 2 (1) of the Criminal Appeal Act 1968, see ante, p. 82.
[44] R. v. Shaw (1974) R.T.R. 458; R. v. Mustafa [1977] Crim. L.R. 282.
[45] See ante, p. 82. This refers not only to the proviso to s. 22 (1) but also the proviso to ss. 13 (2) and 16 (1).
[46] R. v. Haddy (1944) 29 Cr. App. R. 182, cited with approval in Stirland v. D.P.P. (1944) 30 Cr. App. R. 40; R. v. Farid (1945) 30 Cr. App. R. 168; R. v. Whybrow (1951) 35 Cr. App. R. 141; R. v. Brown (1971) 55 Cr. App. R. 473.
[47] The court will not apply the proviso unless it is quite clear that in the absence of the mistake, omission or irregularity, the consequences would have been the same: R. v. Pilcher (1975) 60 Cr. App. R. 1, at p. 6; R. v. Pink (1971) 55 Cr. App. R. 16 at p. 21.
[48] Different considerations apply in the case of an appeal against a verdict of not guilty by reason of insanity (see p. 86, post), or an appeal against a finding of disability (see p. 87, post).
[49] Even where the conviction is the result of a mistrial apparently: see R. v. Thompson, R. v. Klein (1975) 61 Cr. App. R. 108.
[50] See p. 82, post.
[51] See R. v. Cross (1973) 57 Cr. App. R. 660. As to the effect upon orders for the restitution of property and criminal bankruptcy orders, see p. 97, post.
[52] In R. v. Younis [1964] Crim. L.R. 305 the Court of Criminal Appeal purported to act as Justices of the Peace and bind the appellant over to be of good behaviour; see also R. v. Sharp and Johnson (1957) 41 Cr. App. R. 86. Cf. R. v. Finch [1964] Crim. L.R. 179.

of which are the power to order a retrial by reason of evidence received on the appeal[53] and the power to order a *venire de novo*.[54]

In the case of an appeal by a person in whose case the jury returned a special verdict,[55] the court may, instead of allowing the appeal, if it considers that a wrong conclusion was arrived at in the Crown Court on the effect of that verdict, order such conviction to be recorded as appears to be in law required by the verdict, and pass such sentence as may be authorised by law for that passed at the trial.[56]

Where, on an appeal against conviction, the appellant was convicted of an offence and the jury could, on the indictment, have found him guilty of another offence,[57] the court may, if it appears that the jury must have been satisfied of facts which proved him guilty of that other offence,[58] substitute[59] for the verdict of the jury, a verdict of guilty of that other offence, and pass such sentence in substitution for that passed at the trial as may be authorised for the offence, not being a sentence of greater severity.[60]

On an appeal against conviction on an indictment containing two or more counts where the court allows an appeal in respect of part of the indictment, it may, in respect of any count upon which the appellant remains convicted, pass such sentence in substitution for that passed on that count at the trial, as it thinks proper and as is authorised by law for the offence,[61] provided that a sentence may not be passed which would make the appellant's sentence on the indictment as a whole of greater severity than the sentence passed at the trial.[62]

Where on an appeal against conviction, the court is of opinion that the proper verdict would have been one of not guilty by reason of insanity, or that the case is not one where there should have been a verdict of acquittal but that there should have been a finding that the appellant was under disability, the court will make an order that the appellant be admitted to a hospital specified by the Secretary of State.[63]

(6) Ancillary powers

In addition to exercising its principal powers as set out above, the court may, on determining an appeal or, an application for leave to appeal, order *inter alia*

---

[53] See p. 89, *post*.
[54] See p. 99, *post*. The court has no power on appeal to amend the original indictment: *R.* v. *Nelson* (1977) 65 Cr. App. R. 119.
[55] See *R.* v. *Bourne* (1952) 36 Cr. App. R. 125 at p. 127.
[56] Criminal Appeal Act 1968, s. 5.
[57] See, *e.g. R.* v. *Johnson* (1963) 48 Cr. App. R. 25; *R.* v. *Cascoe* (1970) 54 Cr. App. R. 410.
[58] The court will only exercise this power where it appears from the finding of the jury that the facts essential to prove that other offence were established: *R.* v. *Deacon* (1973) 57 Cr. App. R. 688. See also in this respect *R.* v. *Caslin* (1961) 45 Cr. App. R. 47; *R.* v. *Smith* (1962) 46 Cr. App. R. 377; *R.* v. *Jones* (1969) 113 S.J. 86.
[59] Instead of allowing or dismissing the appeal.
[60] Criminal Appeal Act 1969, s. 3. As to what amounts to a sentence of "greater severity," see p. 96, *post*.
[61] Criminal Appeal Act 1968, s. 4 (1), (2).
[62] Criminal Appeal Act 1968, s. 4. See, *e.g. R.* v. *Holley* (1969) 53 Cr. App. R. 19.
[63] Criminal Appeal Act 1968, s. 6., Sched. 1.

the payment of costs,[64] expenses[64] or a contribution towards legal aid,[64a] and may direct loss of time spent in custody.[65]

(7) Notification of determination

The Registrar will, as soon as practicable, serve notice of any determination of the court on an appeal or application for leave to appeal on the appellant, the Home Secretary and any person having custody of the appellant.[66] Notice will also be given to the proper officer of the Crown Court.[67]

(8) Costs

Costs awarded by the court may be either out of central funds[68] or against the appellant. When the court allows an appeal[69] under Part I of the Act against conviction, etc., it may order the payment out of central funds of the appellant.[70] On determining an appeal or application for leave to appeal under Part I of the Act, the court may also order the payment out of central funds of the costs of the prosecutor.[71] In each case, the costs awarded must be such sums as appear to the court to be reasonably sufficient to compensate the party concerned for any expenses properly incurred by him in the appeal or application (including any proceedings preliminary or incidental to it) or in any court below.[72]

When the court dismisses an appeal or an application for leave to appeal under Part I of the Act, it may order the appellant to pay[73] the whole or any part of the costs of the appeal or application.[74]

Where an order for the payment of costs out of central funds is otherwise appropriate, it is generally irrelevant that the appellant is legally aided.[75]

---

[64] See below.
[65] See *ante*, p. 77.
[66] In the case of an appellant detained under the Mental Health Act 1959, to the responsible authority: Criminal Appeal Rules 1968, r. 15 (3).
[67] *Ibid*. r. 15.
[68] See Costs in Criminal Cases Act 1973, s. 13.
[69] The section applies only when an appeal is allowed. Where the court, instead of allowing an appeal, exercises its powers under ss. 3, 4, 5, 6, of the Act (see *ante*, pp. 83–84) no costs are payable.
[70] *Ibid*. s. 7 (1).
[71] *Ibid*. s. 7 (2).
[72] *Ibid*. s. 7 (3). As to taxation, see *ibid*. s. 7 (4). The court may also award out of central funds such sums as appear to be reasonably sufficient to compensate a person properly attending to give evidence on an appeal under Pt. I of the Act, or on any preliminary or incidental proceedings, whether or not he gives evidence, for the expense, trouble or loss of time properly incurred in or incidental to his attendance: Costs in Criminal Cases Act 1973, s. 8 (1). Again, an appellant who is not in custody who appears before the court, either on the hearing of his appeal or in any preliminary or incidental proceedings may have the expenses of his appearance paid out of central funds: *ibid*. s. 8 (2). As to taxation, see *ibid*. s. 8 (3).
[73] To such person as may be named in the order.
[74] *Ibid*. s. 9 (1). These costs may include the costs of any transcript of a record of proceedings: *ibid*. s. 9 (2). As to taxation, see *ibid*. s. 9 (3).
[75] *R*. v. *Arron* (1973) 57 Cr. App. R. 834.

(9) Fines imposed by the Criminal Division

Where the court, on determining an appeal, imposes a fine on an appellant, the court must make an order fixing a term of imprisonment not exceeding 12 months, which the appellant is to undergo if the fine is not paid or recovered. The order may also allow time for the payment of the fine, or may direct payment by instalments of such amounts, on such dates, as may be specified.[76]

10. INSANITY CASES

A person in whose case is recorded a verdict of "not guilty by reason of insanity" may appeal to the Criminal Division of the Court of Appeal on any ground which involves a question of law, and, with the leave of the court on any ground which involves a question of fact alone or a question of mixed law and fact, or on any other ground which appears to the court to be a sufficient ground of appeal.[77] As in the case of an appeal against conviction,[78] an appeal lies without the need for leave if the trial judge grants a certificate that the case is fit for appeal on such a ground.[79]

A person seeking to appeal in such a case initiates his appeal in the same manner as a person seeking to appeal against his conviction.[80]

In general it may be said that similar provisions apply to an appeal under section 12 of the Act as apply to initiating an appeal against conviction[81] but two important differences need to be observed. A legal aid order which may have been in force for the purpose of the proceedings in the Crown Court does not cover the provision of advice and assistance on the prosepcts of an appeal,[82] so that a person seeking such assistance must apply in the first instance to the Registrar.[83] Also, an appellant in custody in consequence of a verdict of "not guilty by reason of insanity" is not entitled to be present at the hearing of his appeal unless the court gives him leave.[84]

The court must allow an appeal under section 12 in the same circumstances as it must allow an appeal against conviction[85] and subject to the same proviso.[86] In addition, however, where an appeal under section 12 is allowed, and the ground, or one of the grounds, is that the finding of the jury as to the appellant's insanity ought not to stand, and the court is of opinion that the proper verdict would have been that he was guilty of an offence,[87] then the court must substitute for the original verdict, a verdict of guilty of that offence,

[76] Criminal Appeal Rules 1968, r. 13.
[77] Criminal Appeal Act 1968, s. 12.
[78] See *ante*, pp. 60–61.
[79] Criminal Appeal Act 1968, s. 12.
[80] See *ante*, pp. 62 *et seq.* Form 2 (N) must be modified to take account of the nature of the appeal. A specimen Form 2 (N) is set out in Appendix F, *post*, No. 2.
[81] See *ante*, pp. 62 *et seq.*
[82] Since the appellant was not "convicted and sentenced" in the Crown Court. See Legal Aid Act 1974, s. 30 (7).
[83] See *ante*, p. 76, note 84.
[84] Criminal Appeal Act 1968, s. 22, see also *ante*, p. 80.
[85] See *ante*, p. 82.
[86] Criminal Appeal Act 1968, s. 13. As to the exercise of the proviso, see *ante*, p. 83.
[87] Whether the offence charged or another offence of which the jury could have found him guilty.

and it has the like powers of punishing or otherwise dealing with the offender, and any other powers, as the Crown Court would have had if the jury had just returned the substituted verdict.[88] In any other case the court must substitute for the verdict of the jury a verdict of acquittal.[88]

Where, on an appeal under section 12, the court is of opinion that the case is not one where there should have been an acquittal, but that there should have been a finding that the defendant was under disability,[89] it must make a hospital order.[90] Where the court substitutes a verdict of acquittal[91] but is of opinion that the appellant is suffering from mental disorder of a nature or degree which warrants his detention in a hospital,[92] for at least a limited period, and is of opinion that he ought to be detained[93] it must make an order that he be admitted to such hospital as the Secretary of State may specify.[94]

Where the court dismisses an appeal, or an application for leave to appeal, by an appellant who is subject to a hospital order, or an order under section 5 of the Criminal Procedure (Insanity) Act 1964, or affirms such an order, and the appellant has been on bail pending the determination of his appeal the court will give such directions as it thinks fit for his conveyance to the hospital from which he was released on bail, and his detention, if necessary in a place of safety pending admission to that hospital.[95]

11. DISABILITY CASES

Where there has been a determination of the question of a person's fitness to be tried[96] and the jury has returned a finding that he is under disability[97] he may appeal to the Criminal Division in the same circumstances as a person in whose case there is returned a verdict of not guilty by reason of insanity.[98] Such a person initiates an appeal in the same manner as a person appealing against conviction.[99]

In general it may be said, as in the case of an appeal by a person in whose case there is returned a verdict of not guilty by reason of insanity,[1] that the same general provisions govern the bringing of an appeal under section 15 as

[88] Criminal Appeal Act 1968, s. 13 (4), (5). Such an order operates as a direction to the Crown Court to amend the record accordingly; *ibid.* s. 13 (6).
[89] See below.
[90] Criminal Appeal Act 1968, s. 14 (1).
[91] *i.e.* under *ibid.* s. 13 (4) (*b*).
[92] With or without medical treatment.
[93] Either in the interests of his own health and safety or with a view to the protection of other persons.
[94] Criminal Appeal Act 1968, s. 14 (2); see also *ibid.* s. 14 (3), Sched. 1 and Criminal Appeal Rules 1968, r. 14.
[95] Criminal Appeal Rules 1968, r. 14.
[96] Under the Criminal Procedure (Insanity) Act 1964, s. 4.
[97] "Under disability" for the purposes of the Criminal Appeal Act 1968, has the meaning assigned to it by the Criminal Procedure (Insanity) Act 1964: Criminal Appeal Act 1968, s. 51 (1). As to the position where the defendant is found not to be under disability and is convicted of an offence and seeks to show that he should never have been tried, see *R.* v. *Podola* (1959) 43 Cr. App. R. 220.
[98] Criminal Appeal Act 1968, s. 15.
[99] See *ante*, p. 62. Form 2 (N) must be modified to take account of the nature of the appeal; see Appendix F, *post*, No. 2.
[1] See *ante*, pp. 62 *et seq.*

govern the bringing of an appeal against conviction.[2] As in an appeal under section 12, so also in the case of an appeal under section 15, the legal aid order in force at the Crown Court does not provide for advice and assistance on the prospect of an appeal[3] and a person seeking such advice and assistance must apply in the first instance to the Registrar.[4] A person in custody in consequence of a finding of disability is not entitled to be present at the hearing of his appeal unless given leave.[5]

The court must allow an appeal under section 15 for the same reasons as apply to an appeal against conviction[6] and subject to the same proviso.[7] In general, the effect of allowing an appeal is that the appellant may be tried[8] for the offence with which he was charged,[9] but where the question of fitness to be tried was determined later than on arraignment, and the appeal is allowed notwithstanding that the finding was properly arrived at because the court is of opinion that the appellant ought to have been acquitted before the question of fitness to be tried was considered, the court must, in allowing the appeal and quashing the finding of disability, also direct that a verdict of acquittal[10] be recorded.[11]

12. HOME SECRETARY'S REFERENCE

The Home Secretary may, if he thinks fit, at any time, in the case of a person convicted on indictment, or tried on indictment and found not guilty by reason of insanity, or found by a jury to be under disability, refer the whole case[12] to the Criminal Division, and the case will then be treated for all purposes as an appeal[13] to the court by that person.[14]

[2] See *ante*, pp. 62 *et seq.*

[3] Since such advice depends upon being "convicted and sentenced" at the Crown Court, see Legal Aid Act 1974, s. 30 (7).

[4] See *ante*, p. 84, note 82.

[5] Criminal Appeal Act 1968, s. 22.

[6] See *ante*, pp. 82 *et seq.*

[7] Criminal Appeal Act 1968, s. 16 (1). As to the exercise of the proviso, see *ante*, p. 83.

[8] The words are "may be tried" and not "will be tried": see *R.* v. *Webb* (1969) 53 Cr. App. R. 360; also *R.* v. *Burles* (1970) 54 Cr. App. R. 196.

[9] Criminal Appeal Act 1968, s. 16 (3). The court may make such orders as appear to be necessary or expedient, pending the trial, for the appellant's release on bail, detention in custody, or continued detention under the Mental Health Act 1959: Criminal Appeal Act 1968, s. 16 (3); Bail Act 1976, Sched. 2.

[10] But not a verdict of not guilty by reason of insanity.

[11] Criminal Appeal Act 1968, s. 16 (2).

[12] In practice the reference is more often than not in terms which restrict it to conviction only, or to sentence only. References on sentence are rare, but see *R.* v. *Forbes* (1968) 52 Cr. App. R. 585. The power to refer the whole case includes the power to refer part of a case: *R.* v. *Bardoe* [1969] 1 W.L.R. 398.

[13] Thus the court may then grant bail, where appropriate (see *ante*, p. 71) or legal aid (see *ante*, p. 74), and the appellant is entitled to be present at the hearing of his appeal (see *ante*, p. 80). The court has, however, no power to direct loss of time (see p. 96, *post*). Appeal to the House of Lords (see p. 105, *post*) lies in the same manner as in any other appeal.

[14] Criminal Appeal Act 1968, s. 17 (1) (*a*). No reference is possible under the section in relation to proceedings in the Crown Court other than on indictment, or in relation to proceedings in the magistrates' courts.

The Home Secretary may, in similar circumstances, if he desires the assistance of the court on any point arising in any such case, refer that point to the court for their opinion on it, and the court will consider the point and furnish him with their opinion on it: *ibid.* s. 17 (1) (*b*). Such a reference is in no sense an appeal, and the opinion may be furnished without any proceedings in public, although the court may give their opinion in open court if the circumstances warrant it:

There is no time limit within which a case must be referred, and a reference may be made at any stage of the proceedings.[15] The Home Secretary's discretion[16] is, as a matter of practice, used sparingly, and the procedure has never been used as a means of achieving a reconsideration of matters already considered by the courts.[17]

A person who seeks to persuade the Home Secretary to refer his case to the Criminal Division, should write to the Home Secretary enclosing, where appropriate, copies of statements of potential witnesses and any other relevant material. If the Home Secretary decides to refer the case to the court he will do so by means of a formal letter to the Registrar.[18] The court, when hearing the appeal, will hear argument on the matters set out in the letter of reference much as though they were grounds of appeal.[19]

On determining an appeal upon a reference by the Home Secretary the court has all the powers exercisable in any other appeal.

13. EVIDENCE ON APPEAL

(1) General

An appeal to the Criminal Division of the Court of Appeal is in no sense a rehearing of the issues which were before the Crown Court. The court may, however, hear evidence in one of three sets of circumstances: (a) in the circumstances, provided by, and under the conditions set out in, section 23 of the Criminal Appeal 1968[20]; (b) informally, in a case where an irregularity is alleged to have occurred in the proceedings of the court of trial[21]; (c) informally, on an appeal, or application for leave to appeal, against sentence, in the same manner as evidence in mitigation is heard in the Crown Court.

(2) Power to receive evidence under section 23

The court[22] may, under section 23 (1) of the Act, if it thinks it necessary or

see *R.* v. *O'Neill* (1948) 33 Cr. App. R. 19; *R.* v. *McCartan* (1958) 42 Cr. App. R. 262; *R.* v. *McMahon*, (1979) 68 Cr. App. R. 18.

[15] In law, although in practice it is unlikely, a case might be referred even before the ordinary rights of appeal were exhausted.

[16] Mandamus does not lie to enforce reference of a case: *ex p. Kinnally* [1958] Crim. L.R. 474.

[17] The fact that case has already been the subject of an appeal does not prevent the Home Secretary from referring it to the court under s. 17 (1) (*a*).

[18] Copies of which will be supplied to the parties by the Home Secretary or by the Registrar.

[19] It is open to the person whose case is referred to ask the court to consider additional "grounds of appeal," when hearing the reference, see Thompson, Morrish and McLean, *op cit.* at p. 115.

The court will, in general, confine itself to the grounds on which the case is referred: see, *e.g. R.* v. *Caborn-Waterfield* [1956] 2 Q.B. 379; *R.* v. *Stones (No. 2)* (1968) 52 Cr. App. R. 624; *R.* v. *Swabey* [1972] 1 W.L.R. 925 C.M.A.C. Where the reference is in respect of sentence the court is not prepared to hear argument in relation to the conviction: *R.* v. *Bardoe* [1969] 1 W.L.R. 398. It is possible that the court is more favourably disposed to receive evidence under s. 23 of the Criminal Appeal Act 1968, when that evidence forms the basis, or part of the basis of a reference under s. 17 (1) (*a*), since otherwise the purpose of the reference might be frustrated: see Thompson, Morrish and McLean, *op. cit.* at p. 75.

[20] See below. An application is made in Form 6 (10), a copy of which is to be found in Appendix F, *post*, No. 8.

[21] See, *e.g.* the "plea bargaining" cases, such as *R.* v. *Turner* [1970] 2 Q.B. 321; *R.* v. *Hall* [1968] 2 Q.B. 787.

[22] The single judge has no power to give leave to call a witness.

expedient in the interests of justice, receive the evidence of any witness who is compellable, or if tendered, who is competent but not compellable.[23]

(3) Duty to receive evidence under section 23

Where the evidence of such a witness is tendered to the court,[24] the court is under a duty to receive it:

(a) if it appears that the evidence is likely to be credible and would have been admissible[25] in the Crown Court on an issue which is the subject of the appeal[26]; and

(b) if the court is satisfied that the evidence was not adduced at the trial, but that there is a reasonable explanation for its not being adduced[27];

unless satisfied that the evidence, if received, would not afford any ground for allowing the appeal.[28]

(4) Court's powers on receiving evidence under section 23

Where evidence is received,[29] or is available to be received,[30] under section 23, the court will consider whether it thinks that the conviction should be set aside on the ground that under all the circumstances it is unsafe or unsatisfactory,[31] in which case it will quash the conviction[32] and whether, if it has allowed the appeal only by reason of the evidence received or available to be received, the interests of justice require the appellant to be retried, in which case it will order a retrial.[33]

(5) Power to appoint examiner

The court[34] may, for the purpose of an appeal, if it thinks it necessary or expedient in the interests of justice, order the examination of any compellable

---

[23] A competent but not compellable witness includes the appellant and the appellant's husband or wife if the appellant makes an application for the purpose and the evidence of the spouse could not have been given at the trial except on such an application: *ibid.* s. 23 (3).

[24] *i.e.* under s. 23 (1).

[25] The court does not hear inadmissible evidence: *R.* v. *Dallas* [1971] Crim. L.R. 90; *R.* v. *Lattimore* (1976) 62 Cr. App. R. 53; and see *R.* v. *Wallace*; *R.* v. *Short* (1979) 68 Cr. App. R. 291.

[26] The court sometimes hears evidence of matters arising since the trial, see, *e.g. R.* v. *Ditch* (1969) 53 Cr. App. R. 627.

[27] As to case where a deliberate decision was made by the defence not to call a witness at the trial, see *R.* v. *Quinton* [1970] Crim. L.R. 91; *R.* v. *Melville* (1976) 62 Cr. App. R. 100; *R.* v. *Lattimore* (1976) 62 Cr. App. R. 53; the unreported case of *R.* v. *Brett and Others* [1975] July 28, C.A. and *R.* v. *Shields and Patrick* [1977] Crim. L.R. 28.

[28] Criminal Appeal Act 1968, s. 23 (2).

[29] The court may order a compellable witness to attend: Criminal Appeal Act 1968, s. 23 (1) (b). The single judge may issue a witness order (*ibid.* s. 31 (2) (b)) but may not give leave for the evidence to be received.

[30] Where the evidence is unimpeachable and is conclusive of the appeal, the court may allow the appeal on the strength of the witness statements without insisting on the witnesses being called: see *R.* v. *Williams* [1956] Crim. L.R. 833; *R.* v. *Gordon* (1963) 47 Cr. App. R. 28; *R.* v. *Gray* (1974) 58 Cr. App. R. 177.

[31] See p. 82, *ante.* The question is whether the *court* is of that opinion: *R.* v. *Stafford* (1973) 58 Cr. App. R. 256.

[32] Criminal Appeal Act 1968, s. 2 (1) (a); Criminal Law Act 1977, s. 44. If a retrial is not ordered a judgment and verdict of acquittal will be entered by the Crown Court: *ibid.* s. 2 (3).

[33] Criminal Appeal Act 1968, s. 7 (1). As to the incidents of such a retrial, see *ibid.* s. 8, Sched. 2. As to the ancillary orders which may be made by the court, or the single judge, see *ibid.*

[34] The single judge has no power to make such an order.

witness to be conducted before a judge[35] or officer of the court or any other person appointed for the purpose[36] and allow the admission of any depositions[37] to be taken as evidence before the court.[38]

(6) Production of documents, etc.

The court[38a] may, for the purposes of an appeal, if it thinks it necessary or expedient in the interests of justice, order the production of any document, exhibit or other thing[39] connected with the proceedings, the production of which appears to be necessary for the determination of the case.[40]

14. APPEALS AGAINST SENTENCE

(1) General

The Criminal Appeal Act 1968 differentiates in dealing with sentence appeals between a sentence passed following conviction on indictment (section 9) and a sentence passed at the Crown Court for an offence of which the offender was not convicted on indictment (section 10).

No appeal lies to the Criminal Division against a sentence passed in any court other than the Crown Court, or against a sentence passed in the Crown Court on appeal to that court from a magistrates' court.

(2) Rights of appeal

The effects of sections 9, 10 and 11 of the Act is that where the Crown Court deals with an offender for an offence of which either he was convicted on indictment, or he was convicted in a magistrates' court and was committed to, or appeared before, the Crown Court for sentence or to be dealt with,[41] he may appeal to the Criminal Division against the sentence passed, or any order made, so long as: (a) the sentence or order is a "sentence" within the meaning of the Act,[42] or is appealable by virtue of some other authority or enactment[43]; and (b) where the conviction was on indictment, the sentence was not one

---

[35] See, e.g. R. v. Saunders (1974) 58 Cr. App. R. 248.
[36] The examiner has a discretion whether to sit in private where the ends of justice would not be served by his sitting in public; he must follow any directions given by the court on the point. The examiner does not reach a decision; the court considers the depositions or notes of evidence taken by him and may decide to receive them in evidence: R. v. Stafford (1973) 57 Cr. App. R. 203. The proceedings before an examiner are "preliminary or incidental to" the appeal or application for leave to appeal, and the appellant, if in custody, is not entitled to be present: Criminal Appeal Act 1968, s. 22 (1).
[37] See Criminal Appeal Rules 1968, r. 9 (2) but cf. R. v. Saunders, supra, at p. 253.
[38] Criminal Appeal Act 1968, s. 23 (4).
[38] The single judge has no power to make such an order.
[39] See R. v. Gordon (1963) 47 Cr. App. R. 282.
[40] Criminal Appeal Act 1968, s. 23 (1) (a).
[41] See pp. 93–94, post.
[42] i.e. within the definition in ibid. s. 50 (1); see pp. 92–93, post.
[43] A conviction in respect of which a probation order is made, or an order for absolute or conditional discharge is disregarded for this purpose, and although such orders are in law within the definition in s. 50 (1) of the Act, appeal does not lie in respect of such a "conviction": but see p. 93, post.

fixed by law[44]; and (c) where the conviction was in the magistrates' court,[45] the sentence passed or other order made is one of those specified in the Act[46]; provided that the court[47] gives leave to appeal, or the sentence is referred to the court by the Home Secretary.[48]

(3) Meaning of "sentence"

The relevant sections of the Criminal Appeal Act 1968,[49] read together, provide for an appeal against any order made by the Crown Court when dealing with an offender for the offence of which he was convicted.[50] By express definition[51] the term "sentence" includes a hospital order made under the Mental Health Act 1959,[52] and a recommendation for deportation.[53]

If the nature of the direction made by the trial court does not amount to an "order" as such,[54] or though amounting to an order, is not contingent upon conviction[55] it is not a sentence against which appeal will lie.

The court treats as part of the sentence orders for the restitution of property,[56] whether restitution orders as such,[57] or compensation orders,[58] but there is no right of appeal by any person other than the appellant.[59]

A sentence for contempt of court imposed upon the appellant, whether in respect of his behaviour at the trial[60] or for absconding from bail[61] is treated as a sentence like any other. A person other than the appellant sentenced for contempt of court has no right of appeal to the Criminal Division of the Court of Appeal.

[44] Appeal does not, therefore, lie against a sentence of life imprisonment imposed for murder, since this is a sentence fixed by law: *Practice Note* [1957] 1 W.L.R. 750.
[45] See p. 93, *post.*
[46] *i.e.* in *ibid.* s. 10 (3), see p. 93, *post.*
[47] Under *ibid.* s. 11 (1), or the single judge under s. 31.
[48] Under *ibid.* s. 17 (1) (*a*); as to which see *ante*, pp. 88 *et seq.*
[49] *i.e.* ss. 9, 10 and 50 (1).
[50] See *R.* v. *Hayden* (1975) 60 Cr. App. R. 204.
[51] Criminal Appeal Act 1968, s. 50 (1).
[52] *i.e.* under *ibid.* s. 60, with or without an order restricting discharge under *ibid.* s. 65.
[53] *i.e.* under the Immigration Act 1971, s. 3 (6). An appeal may be brought against the recommendation even though no appeal is brought against the sentence as a whole: *R.* v. *Edgehill* [1963] 1 Q.B. 593.
[54] Where the trial judge recommends a minimum period to be served by a person convicted of murder (under the Murder (Abolition of Death Penalty) Act 1965, s. 1) such recommendation is not a sentence: *R.* v. *Aitken* [1966] 1 W.L.R. 1076.
[55] An order for costs made under the Costs in Criminal Cases Act 1973, s. 4 is part of the sentence; a legal aid contribution order is not. A legal aid contribution order is not an order contingent on conviction; the power to make it is enjoyed by the court whether the defendant is convicted or acquitted: *R.* v. *Hayden* (1975) 60 Cr. App. R. 300.
[56] See *R.* v. *Hayden* (1975) 60 Cr. App. R. 304; also *R.* v. *Parker* [1970] 1 W.L.R. 1003; *R.* v. *Brogan* [1975] 1 W.L.R. 393. As to the court's power to vary or annul such orders irrespective of whether there is an appeal against the order as such, see Criminal Appeal Act 1968, s. 30, at p. 97, *post.*
[57] *i.e.* under the Theft Act 1968, s. 28 (1).
[58] *i.e.* under the Powers of Criminal Courts Act 1973, s. 35.
[59] *R.* v. *Elliott* [1908] 2 K.B. 452.
[60] See *R.* v. *Aquarius* (1974) 69 Cr. App. R. 165. A person other than the defendant who is committed for contempt in the face of the court has no right of appeal to the Criminal Division, but appeal lies to the Civil Division of the Court of Appeal under the Administration of Justice Act 1960.
[61] See *ante*, p. 59, note 10. A sentence of imprisonment in default of payment of an estreated recognisance is not a "sentence": *R.* v. *Thayne* [1970] 1 Q.B. 141.

A disqualification from holding or obtaining a driving licence is contingent upon conviction and therefore part of the sentence,[62] so also is an order for deprivation of property[63] or an order of forfeiture.[64]

No appeal lies to the Criminal Division against a probation order made by the Crown Court since, although a probation order is a "sentence" within the meaning of section 9 and section 50 of the Criminal Appeal Act 1968, there has not, by reason of the provisions of the Powers of Criminal Courts Act 1973,[65] been a conviction in any relevant sense of the word of the person placed on probation[66]; the same principle applies in the case of a conviction for which an order of conditional discharge, or indeed an order of absolute discharge is made.[67] Where, however, such an order is so defective as to be a nullity, the Criminal Division will declare it so.[68]

By statute, no appeal lies against the making of a criminal bankruptcy order,[69] but where the order is so defective as to be a nullity the court may set it aside.[70]

(4) Appeal after summary conviction: section 10

Although convicted summarily, the effect of section 10 of the Criminal Appeal Act 1968 is to give a right of appeal against sentence to the Criminal Division to a person dealt with at the Crown Court as an incorrigible rogue,[71] to a person convicted of an offence by a magistrates' court and committed to, and dealt with by, the Crown Court for his offence,[72] and to a person convicted of an offence in a magistrates' court who, having been made the subject of a probation order, or an order of conditional discharge, or given a suspended sentence, comes before the Crown Court and is further dealt with for that offence.[73]

---

[62] See *R.* v. *London Sessions Appeals Committee, ex p. Beaumont* [1951] 1 K.B. 557 at p. 561 *per* Hilbery J, and *ante*, p. 5.
[63] Under the Powers of Criminal Courts Act 1973, s. 43. See, *e.g. R.* v. *Lidster* [1976] R.T.R. 240.
[64] *e.g.* under the Misuse of Drugs Act 1971, s. 27. See *R.* v. *Morgan* (1977), February 28, C.A. (unreported).
[65] *Ibid.* s. 13 (1).
[66] *R.* v. *Tucker* (1974) 59 Cr. App. R. 71.
[67] *R.* v. *Wehner* (1977) 65 Cr. App. R. 1.
[68] *R.* v. *Marquis* (1974) 59 Cr. App. R. 228.
[69] Powers of Criminal Courts Act 1973, s. 40 (1).
[70] *R.* v. *Anderson, The Times*, November 22, 1978; *Director of Public Prosecutions* v. *Anderson, The Times*, May 31, 1978, H.L.
[71] *Ibid.* s. 10 (2) (*a*). The Criminal Division is then entitled to examine the circumstances of the case and to quash the sentence if of opinion that there was no valid conviction: *R.* v. *Johnson* [1909] 1 K.B. 439; *R.* v. *Walters* [1969] 1 Q.B. 255; *R.* v. *Jackson* [1974] Q.B. 517.
[72] *Ibid.* s. 10 (2) (*a*), as amended. The subsection covers the cases of a person committed to the Crown Court, (a) with a view to a borstal sentence, under the Magistrates' Courts Act 1952, s. 28; (b) in respect of an offence triable either way tried summarily with the consent of the defendant (*ibid.* s. 29); (c) as a prisoner on licence, under the provisions of the Criminal Justice Act 1967, s. 62 (6); (d) in respect of a summary offence, under the provisions of *ibid.* s. 56 (1) as amended; and (e) with a view to a hospital order being made, coupled with an order restricting discharge (Mental Health Act 1959, s. 67 (1), (3)).
   The validity or otherwise of the committal is not a ground of appeal; this is a matter which may be challenged by an application for judicial review, see *ante*, p. 39.
[73] Criminal Appeal Act 1968, s. 10 (2) (*b*).

As is the case with any sentence appeal to the Criminal Division, appeal lies under section 10 only with leave[74] but in this type of case, the right to apply for leave is restricted[75] to cases where:

(a) the appellant has been sentenced to a term of imprisonment of six months or more[76]; or

(b) the sentence is one which the convicting court had no power to pass[77]; or

(c) where in dealing with the appellant for his offence, the Crown Court made a recommendation for his deportation,[78] an order disqualifying him for holding or obtaining a driving licence[79] or an order dealing with a suspended sentence[80]; or

(d) the Crown Court made an order returning him to borstal[81] on reconviction.[82]

(5) "Subsequent proceedings": section 9

A person convicted on indictment of an offence may appeal to the Criminal Division against any sentence (not fixed by law) passed on him for the offence, whether passed on his conviction or in subsequent proceedings.[83]

Such "subsequent proceedings" include a sentence passed subsequently: (a) on a person who was bound over to be of good behaviour and come up for judgment when called upon; (b) on a person in whose case a probation order was made or a conditional discharge; (c) on a person on whom a suspended sentence of imprisonment was imposed; and where the Crown Court varied or rescinded an order within 28 days or such other appropriate period as the case may be.[84]

(6) Sentences passed in the "same proceeding"

Two or more sentences are passed in "the same proceeding"[85] if they were passed on the same day or, if they were passed on different days, the court in passing any one of them states that it is treating that one together with the other or others as substantially one sentence.[86]

---

[74] Criminal Appeal Act 1968, s. 11 (1).
[75] See *R.* v. *Keelan* (1975) 61 Cr. App. R. 212.
[76] Whether for one offence or for one offence and for other offences for which sentence is passed in the same proceeding: Criminal Appeal Act 1968, s. 10 (3). As to when offences are treated as being passed in the same proceeding, see below. Consecutive terms of imprisonment and terms which are wholly or partly concurrent are treated as a single term: *ibid.* s. 10 (4). A suspended sentence of imprisonment which has not taken effect is treated as a sentence of imprisonment: Powers of Criminal Courts Act 1973, s. 22 (6) (*a*). A sentence of detention in a detention centre is not a sentence of imprisonment: *R.* v. *Moore* [1968] 1 W.L.R. 397.
[77] Criminal Appeal Act 1968, s. 10 (3) (*b*) but see *R.* v. *Keelan* (1975) 61 Cr. App. R. 212.
[78] *i.e.* under the Immigration Act 1971, s. 6.
[79] *i.e.* under the Road Traffic Act 1972, ss. 93, 101.
[80] *i.e.* under the Powers of Criminal Courts Act 1973, s. 23.
[81] *i.e.* under the Criminal Justice Act 1961, s. 12.
[82] Criminal Appeal Act 1968, s. 10 (3).
[83] Criminal Appeal Act 1968, s. 9.
[84] *i.e.* under the Courts Act 1971, s. 11.
[85] See above.
[86] Criminal Appeal Act 1968, s. 10 (4).

An appeal, or application for leave to appeal, against any one of those sentences is treated as being an appeal or application in respect of all of them.[87] If an appellant is subject to a number of sentences passed in the same proceeding and the court quashes one sentence, it may increase the other or others provided the appellant is not more severely dealt with[88] than he was dealt with at the Crown Court[89] and where, for instance[90] a number of short consecutive sentences passed are wrong in principle, but the total sentence overall is proper, the court may substitute longer concurrent sentences, provided the total sentence overall is not increased.[91]

(7) Principal powers in respect of sentence appeals

The powers of the Criminal Division in relation to appeals against sentence[92] are that if they consider that the appellant should be sentenced differently for an offence for which he was dealt with by the Crown Court, they may quash the sentence which is the subject of the appeal and, in place of it, pass such sentence or make such order as they think appropriate for the case[93] and as the Crown Court had power to pass or make[94] when dealing with him for the offence,[95] but must so exercise their powers that, taking the case as a whole, the appellant is not more severely dealt with on appeal than he was in the Crown Court.[96]

The term of any sentence passed by the Criminal Division begins to run, unless the court otherwise directs[97] from the time it would have begun to run if passed in the proceedings from which the appeal lies.[98]

(8) Time spent in custody pending appeal

Subject to any direction which the Criminal Division may give to the contrary, the time during which an appellant is in custody pending the determination of his appeal is reckoned as part of the term of any sentence to which he is for the time being subject.[99] If an appellant is released on bail pending the determination of his appeal, time during which he is at large after being released is disregarded in computing the term of any sentence to which he is

---

[87] *Ibid.* s. 11 (2), but see *R.* v. *Keelan* (1975) 61 Cr. App. R. 212.
[88] See pp. 96–97, *post.*
[89] See *R.* v. *Moore* (1968) 52 Cr. App. R. 180.
[90] As in *R.* v. *Hussain* [1962] Crim. L.R. 712.
[91] And provided the individual sentence does not exceed the maximum authorised for the offence.
[92] Whether under s. 9 or s. 10 of the Criminal Appeal Act 1968. As to the court's special powers under *ibid.* ss. 3, 4, 5, etc., see p. 96, *post.*
[93] Including the power to make a recommendation for deportation where the Crown Court had such power: Criminal Appeal Act 1968, s. 50 (2).
[94] In a case committed to the Crown Court under the Criminal Justice Act 1967, s. 56 (1), the powers of the Criminal Division, like those of the Crown Court, are limited to those possessed by the magistrates' court.
[95] A person who was under 21 when dealt with at the Crown Court is still liable to be dealt with as such even though he is over 21 when dealt with on the appeal.
[96] Criminal Appeal Act 1968, s. 11 (3). As to sentences of "greater severity" see p. 96, *post.*
[97] As to directions for loss of time, see p. 96, *post.*
[98] Criminal Appeal Act 1968, s. 29 (4).
[99] Criminal Appeal Act 1968, s. 29 (1). In relation to suspended sentences, see *Practice Direction* [1970] 1 W.L.R. 259.

subject.[1] Unless the court otherwise directs, the term of any sentence passed by the Criminal Division in substitution for that passed on an appellant in proceedings below, runs from the time when it would have begun to run if passed in the proceedings from which the appeal lies.[2]

(9) Directions for loss of time

Directions for loss of time are intended to result in prompt attention being given to meritorious cases by deterring the unmeritorious cases which stand in their way.[3] They are not intended to discourage an appellant who has arguable grounds. A direction cannot therefore be given where leave to appeal has been granted, or where the trial judge has granted his certificate that a case is fit for appeal[4] or where the appeal is referred to the court by the Home Secretary under section 17 (1) (a) of the Act.[5] The single judge may give a direction for loss of time[6] and, if an application for leave refused by the single judge is renewed before the full court, the court may confirm, cancel or vary the direction.[7]

(10) Other powers in respect of sentence

In addition to its principal powers, referred to above,[8] the Criminal Division may substitute for a sentence imposed on an appellant at the Crown Court a different sentence: (a) where, on an appeal against conviction on an indictment containing two or more counts the court allows an appeal in respect of part of the indictment[9]; or (b) where on an appeal against conviction, the court instead of allowing or dismissing the appeal, substitutes a verdict of guilty of an alternative offence[10]; or (c) where on an appeal against conviction the court orders a different conclusion to be recorded in respect of a special verdict[11]; or (d) where on an appeal against a verdict of not guilty by reason of insanity, the court allows the appeal and substitutes a verdict of guilty of an offence.[12]

(11) Sentences of "greater severity"

The words "greater severity" are not defined in the Criminal Appeal Act 1968 and the court applies the concept to the particular facts of the individual case. Obviously a longer term of imprisonment is more severe than a short term,[13] and a larger fine is more severe than a smaller fine. In respect of other

[1] Criminal Appeal Act 1968, s. 29 (3).
[2] *Ibid.* s. 29 (4).
[3] See *Practice Direction* (1970) 54 Cr. App. R. 280.
[4] See *ante*, p. 60.
[5] See *ante*, p. 88. Criminal Appeal Act 1968, s. 29 (2).
[6] *Ibid.* s. 31 (1). See also "Preparation for Proceedings in the Court of Appeal, Criminal Division" (see *ante*, p. 000, note 0), paras. 15, 15.2. Also *R.* v. *Howitt* [1975] Crim. L.R. 588.
[7] See generally on this topic, Thompson, Morrish and McLean, *op. cit.* under title "Loss of Time."
[8] *Ante*, p. 95.
[9] Under the Criminal Appeal Act 1968, s. 4, see *ante*, p. 84.
[10] Under *ibid.* s. 3, see *ante*, p. 84.
[11] Under *ibid.* s. 5, see *ante*, p. 84.
[12] Under *ibid.* s. 13, see *ante*, p. 88.
[13] See the difficulties involved in cases like, *e.g. R.* v. *Gills* [1967] Crim. L.R. 247; *R.* v. *Whittaker* [1967] Crim. L.R. 431; *R.* v. *Sieh* [1969] Crim. L.R. 99; and *R.* v. *Stofile* [1969] Crim. L.R. 325.

forms of punishment or treatment, the court has, in the past, regarded: (a) a sentence of 18 months imprisonment as not more severe than a sentence of borstal training,[14] (b) a hospital order coupled with a restriction order of indefinite length as not more severe than a fixed term of imprisonment[15]; (c) life imprisonment as more severe than a fixed term; and (d) an extended term of imprisonment as more severe than an ordinary term of the same length.[16]

(12) Compensation, etc., orders; criminal bankruptcy orders

In the case of orders for the restitution of property, and this includes a compensation order,[17] made on indictment, where an order was suspended pending the determination of the appeal, it does not take effect as to the property in question if the conviction is quashed on appeal.[18] The Criminal Division may also annul or vary any such order made by the trial court, even where the conviction is not quashed.[19] If the order is annulled it does not take effect; if it is varied, it takes effect as varied.[20]

Where the Criminal Division allows an appeal against conviction of an offence by virtue of which a criminal bankruptcy order was made[21] the court must rescind the order unless the appellant was convicted in the same proceedings of another offence of which he remains convicted and a criminal bankruptcy order could have been made without reference to the loss or damage caused by the offence in respect of which the appeal is allowed.[22] Where the court does not rescind the order it must amend it by striking out so much of it as relates to that loss or damage.[22] Where the court substitutes a verdict of guilty of another offence, it must rescind the order if such an order could not have been made against the appellant if he had originally been convicted of that other offence.[23] In any other case the court must amend the order so far as may be required in consequence of the substituted verdict.[24]

15. ATTORNEY-GENERAL'S REFERENCE

Where a person tried on indictment has been acquitted, whether in respect of the whole or part of the indictment, the Attorney-General, if he desires the opinion of the court on a point of law[25] which has arisen in the case, may refer that point to the Criminal Division, which will consider it, and give an opinion

[14] *R.* v. *Woods* [1967] Crim. L.R. 601.
[15] *R.* v. *Bennett* (1968) 62 Cr. App. R. 514.
[16] See, *e.g. R.* v. *Duncuft* (1969) 53 Cr. App. R. 495; *R.* v. *Jones* [1970] Crim. L.R. 356.
[17] See *ante*, p. 92.
[18] Criminal Appeal Act 1968, s. 30 (2): Theft Act 1968, s. 33 (3), Sched. 3.
[19] Criminal Appeal Act 1968, s. 30 (4).
[20] *Ibid.* As to the suspension of the operation of an order pending appeal to the House of Lords, see p. 115, *post.*
[21] See above.
[22] Powers of Criminal Courts Act 1973, s. 40 (2).
[23] *Ibid.* s. 40 (3).
[24] *Ibid.* As to the suspension of any order made in the Criminal Division, pending an appeal to the House of Lords, see p. 115, *post.*
[25] A point of law arising in a criminal case is one which, under that mode of trial, falls to be decided by the judge, not by the jury: see *Reference under s. 48A of the Criminal Appeal (Northern Ireland) Act 1968 (No. 1 of 1975), The Times*, July 7, H.L.

on it.[26] A reference of this natures does not affect the trial in relation to which the reference is made, or any acquittal in that trial.[27]

Such a reference must be in writing and must specify the point of law and, where appropriate, such facts of the case as are necessary for the proper consideration of the point.[28] The reference must also summarise the arguments which it is intended to put before the court[29] and must specify any authorities to be cited.[30]

No mention may be made in the reference of the proper name of any person or place which is likely to lead to the identification of the acquitted person in whose case the point of law arises.[31]

The Registrar of Criminal Appeals will cause to be served upon the "respondent," that is the acquitted person, notice of the reference,[32] which will also inform him that the reference will not affect the trial in relation to which it is made or to any acquittal in that trial, and will invite him, within such time as is specified, not being less than 28 days from service of the notice, to inform the Registrar if he wishes to present any argument to the court, and if so, whether he wishes to present that argument in person or by counsel on his behalf.[33]

The Attorney-General is entitled to withdraw or amend the reference at any time before the court has begun to hear the matter, and with the leave of the court, at any time before it gives its opinion,[34] notice of the withdrawal or amendment being served on the acquitted person.[35] The court will not hear argument by or on behalf of the Attorney-General until the time specified in the notice has expired unless the acquitted person agrees or has indicated that he does not wish to present any argument to the court.[36]

At the hearing of the reference the court will hear argument by the Attorney-General or by counsel on his behalf[37] and will hear argument by counsel on behalf of the acquitted person if he so desires, or with the leave of

---

[26] Criminal Justice Act 1972, s. 36 (1). If the definition of a crime as stated in the trial judge's summing-up was too unfavourable to a defendant, and he was convicted, he might appeal to the Criminal Division in the ordinary way, and any error might be corrected and so prevented from gaining currency. If a direction was too favourable to a defendant, there was no way, before the coming into force of this section, of obtaining the opinion of an appellate court to that effect: *Reference under s. 48A of the Appeal (Northern Ireland) Act 1968 No. 1 of 1975, supra.*

[27] Criminal Justice Act 1972, s. 36 (7). There is no right of appeal to the Criminal Division against an acquittal on indictment, see *ante*, p. 59.

[28] Criminal Appeal (Reference of Points of Law) Rules 1973, r. 3 (1) (a). The reference is entitled "Reference under s. 36 of the Criminal Justice Act 1972" together with the year and number: *ibid.*

[29] *Ibid.* r. 3 (1) (b).

[30] *Ibid.* r. 3 (1) (c).

[31] Criminal Appeal (Reference of Points of Law) Rules 1973, r. 3 (1), proviso. It is the duty of the court to ensure that the identity of the acquitted person is not disclosed at the hearing except where he has given his consent to the use of his name in the proceedings: *ibid.* r. 6. See *Attorney-General's Reference (No. 2 of 1975)* [1976] 1 W.L.R. 710.

[32] *Criminal Appeal (Reference of Points of Law) Rules 1973*, r. 4 (1); the term "respondent" is defined in *ibid.* s. 2 (1). As to service of documents, etc., see *ibid.* r. 8 (1).

[33] *Ibid.* r. 4 (1).

[34] *Ibid.* r. 5.

[35] *Ibid.* r. 5. As to service of documents, see *ibid.* r. 8 (1).

[36] *Ibid.* r. 4 (2).

[37] Criminal Justice Act 1972, s. 36 (2) (a).

the court, by the acquitted person himself.[38] Counsel may appear at the hearing at the request of the court as *amicus curiae*, instructed normally by the Treasury Solicitor.[39]

Where the Criminal Division has given its opinion on a point referred to it under section 36 it may, either of its own motion or in pursuance of an application on that behalf, refer the point to the House of Lords, if it appears that the point is one which ought to be considered by the House of Lords.[40] An application for a point to be referred in this manner to the House of Lords is made either orally, immediately after the Criminal Division has given its opinion, or by notice served on the Registrar of Criminal Appeals within the next 14 days following.[41]

Where an acquitted person appears by counsel in the Criminal Division, or on further reference to the House of Lords, he is entitled to payment out of central funds of such sums as are reasonably sufficient to compensate him for the expenses properly incurred for the purpose of being represented.[42] These costs are taxed by the Registrar of Criminal Appeals, or by the officer prescribed by the House of Lords as the case may be.

16. RETRIAL AND VENIRE DE NOVO

Where the Criminal Division of the Court of Appeal allows an appeal against conviction[43] and does so only by reason of evidence received, or available to be received[44] under section 23 of the Criminal Appeal Act 1968[45] and it appears to the court that the interests of justice so require it may order the appellant to be retired.[46] In making such an order, the court[47] may make such orders as appear to be necessary or expedient for the custody or release on bail of the person to be retried, and for the retention pending the retrial of any property or money forfeited, restored or paid by virtue of the original conviction or any order made on that conviction. The court will also, through the Registrar, make any necessary arrangements pending the retrial, for the continued retention in custody of any exhibits, including arrangements for their inspection by any interested party.[48]

If the person ordered to be retried was, immediately before the determination of his appeal, liable to be detained in pursuance of an order or direction

---

[38] *Ibid.* s. 36 (2) (*b*).
[39] In *Attorney-General's Reference (No. 2 of 1975)* [1976] 1 W.L.R. 710 counsel who conducted the prosecution case at the trial appeared as *amicus curiae* at the hearing of the reference.
[40] Criminal Justice Act 1972, s. 36 (3), (4).
[41] Criminal Appeal (Reference of Points of Law) Rules 1973, r. 7.
[42] Criminal Justice Act 1972, s. 36 (5).
[43] The power to order a retrial in such circumstances applies in the case of a reference by the Home Secretary under s. 17 (1) (*a*) of the Criminal Appeal Act 1968, as it applies to any other appeal against conviction.
[44] A retrial can only be ordered in these circumstances: see *R.* v. *Merry* (1970) 54 Cr. App. R. 274. As to a *venire de novo* see p. 101, *post.*
[45] See *ante*, pp. 89–91.
[46] Criminal Appeal Act 1968, s. 7 (1). There may be factors which militate against ordering a retrial, such as the length of time between the commission of the offence and the hearing of the appeal: see, *e.g. R.* v. *Saunders* (1973) 58 Cr. App. R. 248.
[47] Or the single judge: Criminal Appeal Act 1968, ss. 8 (2), 31 (2) (*f*); Bail Act 1976, Sched. 2.
[48] Criminal Appeal Rules 1968, rr. 7 (3), (4).

under Part V of the Mental Health Act 1959, that order or direction continues in force pending the retrial as if the appeal had not been allowed and any order made under section 8 of the Criminal Appeal Act 1968[49] for his custody or release on bail has effect subject to that order or direction.[50]

An application for bail pending a retrial under section 7 should ordinarily be made orally to the court immediately following the order for retrial. If it is not made at that stage, an application is made either by serving notice on the Registrar in the usual form,[51] or more usually, by making an application to the location of the Crown Court at which the appellant is to be retried. Similarly in the case of an application for legal aid for the retrial; it may be made orally immediately following the court's order for retrial, or if it is not made at that time, it may be made to the Crown Court. Where the court orders a person to be retried under section 7, either the Criminal Division or the Crown Court may order that he be given legal aid for the purpose of the retrial.[52]

The retrial takes place upon a fresh indictment preferred at the direction of the Criminal Division.[53] The statute provides that such a person is not to be retried for an offence other than (a) the offence of which he was convicted at the original trial, and in respect of which the appeal was allowed; or (b) an offence of which he could have been convicted on an indictment for the offence of which he was convicted; or (c) an offence charged in alternative count of the indictment in respect of which the jury were discharged from giving a verdict in consequence of convicting him of the offence for which he was convicted.[54]

Certain rules as to the evidence and procedure on a retrial ordered under section 7 of the Act apply by statute. Thus, a transcript of the record of evidence given by any witness at the original trial may, with the leave of the trial judge, be read as evidence, either by agreement between the prosecution and the defence, or if the judge is satisfied that such witness is dead, or is unfit to give evidence or to attend for that purpose, or that all reasonable efforts to find him or to secure his attendance have been made without success.[55]

Where the defendant is again convicted on the retrial, the court before which he is convicted is entitled to pass, in respect of the offence, any sentence authorised by law, not being a sentence of greater severity[56] than that passed on the original conviction.[57] A sentence of imprisonment or other detention

---

[49] See above.
[50] Criminal Appeal Act 1968, s. 8 (3).
[51] See *ante*, pp. 71–74.
[52] Legal Aid Act 1974, s. 28 (11).
[53] Criminal Appeal Act 1968, s. 8 (1); Courts Act 1971, s. 54 (4), Sched. 11, Pt. IV. It is a matter of discretion whether the retrial is held before the same or another judge: *R.* v. *Bogle* [1974] Crim. L.R. 424.
[54] Criminal Appeal Act 1968, s. 7 (2).
[55] Criminal Appeal Act 1968, s. 8 (4), Sched. 2, para. 1. The Criminal Justice Act 1925, s. 13 (3) respecting the reading of depositions or witness statements at the trial does not apply: *ibid*. A transcript may be read without further proof if verified in accordance with rules of court: *ibid*.
[56] As to sentences of greater severity, see *ante*, p. 96.
[57] Criminal Appeal Act 1968, s. 8 (4), Sched. 2, para. 2 (1). This notwithstanding that on the date of the conviction on the retrial the defendant has ceased to be a person of an age at which such a sentence could be passed: *ibid*. para. 2 (2).

passed on conviction on retrial begins to run from the time when a like sentence passed at the original trial would have begun to run.[58]

If the appellant is acquitted on the retrial, the costs of his defence which may be paid out of central funds[59] include any costs which could have been ordered by the court in which he was originally tried, had he been acquitted, and if no order for costs was made in the Criminal Division[60] in respect of the expenses of his appeal, any sums for which such an order could have been made.[61]

Where the court holds that the trial leading to the appellant's conviction[62] was a mistrial and therefore a nullity, there are two courses open. The court may order that the conviction and judgment of the court of trial be simply set aside and annulled,[63] or it may quash the conviction and order a *venire de novo*.[64] On ordering a *venire de novo*, the court may release the defendant on bail[65] or may order that he be detained in custody.[66] The Criminal Division has no power to grant legal aid for the purpose of the trial at the Crown Court.[67]

Following a *venire de novo*, as opposed to a retrial under section 7 of the Act,[68] the parties stand as they did before the original trial, and the evidence is heard again.[69] No special statutory rules as to evidence apply, as they do to a retrial under section 7,[70] nor is there any restriction on the sentence that may be passed if the defendant is convicted.[71]

---

[58] Criminal Appeal Act 1968, s. 8 (4), Sched. 2, para. 2 (3). As to the computation of the term see *ibid.* also the Criminal Justice Act 1967, s. 67.

[59] *i.e.* under the Costs in Criminal Cases Act 1973, s. 3.

[60] *i.e.* under *ibid.* s. 7.

[61] Criminal Appeal Act 1968, s. 8 (4), Sched. 2, para. 3.

[62] There is no power to order a *venire de novo* where the appellant is acquitted, however improperly the verdict may have been obtained: *R.* v. *Middlesex Quarter Sessions (Chairman), ex p. Director of Public Prosecutions* [1952] 2 Q.B. 758.

[63] As was done in *R.* v. *Eyles* (1950) 34 Cr. App. R. 161; *R.* v. *Gash* (1967) 51 Cr. App. R. 37; *R.* v. *Angel* (1968) 52 Cr. App. R. 280. The form of order is such as the court may order: Juries Act 1974, s. 21 (4).

[64] Criminal Appeal Act 1968, s. 1 (2) (*b*) (ii); Criminal Appeal Act 1968, s. 52 (1), Sched. 5, Pt. I. This was done in *R.* v. *Turner* (1970) 54 Cr. App. R. 352.

[65] As in *R.* v. *Hussey* (1924) 18 Cr. App. R. 121.

[66] As in *R.* v. *Golathan* (1915) L.J.K.B. 758.

[67] It may, however, be granted by the trial court, under the Legal Aid Act 1974, s. 28 (7).

[68] See *ante,* p. 100.

[69] *R.* v. *Lloyd* (1924) 18 Cr. App. R. 12.

[70] See *ante,* p. 100.

[71] See, *e.g. R.* v. *Turner (No.* 2) [1971] 1 W.L.R. 901.

PART VI

APPEALS TO THE HOUSE OF LORDS FROM THE DIVISIONAL COURT AND THE CRIMINAL DIVISION OF THE COURT OF APPEAL

1. GENERAL PROVISIONS

(1) Final court of appeal

The House of Lords is the final court of appeal in criminal as in civil matters. Appeals lie to the House in criminal matters from a Divisional Court of the Queen's Bench Division[1] and from the Criminal Division of the Court of Appeal.[2]

(2) Rights of appeal

An appeal lies to the House of Lords, at the instance of the defendant[3] or the prosecutor, from any decision of a Divisional Court of the Queen's Bench Division in a criminal cause or matter.[4] Such a matter includes one by way of case stated from an order or decision of a magistrates' court,[5] or from an order or decision of the Crown Court in the exercise of its appellate jurisdiction,[6] and upon application for judicial review of the decision of a magistrates' court or the Crown Court in the exercise of its appellate jurisdiction.[7]

An appeal lies to the House of Lords, at the instance of the defendant[8] or the prosecutor, from any decision of the Criminal Division of the Court of Appeal on an appeal.[9]

The Criminal Division of the Court of Appeal may refer to the House of Lords a point of law referred to it by the Attorney-General under section 36 of the Criminal Justice Act 1972.[10]

---

[1] Under the provisions of the Administration of Justice Act 1960.
[2] Under the provisions of Pt. II of the Criminal Appeal Act 1968.
[3] In relation to proceedings for an offence, or in relation to an application for an order of mandamus, certiorari or prohibition in connection with such proceedings, a reference to the "defendant" is to be construed as a reference to the person who was, or would be, the defendant in such proceedings: Administration of Justice Act 1960, s. 17 (1) (a).
[4] Ibid. s. 1 (1).
[5] See ante, pp. 24–38.
[6] See ante, pp. 1–24.
[7] See ante, pp. 38–53.
[8] "Defendant" in Pt. II of the Criminal Appeal Act 1968, means, in relation to an appeal, the person who was the appellant before the Criminal Division, and references to the "prosecutor" are to be construed accordingly: ibid. s. 51 (1).
[9] Criminal Appeal Act 1968, s. 33 (1). The right to appeal to the House of Lords exists only in respect of appeals as such, as distinct from applications for leave to appeal. There is no right to appeal to the House of Lords in respect of the refusal of leave to appeal: R. v. Jefferies [1969] 1 Q.B. 120; R. v. Stafford, R. v. Luvaglio (1968) 53 Cr. App. R. 1; R. v. Mealey, R. v. Sheridan [1975] Crim. L.R. 154.
[10] Criminal Justice Act 1972, s. 36 (3).

(3) The need for leave; the certificate

Neither in the case of an appeal from the Divisional Court nor in the case of an appeal from the Criminal Division does an appeal lie without leave. Leave may be granted by the Divisional Court or by the Criminal Division, as the case may be, or it may be granted by the House of Lords,[11] but leave cannot be granted, whether by the court below or by the House, unless the court below certifies[12] that a point of law of general public importance is involved in the decision,[13] *and* it appears that it is one which ought to be considered by the House of Lords.[14]

2. INITIATING AN APPEAL FROM THE DIVISIONAL COURT

(1) Initiating the appeal; applying for the certificate

An application to the Divisional Court for leave to appeal to the House of Lords must be made within the period of 14 days beginning with the date of the decision of that court.[15] An application may be made orally to the Divisional Court, immediately after its decision, when the practice is, as in the case of the Criminal Division of the Court of Appeal, for counsel for the party seeking to appeal to formulate the point of law to be certified forthwith, if he is in a position to do so.[16] If the application is not made orally at that stage it is usual for it to be made by submitting to the Crown Office within the period prescribed a point of law suitable for certification. This will be referred to the judges who composed the court, and the appellant will be informed of the date on which any oral argument as to the application for leave may be heard in open court.

Where the Divisional Court certifies that a point of law of general public importance is involved in the decision[17] but refuses leave to appeal, an application may be made to the House of Lords for leave. Such an application must be made within the period of 14 days beginning with the date on which the application was refused by the Divisional Court.[18]

---

[11] Administration of Justice Act 1960, s. 1 (2); Criminal Appeal Act 1968, s. 33 (1).

[12] The House of Lords has no power to grant a certificate: *Gelberg* v. *Miller* [1961] 1 W.L.R. 459.

[13] A certificate should not be granted unless a point of law of general public importance is involved: *R.* v. *Sinclair* [1968] 1 W.L.R. 1246. The certificate should state what the point of law certified is: *Jones* v. *Director of Public Prosecutions* [1962] A.C. 635. As to the position where no certificate is granted, see *Practice Direction* [1970] 3 All E.R. 70.
 See also, as to whether the House of Lords will go outside the certificate, p. 114, *post.*

[14] Administration of Justice Act 1960, s. 1 (2); Criminal Appeal Act 1968, s. 33 (1). The certificate should not be granted unless the point is one which ought to be considered by the House, although this may be inferred from the fact that the court below granted leave: *Lawrence* v. *Metropolitan Police Commissioner* [1972] A.C. 626, at p. 633, *per* Viscount Dilhorne.

[15] Administration of Justice Act 1960, s. 2 (1).

[16] See p. 106, *post.*

[17] No appeal lies from the refusal of leave by the Divisional Court: *Gelberg* v. *Miller* [1961] 1 W.L.R. 459.

[18] Administration of Justice Act 1960, s. 2 (1). As to the form of such application, see p. 108, *post*, note 1.

(2) Application to extend the time

The House of Lords or the Divisional Court may, upon an application made at any time by the defendant,[19] extend the time within which an application for leave to appeal may be made.[20]

An application made to the Court[21] must be made to a Divisional Court, except in vacation when it may be made to a judge in chambers.[22] If not made in the proceedings before the court from whose order or decision the appeal is brought, it must be made by originating summons in open court.[23] In the case of an application made to a judge in chambers, it is made by summons.[24] Where an application is made in vacation to a judge in chambers, and the judge refuses it, the applicant is entitled to have the application determined by a Divisional Court.[25]

(3) Bail pending appeal

The power of the High Court under, for example, section 37 of the Criminal Justice Act 1948,[26] to grant bail in connection with proceedings before a Divisional Court, includes the power to grant bail to an appellant under section 1 of the Administration of Justice Act 1960, or to a person applying for leave to appeal under that section, pending the appeal.[27] Where application is made to a Divisional Court for leave to appeal to the House of Lords, the court may give such directions as it thinks fit for discharging or enlarging any recognisance entered into by any surety, with reference to the proceedings of that court.[28]

Where the defendant[29] in any proceedings from which an appeal lies under section 1 would be liable, but for the decision of the court below,[30] to be detained, and immediately after that decision, the prosecutor[31] is granted, or gives notice that he intends to apply for, leave to appeal, the court may make an order providing for the detention of the defendant, or directing that he is

---

[19] There is no power to extend the time for an appeal by the prosecutor.
[20] Administration of Justice Act 1960, s. 2 (3).
[21] The procedure for applying to the House of Lords for an extension of time is set out at p. 108, *post*, note 66.
[22] R.S.C., O. 109, r. 1 (1) (*a*).
[23] *Ibid*. r. 1 (2).
[24] *Ibid*. r. 1 (3).
[25] *Ibid*. r. 1 (5).
[26] See *ante*, p. 54. See also Criminal Justice Act 1967, s. 22, *ante*, p. 54.
[27] Administration of Justice Act 1960, s. 4 (2); Bail Act 1976, s. 12, Sched. 2, para. 30. In relation to a recognisance to be entered into under s. 37 of the Criminal Justice Act 1948, a reference to a judgment of the High Court is to be construed as a reference to the judgment of the House of Lords or, if the case is remitted by the House to the court below, to the judgment of that court on the case as remitted: *ibid*.
[28] *Ibid*. s. 4 (3); Bail Act 1976, s. 12, Sched. 3.
[29] A reference to the "defendant" is to be construed in relation to proceedings for an offence, and in relation to an application for an order of mandamus, certiorari or prohibition in connection with such proceedings, as a reference to the person who was or would have been the defendant in those proceedings, and reference to the prosecutor is to be construed accordingly: *ibid*. s. 17 (1).
[30] A reference to the "court below" is to be construed, in relation to any function of a Divisional Court, as a reference to the Divisional Court or to a judge, according as the function is exercisable by a court or a judge by virtue of Rules of Court: *ibid*. s. 17 (3).
[31] See note 29, *infra*.

not to be released except on bail, which the court may grant, so long as any appeal is pending.[32]

(4) Legal aid

The House of Lords does not grant legal aid.[33] In the case of appeals from a Divisional Court and applications relating to them, application for legal aid should be made to the appropriate Area Committee of the Law Society.[33]

(5) Presence of the defendant

A defendant who is detained pending an appeal from the Divisional Court is not entitled to be present on the hearing of his appeal or of any proceedings preliminary or incidental to the appeal, except where an order of the House of Lords or Rules of Court, as the case may be, authorise him to be present, or where the House or the court below, as the case may be, gives him leave to be present.[34]

An application by a defendant to the Divisional Court for leave to be present is made to a Divisional Court except in vacation when it may be made to a judge in chambers.[35] If the application is made to a Divisional Court, then, if not made in the proceedings before the court from whose decision or the appeal in question is brought, it must be made by originating motion in open court.[36] Any such application to a judge in chambers must be made *ex parte* unless the judge otherwise directs.[37] If such an application is made in vacation to a single judge and the judge refuses the application, the applicant is entitled to have the application determined by a Divisional Court.[38]

3. INITIATING AN APPEAL FROM THE CRIMINAL DIVISION

(1) Applying for leave; the certificate

A person seeking the leave of the Criminal Division to appeal to the House of Lords under Part II of the Criminal Appeal Act 1968, gives notice of that application either orally, immediately after the determination of the court is given[39] or in writing, in Form 17 (HL)[40] served on the Registrar within 14 days

---

[32] As to when an appeal is "pending," see *ibid*. s. 17 (4). Such an order ceases to have effect (unless the appeal has previously been disposed of) at the expiration of the period for which the defendant would have been liable to be detained but for the decision of the court below: *ibid*. s. 5 (1). Where no order is made, although the court had power to make it, or the defendant is released or discharged before the appeal is disposed of, he is not liable to be detained again as a result of the decision of the House of Lords on the appeal: *ibid*. s. 5 (5). As to persons liable to be detained under Pt. V of the Mental Health Act 1959, see *ibid*. s. 5 (4).
[33] Directions as to Procedure 1979, Dir. 34.
[34] Administration of Justice Act 1960, s. 9 (3).
[35] R.S.C., O. 109, r. 1. (1) (*b*).
[36] *Ibid*. O. 109 (1) (2).
[37] *Ibid*. O. 109, r. 1 (3). Notwithstanding anything in O. 8, r. 2 (1), no notice of motion need be given to any party affected by such an application unless the Divisional Court otherwise directs: *ibid*. O. 109, r. 1 (4).
[38] *Ibid*. O. 109, r. 1 (5).
[39] In practice the application will be made after the court gives its reasons for its decision.
[40] As amended by the Criminal Appeal (Amendment) Rules 1978, r. 7 (*d*). A copy of the Form appears in Appendix F, *post*, No. 9.

beginning with the day of the court's decision.[41] The time may be extended by the court.[42]

Where application is made orally, immediately after the court's decision, it is the practice for counsel for the party seeking to appeal[43] to formulate the point of law forthwith if he is in a position to do so, and to hand a written draft of it to the court for acceptance or amendment.[44] Although such an application is ordinarily made *ex parte*, counsel for the other side may assist in the formulation of the point of law. There is nothing to prevent counsel asking for an adjournment for the purpose of formulating the point.

Where application for leave to appeal is made subsequently, in Form 17 (HL), the form must state the point involved in the decision which the applicant wishes the court to certify as a point of law of general public importance. Where such an application is made, the Registrar will list the application for hearing as soon as practicable, but if there does not seem to be a point, the court may deal with the application on the papers without granting legal aid or leave to be present.[45]

If the Criminal Division refuses to certify that a point of law of general public importance is involved in the decision, that is an end of the matter.[46] If the court does certify, an application for leave to appeal must then be made to the court, and if that is refused, an application for leave may be made to the House of Lords.

On dismissing an application, the court may order the payment out of central funds of the costs of the appellant or the prosecutor, such costs being those sums appearing to the court to be reasonably sufficient to compensate the party concerned for any expenses properly incurred by him in the expenses of the application.[47] Where the court dismisses an application by the defendant for leave to appeal to the House of Lords it may order him to pay the whole or any part of the costs of the application.[48]

An application for leave is made to the House of Lords by giving notice in Form 17 (HL) within the period of 14 days beginning with the date on which the application was refused by the Criminal Division.[49]

---

[41] Criminal Appeal Rules 1968, r. 23 (1) (*a*); Criminal Appeal (Amendment) Rules 1978, r. 7 (*d*); Criminal Appeal Act 1968, r. 34 (1).

[42] Or by the single judge: Criminal Appeal Act 1968, ss. 34 (2), 44 (*a*). An application for extension of time is also made in Form 17 (HL).

[43] Whether the defendant or the prosecutor, see *ante*, p. 102.

[44] See Thompson, Morrish and McLean *op.cit.* under the title "House of Lords."

[45] *R*. v. *Daines, R*. v. *Williams* [1961] 1 W.L.R. 52.

[46] It has been held under the corresponding provisions of the Administration of Justice Act 1960, s. 1 (see *ante*, p. 103) that no appeal lies from the refusal of a certificate: *Gelberg* v. *Miller* [1961] 1 W.L.R. 459. The court does not normally give its reasons for refusal: *R*. v. *Jones* (1975) 61 Cr. App. R. 120; *R*. v. *Cooper, R*. v. *McMahon* (1975) 61 Cr. App. R. 215.

[47] Costs in Criminal Cases Act 1973, s. 10 (1), (2). See, as to taxation, *ibid*. s. 10 (3).

[48] *Ibid*. s. 11 (1), (2).

[49] Criminal Appeal Act 1968, s. 34 (1); Criminal Appeal Rules 1968, r. 23 (1) (*a*). The time may be extended by the Criminal Division or by the House of Lords: Criminal Appeal Act 1968, s. 34 (2). A single judge may grant the extension: *ibid*. s. 44 (*a*). An application for extension of time is included in Form 17 (HL): Criminal Appeal Rules 1968, r. 23 (1) (*a*); Criminal Appeal (Amendment) Rules 1978, r. 7 (*d*). A specimen of Form 17 (HL) appears in Appendix F, *post*, No. 9.

(2) Bail

The Criminal Division may, if it seems fit, on the application of a person appealing, or applying for leave to appeal, to the House of Lords, grant him bail pending the determination of his appeal.[50] The House of Lords has no power to grant bail to an appellant. Where the application for leave to appeal is not made orally to the court after the determination of the appeal,[51] an application for bail may be included in Form 17 (HL),[52] details of proposed sureties being given in Form 4 (B).[53]

(3) Detention of defendant on prosecutor's appeal

Where, immediately after a decision of the Criminal Division from which an appeal lies, the prosecutor is granted leave to appeal, or gives notice that he intends to apply for leave to appeal, and, but for the decision of the Criminal Division the appellant would be liable to be detained, the court may make an order[54] for his detention, or may direct that he is not to be released except on bail, so long as the appeal is pending.[55]

(4) Legal aid

Where either party to an appeal to the Criminal Division desires to appeal to the House of Lords under Part II of the Criminal Appeal Act 1968 the court may order that the person to whose conviction or sentence the appeal relates be given legal aid for the purpose of the appeal and of any preliminary or incidental proceedings.[56] Where the prosecutor appeals, or applies for leave to appeal, from the Criminal Division to the House of Lords, legal aid must be given to the defendant if his means warrant it.[57]

An application for legal aid in such circumstances is made either orally to the court at the conclusion of the hearing of the appeal in the Criminal Division, or subsequently, in writing, by giving notice to the Registrar in Form 17 (HL). Where the second procedure is adopted, the application will be considered in the same manner[58] as an application for legal aid in relation to an appeal under Part I of the Criminal Appeal Act 1968.

(5) Presence of the defendant

A defendant detained pending an appeal to the House of Lords is not entitled to be present at the hearing of the appeal, or of any proceedings

---

[50] Criminal Appeal Act 1968, s. 36. Bail may be granted by the single judge: *ibid.* s. 44 (*b*).
[51] See *ante*, p. 106.
[52] Criminal Appeal Rules 1968, r. 23 (1) (*d*); Criminal Appeal (Amendment) Rules 1978, r. 6 (*a*).
[53] See *ante*, p. 72. A copy of Form 4 (B) appears in Appendix F, *post*, No. 5.
[54] But see Criminal Appeal Act 1968, s. 37 (4) in relation to persons detained under an order or direction under Pt. V of the Mental Health Act 1959; see also *Director of Public Prosecutions* v. *Merriman* [1973] A.C. 584, H.L.
[55] CriminalmAppeal Act 1968, s. 37 (2). As to the lapse of the order, see *ibid.* s. 37 (3). As to the meaning of "pending," see *ibid.* s. 34 (3).
[56] Legal Aid Act 1974, s. 28 (10). Legal aid may be granted by the Registrar or by the single judge (see *ante*, pp. 74–78) but not by the House of Lords.
[57] Legal Aid Act 1974, s. 29 (1) (*b*), (2).
[58] See *ante*, p. 69.

preliminary or incidental to it, except where authorised by the House of
Lords, or with the leave of the Criminal Division.[59] A defendant who desires
to be present should give notice in Form 1 / (HL).[60]

(6) Powers of the single judge

In relation to an appeal under Part II of the Criminal Appeal Act 1968, the
single judge[61] may exercise the powers of the Criminal Division of the Court of
Appeal to: (a) extend the time for making an application for leave to appeal;
(b) make an order for or in relation to bail; (c) give leave for a person to be
present at the hearing of any proceedings preliminary or incidental to the
appeal.[62]

The single judge may also exercise the powers of the court to make an order
for costs under section 10 of the Costs in Criminal Cases Act 1973.[63] Where
the judge refuses an application to exercise any of these powers the applicant
is entitled to have the application determined by the Court.[64] Again, the
court's power to suspend a person's disqualification under section 94A of the
Road Traffic Act 1972 may be exercised by the single judge, and if he refuses
the application the applicant is entitled to have the application determined by
the court.[65]

4. PETITION FOR LEAVE TO APPEAL

(1) Form of petition

An application to the House of Lords for leave to appeal is made by a
petition in the prescribed form[66] which should set forth shortly the facts and
points of law, and should conclude with summarised reasons why leave to
appeal should be granted.[67] The petition may not be lodged[68] with the Judicial
Office for presentation to the House of Lords unless the certificate required
by statute[69] has been granted by the court below.[70]

(2) Service of petition

The petition for leave to appeal must be served by the petitioner or his
agents and must be served together with a copy and with two clear days notice

[59] Criminal Appeal Act 1968, s. 38. Leave may be given by the single judge: *ibid*. s. 44 (*c*).
[60] Criminal Appeal Rules 1968, r. 23 (1) (*c*); Criminal Appeal (Amendment) Rules 1978, r. 7 (*d*).
[61] See *ante*, p. 69, note 2.
[62] Criminal Appeal Act 1968, s. 44.
[63] *Ibid*. s. 44; Costs in Criminal Cases Act 1973, Sched. 1.
[64] Criminal Appeal Act 1968, s. 44.
[65] *Ibid* s. 44 (2); Road Traffic Act 1974, Sched. 6.
[66] A form of petition, taken from Appendix A to the House of Lords Directions as to Procedure,
1979, is to be found, for the sake of convenience, in Appendix G, *post*, No. 1. An application to
the House for an extension of time may be made on the petition for leave, setting out the reasons
why the petition is out of time: Dir. 12.
[67] *Ibid*. Dir. 5 (i).
[68] "Lodgment" and "lodging" mean deposit or depositing in the Judicial Office of the House of
Lords: *Ibid*. Dir. 39.
[69] *i.e.* by the Administration of Justice Act 1960, s. 1 (2) (see *ante*, p. 103), and the Criminal
Appeal Act 1968, s. 33 (2) (*ante*, p. 105).
[70] Directions as to Procedure 1979, Dir. 5 (ii).

of intention to present the petition, on the respondents or their agents.[71] A copy of the order complained of must be lodged with the petition.[72]

(3) Entering appearance

The respondents or their London agents should enter appearance to the petition for leave as soon as they have received service. They should attend at the Judicial Office of the House of Lords to enter their name and address. No fee is payable. There is no obligation on parties who intend to take no part in the proceedings before the House to enter an appearance, but the Judicial Office will not send communications to those who have not entered their names.[73]

(4) Papers for the Appeal Committee

A petition for leave to appeal to the House is referred to an Appeal Committee.[74] Within 14 days of the refusal of the court below of an application for leave to appeal, there must be lodged,[75] that is deposited with the Judicial Office, the original petition, endorsed with a certificate of service, and signed by the petitioner or his agents, a copy of the order of the court below, or if leave to appeal and/or a certificate[76] was requested at a later date, a copy of the supplementary order of the court below.[77] Within one week of lodgment of the petition, the following documents are required: (a) four copies of the petition for leave to appeal; (b) four additional copies of the order of the court below; (c) four additional copies of any supplementary order; (d) five copies of the transcript of the judgments of the court below; (e) five copies of the order of the court of first instance; (f) five copies of the transcript of the judgment of the court of first instance, or of the case stated; and (g) one set of any other documents considered necessary.[78]

All petitions and supporting documents lodged in the Parliamentary Office for the use of the Appeal Committee become the property of the House.[79]

---

[71] A certificate of such service must be endorsed on the original petition: *ibid*. Dir. 7 (1). A form of certificate, taken from Appendix B to the Directions as to Procedure, is to be found in Appendix G, *post*, No. 1.

[72] *Ibid*. Dir. 7 (1). Petitions for leave to appeal to the House of Lords carry the same title as in the court of first instance. The prosecutor is therefore shown first in the title and on the petition whether he is the petitioner or the respondent in the House of Lords. "Regina" is used in the title. In the petition the prosecuting authority should be cited as follows: "Director of Public Prosecutions *or other prosecuting authority* (on behalf of Her Majesty)": Dir. 6.

[73] Directions as to Procedure, 1979, Dir. 7 (ii).

[74] See p. 110, *post*.

[75] See *ante*, p. 108, note 68.

[76] *i.e.* the certificate under the Administration of Justice Act 1960, s. 1 (2) and the Criminal Appeal Act 1968, s. 33 (2).

[77] Directions as to Procedure, 1979, Dir. 8 (i).

[78] *Ibid*. Dir. 8 (ii). In the case of an appeal from the Criminal Division of the Court of Appeal, arrangements may be made for the copying of certain of the above documents upon application to the Registrar. *Ibid*. It is essential that all copies of documents lodged be clearly legible. Copies which do not conform to the required standard will not be accepted: *ibid*.

[79] At the discretion of the Clerk of the Parliaments, documents other than the original petition may be released provided that application is made within 14 days of the Committee's decision: Dir. 8.

(5) Reference to Appeal Committee

The procedure of the House of Lords is regulated by Standing Orders, by which are set up two Appeal Committees, their duty being to consider any petition or application for leave to appeal that is referred to them, and any other matter relating thereto, and to report to the House on them.[80] In a criminal matter, or in any matter concerning extradition, an Appeal Committee may take decisions and give directions on behalf of the House.[81] The Lord Chancellor, if present, or in his absence the senior Lord of Appeal in Ordinary, takes the chair.[82]

The Appeal Committee to whom a petition for leave to appeal is referred will consider whether it should be referred for an oral hearing. A petition will be referred for an oral hearing if any member of the Committee considers that it is fit for such a hearing.[83]

Where a petition is not considered fit for an oral hearing, the Clerk of the Parliaments will notify the parties that the petition is dismissed.[84] Where a petition is not referred for an oral hearing, costs may be awarded as follows: (a) to a legally aided petitioner, reasonable costs in preparing the papers for the Appeals Committee[85]; (b) to a legally aided respondent, only those costs necessarily incurred in attending on the client, petitioner's agents, perusing petition and entering attendance[86]; (c) to an unassisted respondent where the petitioner is legally aided, payment out of the legal aid fund of costs incurred by him, as at (b) above[87]; (d) where neither party is legally aided, the respondent will be allowed only those costs as at (b) above.[88]

Applications for such party and party costs must be made in writing to the Judicial Office.[88]

(6) Oral hearing of petition for leave

In the event of a petition for leave to appeal being referred for an oral hearing the petitioner's agents and the agents for the respondents, or all those who have entered appearance[89] will be given notice of the meeting of the Appeal Committee before whom all parties are directed to attend.[90] Only one counsel on each side will be heard.[91]

Any application for costs should be made at the conclusion of the hearing, immediately after the Appeal Committee has announced its decision.[92]

---

[80] See Standing Order No. 81.
[81] *Ibid.* para. 81 (3).
[82] *Ibid.* para. 81 (4). Seniority is determined by reference to the date of first appointment to the office of Lord of Appeal in Ordinary, without regard to rank in the Peerage: *Ibid.* para. 81 (5).
[83] Directions as to Procedure, 1979, Dir. 9.
[84] *Ibid.* Dir. 10 (1).
[85] See scale items in *Forms of Bills of Costs in the House of Lords*, p. 5.
[86] See *ibid.* scale items (ii), (iii), (x) and (xi).
[87] Subject to the Legal Aid Act 1974, s. 13.
[88] Directions as to Procedure 1979, Dir. 10 (ii).
[89] See *ante*, p. 109.
[90] Directions as to Procedure, 1979, Dir. 11 (i). As soon as such notice has been given, the parties should inform the Judicial Office in writing of the names of the counsel or agents whom they propose to brief: *ibid.* Country solicitors should appoint London agents, *ibid.* Dir. 11 (iv).
[91] *Ibid.* Dir. 11 (i). Unless the legal aid order otherwise provides, only a junior counsel's fee will be allowed on taxation: *ibid.*
[92] *Ibid.* Dir. 11 (iii).

On determining an application for leave to appeal under Part II of the Criminal Appeal Act 1968, the House may order the payment out of central funds of the costs of the defendant or the prosecutor[93] and when dismissing an application for leave by the defendant may order him, if the House thinks fit, to pay the whole or any part of the costs of the application.[94]

5. PETITIONS OF APPEAL

(1) Time for lodging petition

In cases where the Divisional Court or the Criminal Division of the Court of Appeal has granted leave to appeal to the House,[95] there is no statutory time limit within which the petition of appeal is to be lodged. It is, however, recommended that an appellant observe the time limit of three months applicable to civil appeals.[96] Where leave to appeal is granted by an Appeal Committee of the House, the committee may set a time limit within which the petition must be lodged.[96]

(2) Form of petition; consolidation

A petition of appeal must be in the prescribed form[97] and should be signed by the appellants or their agents.[98]

An application to consolidate appeals and to lodge one record in respect of more than one appeal, and other incidental applications must also be made by petition. The form of such petition[99] should follow, as far as applicable, that given for petitions for leave to appeal.[1]

(3) Service of petition

The petition of appeal must be served, together with a copy, and with two clear days notice of intention to present an appeal, on the respondents and their agents.[2]

---

[93] Costs in Criminal Cases Act 1973, s. 10.

[94] *Ibid.* s. 11.

[95] See *ante*, pp. 103, 106.

[96] Directions as to Procedure 1979, Dir. 14.

[97] The form of petition of appeal is shown in Appendix G to the Directions as to Procedure 1979, a specimen of which appears for convenience in Appendix G, *post*, No. 3.

The original petition should be duplicated on parchment substitute, or good quality service paper. A double sheet folded bookwise should be used, to give a page size of foolscap or A4 ISO. Pages should be duplicated on both sides without intervening blank pages: *Ibid.* Dir. 13. In certain circumstances the original petition may be typed. Copies may be accepted provided that they are clearly legible: *ibid.*

Petitions of appeal to the House carry the same title as that in the court of first instance. The prosecutor is therefore shown first in the title and on the petition whether he is the appellant or the respondent in the House. "Regina" is used in the title. In the petition the prosecuting authority should be cited as follows "Director of Public Prosecutions *or other prosecuting authority* (on behalf of Her Majesty)": *ibid.* Dir. 17.

[98] *Ibid.* Dir. 15. Country solicitors should appoint London agents: *ibid.* Dir. 16.

[99] A draft of which should first be submitted to the Judicial Office.

[1] Dir. 31. For form of petition for leave to appeal, see note 97, *infra*.

[2] Directions as to Procedure, 1979, Dir. 18. A certificate of such service must be endorsed on the original petition: *Ibid.* A form of certificate, taken from Appendix C to the Directions as to Procedure, 1979, appears at Appendix G *post*, No. 3.

(4) Presentation of appeal

The petition of appeal, together with four copies, must be lodged[3] in the Judicial Office, and will be presented[4] to the House of Lords forthwith. If the House is not sitting, the presentation will be made on the next sitting day.[5]

No security for costs is required to be lodged in criminal appeals to the House and no fees are payable except on taxation.[5]

A copy of any legal aid certificate should also be lodged in the Judicial Office.[6]

(5) Entry of appearance

London agents for all respondents should enter appearance on behalf of their clients to an appeal as soon as they, or their professional clients, have been served with the petition. The London agents must attend at the Judicial Office to record the name and address of their firm. No fee is payable.[7]

While there is no obligation on parties who intend to take no part in the proceedings before the House to enter appearance, the Judicial Office does not send communications to respondents' agents who have not entered their names.[8]

(6) Preparation of documents; record

The preparation and lodgment[9] of the documents to be used in the appeal are primarily the responsibility of the appellants, although preparation should be undertaken after consultation with the respondents.[10]

After the petition of appeal has been lodged, the appellants must prepare and lodge in the Judicial Office 12 copies of the record.[11] In Criminal Appeals no "cases" for the appellants or respondents are normally required and no unbound appendix is lodged. In the event of the House requiring "cases" to be lodged, the Clerk of the Parliaments will notify the parties.[12]

The documents required to be included in the record are: (a) the petition of appeal; (b) summonses, indictments, etc., (c) the case stated (if any); (d) the judgment of the court of first instance; (e) the judgments of the court below; (f) the orders of all the courts; (g) "cases" (if required); and (h) any other documents considered necessary.[13]

---

[3] See *ante*, p. 108, n. 68.
[4] Presentation is effected by publication in the Minutes of Proceedings of The House: Directions as to Procedure, 1979, Dir. 19.
[5] *Ibid*. Dir. 20. See, as to taxation, Dir. 38.
[6] *Ibid*. Dir. 34.
[7] *Ibid*. Dir. 21.
[8] *Ibid*.
[9] See *ante*, p. 108, note 68.
[10] Directions as to Procedure 1979, Dir. 22.
[11] The record should be bound with plastic comb binding, in limp red covers of fibrex board substance: *ibid*. Dir. 23.
[12] *Ibid*. The Judicial Office should then be consulted as to procedure.
[13] *Ibid*. Dir. 24. A table showing the total number of documents normally required for the hearing of an appeal, taken from Appendix D to the Directions as to Procedure 1979 (see *ibid*. Dir. 30), is included in Appendix G, *post* No. 4.
　　Documents may be reproduced in such form as may be approved by the Clerk of the

If any of the parties intend to invite the House to depart from one of its own previous decisions, this intention must be clearly stated in the form of a tabulated statement on the top right hand side of the index to the record.[14]

The appellants must supply free of charge to the respondent sufficient copies of the record to meet the minimum needs of the respondents' counsel and agents.[15]

As soon as 12 copies of the record have been lodged, the appeal is set down for hearing.[16] The lodgment of the record carries the right of both parties to be heard by leading and/or junior counsel.[17]

(7) Notice of hearing

As soon as an appeal is shown in the term's Cause List, agents should keep themselves informed, by enquiry at the Judicial Office, of the probable date of the hearing. It is the practice to give advance notice of expected dates of hearings.[18] Agents receive a formal notification shortly before the hearing.[19]

(8) List of authorities

At least two clear days before the hearing of the appeal,[20] agents for all parties must forward to the Judicial Office a list, drawn by junior counsel, of the law reports, text books and other authorities. The list should be divided into two parts, the first containing only those authorities which counsel definitely intend to cite in submissions to the House, the second containing those authorities which in the opinion of counsel might be called for during the course of the appeal, but which counsel themselves do not intend to cite.[21] Five

Parliaments, quarto (or A4 ISO) or foolscap. Documents of an unsuitable size or form for binding in with the other documents, *e.g.* booklets, statutes, etc., should be included in a pocket attached to the inside of the back cover. Legible copies of documents used in the courts below may be accepted at the discretion of the Judicial Office. In exceptional cases, where documents are difficult and costly to reproduce and a small number only are available, a reduced number of them may be accepted: *ibid.* Dir. 24.

All documents in the record should be paginated throughout the record in one series. Where the pages of the documents have been numbered in separate series, the page number in the record should be clearly stamped on each sheet. Cut-out stiff buff-coloured separation indices, tabbed with the description of the name of the document, should be provided to distinguish each category of document, *e.g.* "petition of appeal," "indictment," "judgments of Court of Appeal," etc. A list of contents indicating the page numbers of documents should form the first page of the record. The record should contain some blank pages at each end: *ibid.* Dir. 25.

[14] Directions as to Procedure, 1979, Dir. 26.
[15] *Ibid.* Dir. 28. Documents to be held in readiness at the hearing of the appeal may be reproduced in such form as may be approved by the Clerk of the Parliaments, six copies being required of any documents likely to be handed in and examined by the House. All such documents must be made available to the other parties for prior examination if required. Except in cases where the House might wish to scrutinise them, originals of documents need not be brought to the hearing: *ibid.* Dir. 29.
[16] *Ibid.* Dir. 23.
[17] *Ibid.* Dir. 27.
[18] The dates notified in advance are provisional only. Counsel, agents and parties concerned should hold themselves in readiness during the week prior to, and the week following, the date given: *Ibid.* Dir. 32 (i).
[19] *Ibid.* Dir. 32 (i). Briefs should be delivered as early as possible and the Judicial Office should be informed of the names of counsel briefed: *ibid.* Dir. 32 (ii).
[20] Excluding Saturdays, Sundays and Bank Holidays.
[21] Directions as to Procedure, 1979, Dir. 33. Where a case is not reported in the Law Reports, the list must include a reference to the case in other recognised reports. The House of Lords Library will normally arrange for copies of these authorities to be available at the hearing: Dir. 33. See also Appendix G, *post*, No. 5.

copies of the authorities listed in the first part will be available at the hearing; only one copy of the authorities listed in the second part will be made available.[22]

6. THE HEARING; POWERS OF THE HOUSE OF LORDS

(1) The hearing

An appeal to the House of Lords in a criminal cause or matter is normally heard by an Appellate Committee, of which two are established by Standing Orders.[23] An appeal or a reference under section 36 of the Criminal Justice Act 1972, may not be heard and determined unless there are present at the hearing and determination not less than three Lords of Appeal.[24] The proceedings are regulated by Standing Orders of the House.[25]

(2) Powers of the House

For the purpose of disposing of an appeal, the House may exercise any powers of the court below, that is to say in the case of the Divisional Court, the powers of the magistrates' court or the Crown Court whose decision is challenged,[26] and in the case of the Criminal Division of the Court of Appeal, the powers of that court.[27] In either case, the House has power to remit the case to the Divisional Court or to the Criminal Division, as the case may be.[28]

The House is not confined in a criminal case to considering the question or questions certified and matters relating to those questions only. If, in order to dispose of an appeal, the House ought to consider other matters, it will do so.[29]

If a point is referred to the House under section 36 of the Criminal Justice Act 1972,[30] the House will consider the point and give their opinion on it accordingly.[31]

Any sentence passed on an appeal to the House, in substitution for another sentence, will begin to run from the time when the other sentence would have begun to run, unless the House otherwise directs.[32] Any time during which a defendant was on bail pending the hearing of the appeal, will not count towards the sentence.[33]

---

[22] *Ibid.* Dir. 33.
[23] See House of Lords Standing Orders (1972) (Public Business), No. 80 made under the Appellate Jurisdiction Act 1876, s. 11.
[24] *Ibid.* s. 5; also the Criminal Appeal Act 1968, s. 39 (1). Criminal Justice Act 1972, s. 36 (4). As to the powers of the House to hear appeals during the prorogation or dissolution of Parliament, see Appellate Jurisdiction Act 1876, ss. 8, 9.
[25] See House of Lords Standing Orders (Judicial Business) (1971).
[26] Administration of Justice Act 1960, ss. 1 (4), 17 (3).
[27] Criminal Appeal Act 1968, s. 35 (3).
[28] Administration of Justice Act 1960, s. 1 (4); Criminal Appeal Act 1968, s. 35 (3).
[29] *Attorney-General for Northern Ireland* v. *Gallagher* [1963] A.C. 349. But in *Jones* v. *Director of Public Prosecutions* [1962] A.C. 635 the House held that where the certificate was granted in relation to conviction only, the House would not deal with matters relating to sentence.
[30] See *ante*, pp. 97–99.
[31] Criminal Justice Act 1972, s. 36 (4).
[32] Administration of Justice Act 1960, s. 6 (3); Criminal Appeal Act, 1968, s. 43 (2).
[33] Administration of Justice Act 1960, s. 6 (1); Criminal Appeal Act 1968, s. 43 (1).

Where an order for the restitution of property[34] was suspended until the determination of an appeal to the Criminal Division of the Court of Appeal, and the conviction was not quashed, the operation of the order continues to be suspended until the expiration of the time within which an application for leave to appeal to the House of Lords may be made, and if it is made, so long as the appeal is pending. If the conviction is quashed by the House of Lords, the order will not take effect.[35] If the Criminal Division quashed the conviction but it is restored by the House, the House of Lords may make any order for the restitution of the property which could be made on the defendant's conviction by the court that convicted him.[36]

Where the Criminal Division rescinds or amends a criminal bankruptcy order,[37] that rescission or amendment does not take effect until the time for applying for leave to appeal to the House of Lords has expired, or, if an application is made, so long as an appeal is pending, or if, on that appeal, the conviction to which it relates is restored.[38]

(3) Costs

The House of Lords, on determining an appeal from a Divisional Court in a criminal cause or matter,[39] or on determining an appeal, or an application for leave to appeal under Part II of the Criminal Appeal Act 1968,[40] may order the payment out of central funds of the costs of the accused[41] or the prosecutor. Those costs are such sums (a) in the case of an appeal from the Divisional Court, as appear to the House reasonably sufficient to compensate the party concerned for any expenses properly incurred by him in the appeal to the House (including any application for leave) or in any court below[42]; and (b) in the case of an appeal from the Criminal Division of the Court of Appeal, such sums as appear to the House to be reasonably sufficient to compensate the party concerned for any expenses incurred by him in the case, being (i) where the order is made on the dismissal of an application for leave to appeal, any expenses of application, and (ii) where it is made on the determination of the appeal, any expenses of the appeal (including any application for leave) or incurred in the court below.[43]

Where the House of Lords dismisses an application by the accused[44] for leave to appeal from the Criminal Division under Part II of the Criminal Appeal Act 1968, it may, if it thinks fit, order him to pay to such person as may be named in the order, the whole or any part of the costs of the application.[45]

[34] See *ante*, p. 97.
[35] Criminal Appeal Act 1968, s. 42 (1), (2).
[36] *Ibid.* s. 42 (3).
[37] See *ante*, p. 97.
[38] Powers of Criminal Courts Act 1973, s. 40 (4).
[39] Under Costs in Criminal Cases Act 1973, s. 6.
[40] Under *ibid.* s. 10.
[41] "Accused" is the word used in the Act; presumably it is intended to be synonymous with "defendant," as to which see *ante*, p. 102, note 3, p. 102, note 8.
[42] Costs in Criminal Cases Act 1973, s. 6 (2); as to taxation, see *ibid.* s. 6 (3).
[43] *Ibid.* s. 10 (2); as to taxation, see *ibid.* s. 10 (3).
[44] See note 41, *supra*.
[45] *Ibid.* s. 11 (1); as to taxation, see *ibid.* s. 11 (2).

Where, on a point being referred to the House under section 36 of the Criminal Justice Act 1972, the acquitted person appears by counsel for the purpose of presenting argument to the House, he is entitled to his costs, that is to say payment out of central funds of such sums as are reasonably sufficient to compensate him for expenses properly incurred by him for the purpose of being represented on the reference.[46]

---

[46] Criminal Justice Act 1972, s. 36 (5), in which taxation is also dealt with.

APPENDIX A
APPEALS FROM THE CROWN COURT AND MAGISTRATES' COURTS IN CRIMINAL CASES

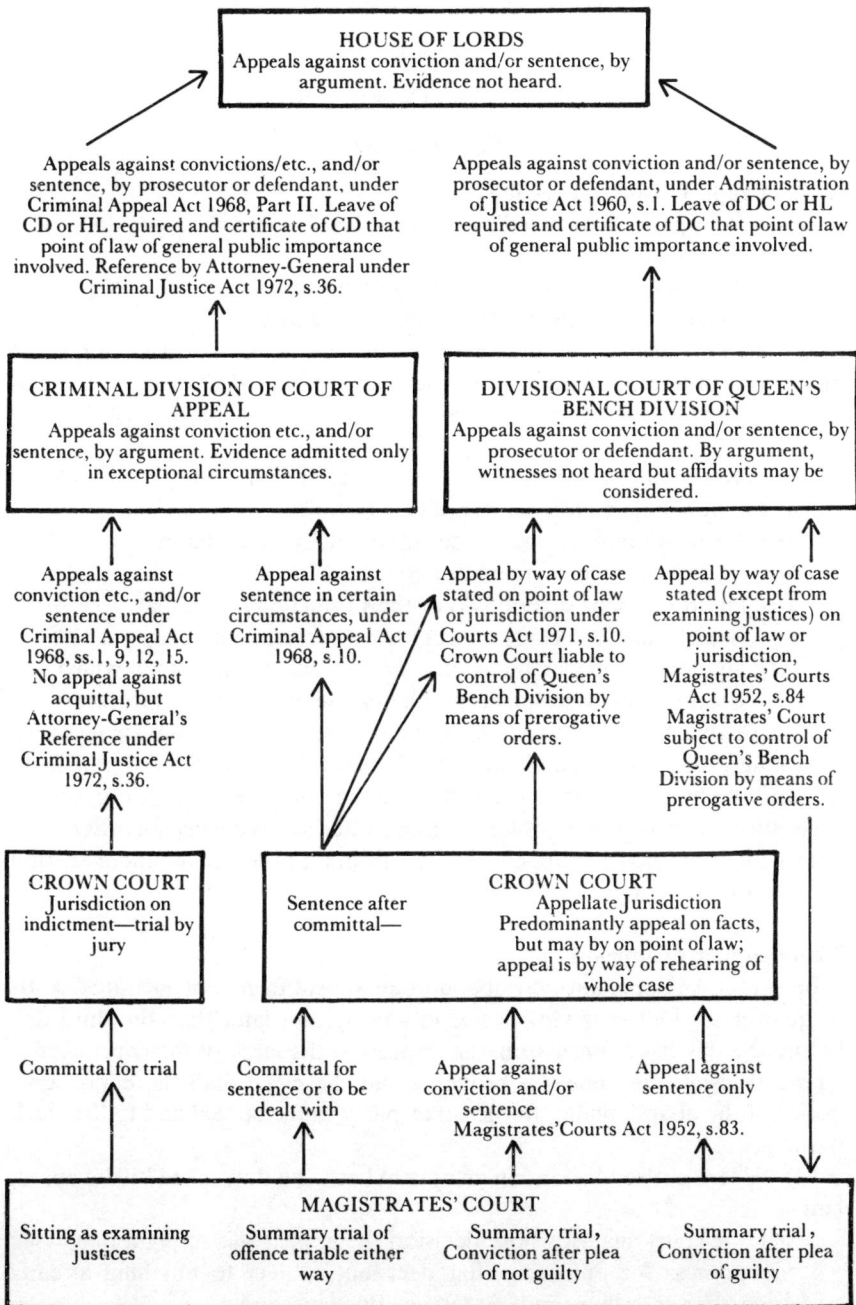

HOUSE OF LORDS
Appeals against conviction and/or sentence, by argument. Evidence not heard.

Appeals against convictions/etc., and/or sentence, by prosecutor or defendant, under Criminal Appeal Act 1968, Part II. Leave of CD or HL required and certificate of CD that point of law of general public importance involved. Reference by Attorney-General under Criminal Justice Act 1972, s.36.

Appeals against conviction and/or sentence, by prosecutor or defendant, under Administration of Justice Act 1960, s.1. Leave of DC or HL required and certificate of DC that point of law of general public importance involved.

CRIMINAL DIVISION OF COURT OF APPEAL
Appeals against conviction etc., and/or sentence, by argument. Evidence admitted only in exceptional circumstances.

DIVISIONAL COURT OF QUEEN'S BENCH DIVISION
Appeals against conviction and/or sentence, by prosecutor or defendant. By argument, witnesses not heard but affidavits may be considered.

Appeals against conviction etc., and/or sentence under Criminal Appeal Act 1968, ss.1, 9, 12, 15. No appeal against acquittal, but Attorney-General's Reference under Criminal Justice Act 1972, s.36.

Appeal against sentence in certain circumstances, under Criminal Appeal Act 1968, s.10.

Appeal by way of case stated on point of law or jurisdiction under Courts Act 1971, s.10. Crown Court liable to control of Queen's Bench Division by means of prerogative orders.

Appeal by way of case stated (except from examining justices) on point of law or jurisdiction, Magistrates' Courts Act 1952, s.84 Magistrates' Court subject to control of Queen's Bench Division by means of prerogative orders.

CROWN COURT
Jurisdiction on indictment—trial by jury

Sentence after committal—

CROWN COURT
Appellate Jurisdiction Predominantly appeal on facts, but may by on point of law; appeal is by way of rehearing of whole case

Committal for trial

Committal for sentence or to be dealt with

Appeal against conviction and/or sentence Magistrates' Courts Act 1952, s.83.

Appeal against sentence only

MAGISTRATES' COURT

Sitting as examining justices

Summary trial of offence triable either way

Summary trial, Conviction after plea of not guilty

Summary trial, Conviction after plea of guilty

PART V

APPEAL AND CASE STATED

Right of appeal

Right of appeal to quarter sessions.

83.—(1) A person convicted by a magistrates' court may appeal to a court of quarter sessions—

(*a*) if he pleaded guilty, against his sentence;

(*b*) if he did not, against the conviction or sentence.

(2) A person sentenced by a magistrates' court for an offence in respect of which a probation order or an order for conditional discharge has been previously made may appeal to a court of quarter sessions against the sentence.

(3) In this section the expression "sentence" includes any order made on conviction by a magistrates' court, not being—

(*a*) a probation order or an order for conditional discharge;

(*b*) an order for the payment of costs;

(*c*) an order under section two of the Protection of Animals Act, 1911 (which enables a court to order the destruction of an animal); or

(*d*) an order made in pursuance of any enactment under which the court has no discretion as to the making of the order or its terms.

(4) An appeal shall lie to a court of quarter sessions from any order made by a magistrates' court under the enactments relating to bastardy, or from any refusal by a magistrates' court to make such an order, or from the revocation, revival, or variation by a magistrates' court of such an order:

Provided that no such appeal shall lie from an order made under section seventy-four of this Act.

Abandonment of appeal.

85.—(1) An appellant may abandon an appeal from a magistrates' court to quarter sessions by giving notice in writing, not later than the third day before the day fixed for hearing the appeal, to the clerk of the court against whose decision the appeal is brought; and the clerk shall thereupon give notice of the abandonment to the other party to the appeal and to the clerk of the peace.

(2) Where notice to abandon an appeal has been duly given by the appellant—

(*a*) the court against whose decision the appeal was brought may issue process for enforcing that decision, subject to anything already suffered or done under it by the appellant; and (*b*) the said court may, on the application of the other party to the appeal, order the appellant to pay to that party such costs as appear to the court to be just and reasonable in respect of expenses properly incurred by that party in connection with the appeal before notice of the abandonment was given to that party.

(3) Costs ordered to be paid under this section shall be enforceable as a civil debt.

Enforcement of decision of quarter sessions.

86. After the determination by a court of quarter sessions of an appeal from a magistrates' court the decision appealed against as confirmed or varied by the court of quarter sessions, or any decision of the court of quarter sessions substituted for the decision appealed against, may, without prejudice to the powers of the court of quarter sessions to enforce the decision, be enforced—

(*a*) by the issue by the court by which the decision appealed against was given of any process that it could have issued if it had decided the case as the court of quarter sessions decided it;

(*b*) so far as the nature of any process already issued to enforce the decision appealed against permits, by that process;

and the decision of the court of quarter sessions shall have effect as if it had been made by the magistrates' court against whose decision the appeal is brought.

APPENDIX C
CROWN COURT FORMS

IN THE INNER LONDON AREA AND IN THE METROPOLITAN POLICE DISTRICT

NOTE.—The attention of the appellant is called to the notice on the back hereof.

Notice of Appeal

TO the Clerk of the

Magistrates' Court in the said Area and District

and TO

of

I,

of

hereby notify you that it is my intention to appeal to the Crown Court
sitting at

against a certain conviction of me

sentence which was passed upon me

order

determination

made against me

by   Magistrates' Court

in the said Area on   , for having on

                                                                      in the said Area and District

the general grounds of such appeal are:—

and that I am not guilty of the said offence.

DATE:

S.9
—
Notice of Appeal

(Signed) ....

N.B.—The Court Administrator will in due course give you and each of you notice as to the date,
time and place fixed for the hearing of such appeal.

(P.T.O.)

THE CROWN COURT
Inner London Sessions House
Newington Causeway London SE1 6AZ

Telephone 01-407 7111 ext 204

Your reference

Our reference   Appeals

Date

Dear Sir/Madam,

Crown Court Rules 1971 - Rule 7

I refer to your letter of the   in which
you expressed your intention to appeal against a conviction/sentence
passed upon you at the Magistrates' Court on the

Upon examination of the relevant dates, I find that your
notice in this respect has not been given within the prescribed
period of 21 days from the date of conviction and that your appeal
is out of time.

If you wish to apply for leave to appeal out of time, you
may do so by completing the enclosed form and returning same to this
Court as soon as possible.

The form must be completed in full.

Yours faithfully,

An Officer of the Crown Court

The Crown Court
Inner London Sessions House
Newington Causeway,
London SE1 6AZ

Tel: 01-407-7111 Ext. 202

Information in support of
AN APPLICATION FOR LEAVE TO APPEAL OUT OF TIME
Please complete in detail and up to Item No. 8 in Capitals.

1. Full Name. ....

2. Address where Appeal's ....
    Hearing Notice and other ....
    papers can be served.

3. Name of Magistrate' Court concerned ....

4. Date of Conviction ....

5. Offence or offences ....
    of which you were ....
    convicted.
    ....
    ....

6. The Sentence or ....
    Sentences imposed ....
    ....

7. Did you Plead guilty ....
    or found guilty after Trial ....

8. Appealing against Conviction or Sentence ....

9. Reasons for failing to Lodge Notice of ....
    Appeal within 21 days of the decision.
    (Please set out your reasons as ....
    fully as possible.) ....

....
....
....
....
....
....
....
....
....
....

(Please write legibly)   Signature. _____

                                    Date. _____

Note:- If you pleaded guilty at the Magistrates' Court
       you cannot appeal against conviction to this Court.
       You may, however, appeal against sentence.

THE CROWN COURT

Inner London Sessions House
Newington Causeway London SE1 6AZ

Telephone 01-407 7111 ext   204

Your reference	
Our reference	Appeals
Date	

Dear Sir,

        Papers were forwarded to us in respect of an Appeal against a conviction at your Court on

        As this Appeal was out of time a letter was sent to the Appellant informing him/her that, should he/she wish to apply for permission for an extension of time in which to appeal, it would be necessary to complete and return to us the enclosed questionnaire.

        To date there has been no response.

                 Yours faithfully,

             Appeals Clerk.

"SCHEDULE 2

FORM OF NOTICE OF APPLICATION RELATING TO BAIL

IN THE CROWN COURT

Take notice that an application relating to bail will be made to the Crown Court

at

on   at   a.m./p.m.

on behalf of the defendant/appellant/prosecutor/respondent.

Name of defendant/appellant: Crown Court No.
(Block letters)

Solicitor for the *Applicant:*

Address:

If defendant/appellant is in custody:
state place of detention and
give Prison No. if applicable

State particulars of proceedings
during which defendant/appellant)
was committed to custody or
bailed [un]conditionally:

Enter details of any relevant previous
applications for bail or variation of
conditions of bail:

Nature and grounds of application:
(State fully facts relied on and list
previous convictions (if any). Give
details of any proposed sureties and
answer any objections raised
previously):

Notes
The appropriate officer of the Crown Court should be consulted about the
time and place of the hearing before this notice is sent to the other party to
the application.
A copy of this notice should be sent to the Crown Court.".

THE CROWN COURT
Inner London Sessions House
Newington Causeway London SE1 6AZ

Telephone 01-407 7111 ext

Your reference

Our reference

Date

Dear Sir/Madam,

APPEAL OF: _____

I write to inform you that this Court has issued the attached Direction, the effect of which is to accept the notice of appeal you have submitted as if it had been served within the prescribed period.

Copies of this Direction have been sent to the Respondent and to the Magistrates Court.

It will however, be necessary for you to serve a copy of the Direction on any other party whom you know to be concerned with this case and an extra copy is enclosed for that purpose.

Your appeal has been registered at this Court and you will shortly be given notice of the date on which you are required to attend this Court to make your appeal. Such notice will be sent to you by Recorded Delivery post and it is important that you should make arrangements to receive that communication. If you change your address before your appeal is heard you must inform this Court at once.

Should you wish in due course to abandon your appeal you will be required to give notice in writing to the Magistrates Court, to any other party to the appeal and to this Court. Such notice must be received by all parties not later than the third day before the date fixed for the hearing of the appeal; for this purpose any Saturday, Sunday or Bank Holiday is to be disregarded.

Yours faithfully,

For Courts Administrator.

(existing Notice accepted)

THE CROWN COURT AT INNER LONDON SESSIONS HOUSE,

NEWINGTON CAUSEWAY, LONDON, S.E.1

DIRECTION GIVEN UNDER RULE 7 OF THE CROWN COURT
RULES 1971 FOLLOWING AN APPLICATION FOR AN
EXTENSION OF TIME FOR GIVING NOTICE OF APPEAL

NOTICE is hereby given that upon application

by   (appellant)

of

this Court has extended the time for giving

notice of appeal against a decision of the

                    Magistrates' Court

on the   day of   19

so that the notice of appeal already given may be

treated as if it had been given within the prescribed

period.

Date _____

                              for Courts Administrator

TO: The Appellant (2 copies)
    The Appellant's Solicitors
The Chief Clerk   Magistrates' Court
The Respondent

(NOTE) The appellant is required to give notice of this
       extension of time to any other party to the appeal).

THE CROWN COURT
Inner London Sessions House
Newington Causeway London SE1 6AZ

Telephone 01-407 7111 ext

Your reference	
Our reference	
Date	

Dear Sir/Madam,

NOTICE OF APPEAL

APPLICATION FOR EXTENSION OF TIME

I write to inform you that this Court has granted you an extension of time to serve formal Notice of your proposed appeal.

You should now obtain copies of the appropriate form from the Magistrates Court and, after completion, send copies to:-

    1.   The Magistrates' Court

    2.   The Respondent and

    3.   Any other party to the appeal

All posted in time to arrive not later than the date mentioned in the attached Direction.

You must also enclose with your Notices copies of the Direction which are attached hereto.

If your Notices are served as required your appeal will be registered at this Court and you will, in due course, be informed of the date upon which you must attend to make your appeal. This Notice will be sent to you by Recorded Delivery post and you should arrange to receive same at the address you have given. If you change your address before your appeal is heard you must inform this Court without delay.

Should you afterwards wish to abandon your appeal you are required to give Notice in writing to the Magistrates' Court, to any other party to the appeal and also to this Court. Such Notice must be received in each case no later than the third day before the date fixed for the hearing of the appeal and for this purpose any Saturday, Sunday or Bank Holiday is to be disregarded.

Yours faithfully,

For Courts Administrator.

(Notices still to be served)

THE CROWN COURT AT INNER LONDON SESSIONS HOUSE

NEWINGTON CAUSEWAY, LONDON, S.E.1

DIRECTION GIVEN UNDER RULE 7 OF THE CROWN COURT
RULES 1971 FOLLOWING AN APPLICATION FOR AN
EXTENSION OF TIME FOR GIVING NOTICE OF APPEAL

NOTICE is hereby given that upon application

by   (appellant)

of

this Court has extended until the   day of

          19   , the time for giving notice of

appeal against a decision of the

Magistrates Court

on the   day of   19

Date: _____

                              for Courts Administrator

TO: The Appellant. (2 copies)
      The Appellant's Solicitors
      The Chief Clerk,   Magistrates Court.

(NOTE) The appellant is required to give notice of this
        extension of time to any other party to the appeal).

NOTICE OF APPLICATION RELATING TO

BAIL IN THE CROWN COURT AT

....

Notes: The appropriate office of the Crown Court should be consulted about the time and place of the hearing before this notice is sent to the other party to the application.
A copy of this notice should be sent to the Crown Court.

Take notice that an application relating to bail will be made to the Crown Court

at

on   at   am/pm.

on behalf of the defendant / appellant / prosecutor / respondent.

Name of Defendant / Appellant: Crown Court No.
(Block letters)

Solicitor for the **Applicant:**
Address:

If Defendant / Appellant is in custody:
state place of detention and
give Prison No. if applicable

State particulars of proceedings
during which Defendant / Appellant
was committed to custody or
bailed [un]conditionally:

Enter details of any relevant previous
applications for bail or variation of
conditions of bail:

Nature and grounds of application:
(State fully facts relied on and list
previous convictions (if any). Give
details of any proposed sureties and
answer any objections raised
previously):

APPENDIX C

In the Crown Court (Code No.   )

at

on

No.

NOTE: *Delete alternatives as appropriate.*

WHEREAS the defendant/appellant   Date of birth:

of

being before the Crown Court for the purposes of criminal proceedings

AND the Court having considered bail in accordance with the provisions of the Bail Act 1976

IT IS ORDERED that the defendant/appellant be granted bail
unconditionally
OR
subject to the following conditions:—

A.   To be complied with BEFORE release on bail:

to provide surety / sureties in the sum of £
to secure the surrender of the defendant/appellant to custody at the time and place directed
[NOTE: Recognizance(s) of surety / sureties endorsed overleaf.]

AND/OR

B.   To be complied with AFTER release on bail:

The above conditions having been imposed for the following reasons:

AND that the defendant / appellant shall appear at the Crown Court at
[or such other place as shall be notified]
on

[on such day and at such time as the Court may direct]

THERE to surrender himself/herself into custody.

An Officer of the Crown Court

Date:

FORM 5102
Bail: Record of decision—conditional or unconditional grant.

MCR 2/78 TCLB

Recognizance(s) of Surety/Sureties

I,

of

acknowledge my obligation to forfeit the sum specified opposite my signature if the defendant/ appellant fails to surrender to the custody of the Crown Court.

Signature:

I,

of

acknowledge my obligation to forfeit the sum specified opposite my signature if the defendant/ appellant fails to surrender to the custody of the Crown Court.*

Signature:

Taken before me on the

An Officer of the Crown Court

In the Crown Court (Code No.   )

at

on   No.

NOTE: Delete alternatives as appropriate.

WHEREAS the defendant/appellant   Date of birth:

of

being before the Crown Court for the purposes of criminal proceedings

AND the Court having considered bail in accordance with the provisions of the Bail Act 1976

AND having found that the exception(s) to the right to bail applies/apply
withholds bail for the reason(s) stated below,
in accordance with Section 5(3) and Schedule 1 to the Bail Act 1976:-

Exceptions to the right to bail (tick appropriate box(es))   **Reasons for withholding bail:**

☐   1. Belief that he/she would:-
        (a) fail to surrender to custody

☐   (b) commit an offence whilst on bail

☐   (c) interfere with witnesses

☐   (d) obstruct the course of justice

☐   2. For his/her own:-
        (a) protection

☐   (b) welfare (child or young person only)

☐   3. Already detained in custody in pursuance of
        sentence.

☐   4. Not been practicable to obtain sufficient
        information for a decision on bail.

☐   5. Has been arrested for absconding from bail
        (in these proceedings).

☐   6. Impracticable to complete inquiries or
        reports other than in custody.
            NOTE: Only applicable to adjournments for
                  inquiries or a report.

An Officer of the Crown Court
Date:

FORM 5102A
Bail: Record of decision—bail withheld

MCR 2/78 TCLB

In the Crown Court (Code No.   )

at

on

No.

NOTE: Delete alternatives as appropriate.

WHEREAS the defendant/appellant   Date of birth:

of

being before the Crown Court for the purposes of criminal proceedings

AND having been granted bail
unconditionally
OR
subject to the following conditions (Conditions of bail first imposed):-

1.

2.

3.

by   Court   on the
to appear at the Crown Court

on

[on such day and at such time as the Court may direct]
there to surrender himself/herself into custody

UPON application by
under Section 3(8) of the Bail Act 1976 for
conditions imposed thereon to be varied
OR
conditions to be imposed thereon

IT IS ORDERED that
the original conditions be removed (varied to those specified below)
OR
the conditions specified below shall be complied with in respect of the said bail

CONDITIONS OF BAIL IMPOSED (AS VARIED):

1.

2.

3.

The above conditions were imposed for the following reasons:

An Officer of the Crown Court

Date:

FORM 5102B
Bail: Record of decision—variation of conditions
    or subsequent imposition of conditions on bail granted unconditionally

MCR 2/78 TCLB

In the Crown Court (Code No.   )

at

No.

on

_____

To   The Governor

of

_____

WHEREAS   (Hereinafter called the defendant/appellant)

being now in your custody under a warrant of the

Magistrates' Court

(The Crown Court at   ) dated

and bail having been granted by the Crown Court on   subject

to the conditions set out in the attached record of decision on bail

IT IS ORDERED that, upon the defendant/appellant complying with the conditions required to be complied with before release, as therein set out, he/she shall be discharged out of your custody in respect of his/her commitment as aforesaid.

An Officer of the Crown Court

Date:

In the Crown Court (Code No.   )

at

on

No.

To   The Governor

of

WHEREAS   (Hereinafter called the defendant/appellant)

being now in your custody under a warrant of the

Magistrates' Court

(The Crown Court at   ) dated

and bail having been granted by the Crown Court unconditionally [subject to the conditions set out

in the record of decision on bail dated   (copy attached)

and such conditions as require compliance before release having been duly complied with].

IT IS ORDERED that the defendant/appellant shall be discharged out of your custody in respect

of his/her commitment as aforesaid.

An Officer of the Crown Court

Date:

FORM 5048A. Bail: Order for releases from custody.   MCR 2/78 TCLB

In the Crown Court (Code No.   )

at

on

To

of

NOTE: *Delete alternatives as appropriate.*

WHEREAS on the
you acknowledged your obligation to forfeit the sum of £

if the defendant/appellant

of

failed to surrender to the custody of the Crown Court

AND WHEREAS the defendant/appellant failed to surrender to custody

on

IT IS ORDERED that you appear at the Crown Court at

on the

to show cause why the said sum should not be forfeited.

An Officer of the Crown Court

Date:

In the Crown Court (Code No.   )

at

on

No.

To

of

Note: delete alternatives as appropriate.

WHEREAS

of

gave security in the sum of/in the form of

before

for his   surrender to custody (the surrender to custody of

I HEREBY GIVE NOTICE THAT

the said   duly surrendered to custody as required

on

or

Notwithstanding that the said   failed to surrender to custody

as required on   the Court made no order as to forfeiture of the security

AND (the amount of) the security shall therefore be returned to

An Officer of the Crown Court

Date:

In the Crown Court (Code No.   )

at

No.

on

NOTE: *Delete alternatives as appropriate.*

ALL CONSTABLES ARE ORDERED

To arrest

of

who, having been released on bail subject to a duty to surrender to the custody of the Crown Court, has failed to surrender as required
and

EITHER

1. bring him/her forthwith before the Crown Court or a Magistrates' Court

OR

2. release him/her on bail unconditionally (subject to the following condition (s)):-

   A. To be complied with BEFORE release on bail:

      to provide surety / sureties in the sum of £

      to secure the surrender of the defendant to custody at the time and place directed

      AND (OR)

   B. To be complied with AFTER release on bail:

to appear at the Crown Court at
(or such other place as shall be notified)

on

[on such day and at such time as the Court may direct]

THERE to surrender himself/herself into custody.

Judge of the Crown Court

Date:

FORM 5061
Warrant for arrest

MCR 2/79 TL

In the Crown Court

at

No.

To

of

NOTICE OF HEARING OF APPEAL

The appeal of

against

by the   Magistrates Court

on the

will be heard at the Crown Court

at

on

An Officer of the Crown Court

Date:

Copy to Appellant
      Respondent

   Clerk to Justices

Form 5011 – Notice of Hearing of Appeal   RM 7/71

THE CROWN COURT
Inner London Sessions House
Newington Causeway London SE1 6AZ

Telephone 01-407 7111 ext

Your reference

Our reference

Date

Dear Sir/Madam,

Re: Your Appeal

Your appeal has been received at this Court and registered under the above reference number.

The hearing is likely to take place during the two weeks beginning on   and you will receive a recorded delivery formal notice specifying the actual date and time of the hearing at this Court.

You should understand that it is necessary for you to be present at Court to prosecute your appeal, together with any witnesses you may wish to call.   Failure to attend may result in the appeal being dismissed and an order made against you for costs.

Accordingly you should so arrange your affairs that you may come to Court on the day fixed.

If you change your address to one different from that to which this letter is addressed, you must advise me in writing immediately.

Yours faithfully,

Deputy Courts Administrator

THE CROWN COURT,
INNER LONDON SESSIONS HOUSE,
NEWINGTON CAUSEWAY,
LONDON SE1 6AZ

Telephone Number: 01-407 7111 Ext.

Your Ref:

Our Ref:

Date:

Dear Sir or Madam,

                    Appeal of _____

        I refer to your letter to this Court dated
concerning your appeal in respect of the proceedings against you at the
                    Magistrates' Court on the

        I am directed to inform you that, after considering the submissions
you have made, the Court has allowed your appeal to be reinstated in the
List for hearing.

        You will shortly be advised by Notice form this Court of the new
date fixed for the hearing of your appeal and you should make arrangements
for such notice to be received at your address by Recorded postal delivery.

                    Yours faithfully,

                    An Officer of the Crown Court.

Copies for information to:

(i)   The Chief Clerk,   Magistrates' Court

(ii)   The Respondent(s)

(iii)   I.L.S.H. List Office

APPENDIX D
CASE STATED

148. Case stated
(*M. C. Act* 1952, *s.* 87; *M. C. Rules* 1968, *rr*, 66, 68)

In the High Court of Justice
  Queen's Bench Division
  Between A. B., Appellant

and

  C. D., Respondent.
Case stated by Justices for the [county of   , acting in and for the
Petty Sessional Division of   ], in respect of their adjudication as a
Magistrates' Court sitting at

CASE

1. On the   day of   , 19 , an information [*or* complaint]
was preferred by the appellant [*or* respondent] against the respondent [*or*
appellant] that he/she (*state shortly particulars of information or complaint
and refer to any relevant statutes*).

2. We heard the said information [*or* complaint] on the   day
of   , 19 , and found the following facts:—(*set out in separate
lettered paragraphs*).

*[The following is a short statement of the evidence:—(*set out so as to
show relevant evidence given by each witness*)].

†3. It was contended by the appellant that

†4. It was contended by the respondent that

5. We were referred to the following cases

6. We were of opinion that (*state grounds of decision*) and accordingly
(*state decision including any sentence or order*).

PART V.—Forms

QUESTION

7. The question for the opinion of the High Court is
  Dated the   day of   , 19
E. F.,
G. H.,
Justice of the Peace for the [county] aforesaid [on
behalf of all the Justices adjudicating].

[Signed (a), on behalf of the above-
mentioned Justices, at their direction
J. C.
Justices' Clerk for the Petty
Sessional Division of . . . .]

* Insert only if the opinion of the High Court is sought, whether there was evidence upon
which the Magistrates' Court could come to its decision.
† Only a brief summary should be given.

FORMS RELATING TO APPLICATIONS
TO THE HIGH COURT FOR BAIL

No. 97
Summons to grant bail
(0.79, r.9)

In the High Court of Justice,

Queen's Bench Division.

Let all parties concerned attend the judge in chambers on the
day of 19 at o'clock on the hearing
of an application on behalf of A.B. to be granted bail as to his commitment on the day of by a magistrates'
court sitting at [*or* by the Crown Court at]
[*or* by the High Court].

Dated the day of 19

This summons was taken out by of
[agent for of] solicitor for the said A.B."

"No. 97A
Summons to vary arrangements for bail in a criminal proceeding
(0.79, r.9)

In the High Court of Justice,
Queen's Bench Division.

Let all parties concerned attend the judge in chambers on the
day of 19 at o'clock on the hearing
of an application [on behalf of A.B.] [by] that the terms
on which A.B. was granted bail by on
should be varied as follows—

Terms on which A.B. was granted bail—
Proposed variation—

Dated the day of 19

This summons was taken out by [of
[agent for of] solicitor for the said A.B.]
[[as prosecutor] [a constable of Police
Force]].".

"No. 98
Order of judge in chambers to release prisoner on bail
(0.79, r.9)

In the High Court of Justice,
Queen's Bench Division.

The Honourable Mr Justice   Judge in chambers.

Whereas on the   day of   19   A.B.
[*state the circumstances in which the applicant was committed as, for
example*, was remanded in custody *or* was committed in custody by a
magistrates' court sitting at   for trial at the Crown Court
at   on a charge of   *or* was convicted by a
magistrates' court sitting at   of   and
sentenced to   and the said A.B. has given notice of
appeal to the Crown Court against such conviction *or* sentence]:

And whereas the said A.B. is in the custody of the Governor of Her
Majesty's prison at   and has applied to the judge in
chambers to be granted bail:

Upon hearing counsel [*or* the solicitor] for the said A.B. and upon
reading the affidavit of   filed the   day
of   19   :

It is ordered that the said A.B., after complying with the condition(s)
specified in Schedule I hereto, shall be released on bail, subject to the
condition(s) specified in Schedule II hereto, and with a duty to surrender
to the custody of [the magistrates' court at   on the
                    day of   19   at   a.m./p.m.]
[the Crown Court on such day and at such time and place as may be
notified to the said A.B. by the appropriate officer of that court].

Dated the   day of   19   .

SCHEDULE I

Conditions to be complied with before release on bail

To provide   suret[y][ies] in the sum of £   [each]
before a justice of the peace [*or as may be*] to secure A.B.'s surrender to
custody at the time and place appointed.

†

SCHEDULE II

Conditions to be complied with after release on bail

†

†Insert condition(s) as appropriate (including in Schedule I directions
under 0.79, r.9(6B), in respect of any pre-release conditions).

No. 98A

Order of judge in chambers varying arrangements for bail

(0.79, r.9)

In the High Court of Justice,

    Queen's Bench Division.

The Honourable Mr Justice   Judge in chambers.

Whereas on the   day of   19
[*state the circumstances in which the committal was made as, for example*, A.B. was remanded in custody *or* was committed in custody by a magistrates' court sitting at   for trial at the Crown Court at   on a charge of   *or* was convicted by a magistrates' court sitting at   of   and sentenced to   and the said A.B. has given notice of appeal to the Crown Court against such conviction *or* sentence] :

And whereas the said A.B. was granted bail with a duty to surrender to the custody of [the magistrates' court at   **on** at   a.m./p.m.] [the Crown Court on a day and at a time and place to be notified by the appropriate officer of that court] and subject to the following conditions—[*state conditions imposed on the grant of bail*]

And whereas [the said A.B.] [[as prosecutor] [a constable of   Police Force]] has applied to the judge in chambers for a variation in the said arrangements for bail :

Upon hearing counsel [or the solicitor] for the applicant and upon reading the affidavit of   filed the   day of   19   :

It is ordered that the said arrangements for bail be varied as follows—

Dated the   day of   19   .

No. 100

Notice of bail

(0.79, r.9)

Whereas on the   day of   19   A.B. was
[*state circumstances in which A.B. was committed, as in No. 98 or 99*]:

And whereas the Honourable Mr Justice   [*or* the Court of Appeal] has made an order dated the   day of
19   that [*recite order for bail*]

Take notice that in pursuance of the said order [
sufficient suret[y][ies] will enter into such recognizance] [
will give security] as aforesaid before   at
            on the   day of   19   at
a.m./p.m. [And that the names and descriptions of such suret[y][ies]
are—]

Dated the   day of   19   .

                              (Signed)
                              Solicitor for the said A.B.

R.1.   FORM 1

CRIMINAL APPEAL ACT 1968

Judge's certificate
R.v.

Particulars of trial

Full name of person tried..............

Name of court ....

Offences for which person tried........

Decision of court —

*Delete   *convicted of ....
if   *unfit to plead
inapplicable   *verdict of not guilty by reason of
                  insanity

Date of decision of court ....

I certify that the case is a fit case for
appeal on the ground that:—

                  Signed....................
                  Judge of the court.

Date..............

SEE NOTES
ON BACK

CRIMINAL APPEAL ACT, 1968

No. 2
(See R2 Form 2)

COURT OF APPEAL
CRIMINAL DIVISION **N**

NOTICE OF APPLICATION
FOR LEAVE TO APPEAL
AND OF OTHER APPLICATIONS
(See Note 7)

To the Registrar, Criminal Appeal Office
REF. No.

Royal Courts of Justice, Strand, LONDON, W.C.2A 2LL

Write legibly in black

PART 1

Particulars of APPELLANT	FULL NAMES Block letters	FORENAMES	SURNAME	Age on Conviction
	ADDRESS If detained give address where detained		Index number if detained	

| COURT where tried and/or Sentenced. (see note 3) | DATES of appearances at the Court including dates of conviction (if convicted at the Court) and sentence. | Name of Court |
| | | Name of Judge |

Particulars of OFFENCES of which convicted. (State whether convicted on indictment or by a magistrates Court) and particulars of SENTENCES and ORDERS.	OFFENCES	Convicted on INDICTMENT or by MAGISTRATES COURT	SENTENCES AND ORDERS

Offences TAKEN INTO CONSIDERATION when sentenced.   TOTAL SENTENCE

PART 2

The appellant is applying for:— (*Delete if inapplicable)

*EXTENSION of time in which to give notice of application for leave to appeal.

*LEAVE to appeal against CONVICTION.   *BAIL.

*LEAVE to appeal against SENTENCE.   *LEAVE to be present at hearing.
                                          see
                                          note
                                          8
*LEGAL AID.   *LEAVE to call WITNESSES.

	Date	Address of person signing on behalf of Appellant. (See Note 6)
(Signed) (Appellant)		

This notice was handed in by the appellant today.   Date   **N**   Received in the Criminal Appeal Office.
                                                              FORMS N.G.   Date
(Signed)   (Officer)

E.D.R.

Form 1458 31431—5-5-70 XBD

L17

SEE NOTES ON BACK	**CRIMINAL APPEAL ACT, 1968**	(See R2 Form 3)

| COURT OF APPEAL CRIMINAL DIVISION **G** | Grounds of Application for Extension of Time Leave to Appeal Against Conviction Leave to Appeal Against Sentence | To the Registrar, Criminal Appeal Office REF. No. Royal Courts of Justice, Strand, LONDON, W.C.2A 2LL |

Write Legibly in Black

FULL NAMES OF APPELLANT   FORENAMES   SURNAME
Block letters

Give the Name and Address of the Solicitor and/or Counsel (if any) who represented the Appellant at the Trial

SOLICITOR   COUNSEL

List of Documents sent with this Form which the Appellant wishes to be returned. Criminal Appeal Forms will **NOT** be returned

THE APPLICATIONS ARE FOR:—

EXTENSION of time in which to give notice of application for leave to appeal against:—

   *CONVICTION   and   *SENTENCE
   (*Delete if inapplicable)

> Delete this section if no extension required

LEAVE TO APPEAL AGAINST CONVICTION for the following offences:—

> Delete this section if there is no application against conviction

LEAVE TO APPEAL AGAINST THE FOLLOWING SENTENCES OR ORDERS:—

> Delete this section if there is no application against sentence

THE GROUNDS ARE AS FOLLOWS:— (Include reasons for delay if extension asked for)

If Grounds of Appeal have been settled and signed by Counsel they should be sent with this Form (see note 14)

Continue (and sign) on Page 3 if necessary.

I HAVE READ FORM A A	Date	Address of person signing on behalf of Appellant (See Note 13)
(Signed) (Appellant)		

	G	FOR USE IN THE CRIMINAL APPEAL OFFICE Received

Form 1457 31430—4-5-70 XBD

G

FULL NAME OF APPELLANT   FORENAMES   SURNAME
Block letters

Page 3

Continue (and sign) on Page 4 if necessary.

I HAVE READ FORM A A		Date	**G**	SEE NOTE 13
(Signed)	(Appellant)			

| COURT OF APPEAL CRIMINAL DIVISION | **FORM** **FG** | Further Grounds of Application for Extension of Time Leave to Appeal Against Conviction Leave to Appeal Against Sentence | To the Registrar, Criminal Appeal Office REF. No. Royal Courts of Justice, Strand, LONDON, W.C.2A 2LL |

Write Legibly in **Black**

APPELLANT FULL NAMES Block letters	FORENAMES	SURNAME
ADDRESS If detained give address where detained		INDEX NUMBER if detained
Court of Assize or Quarter Sessions	Before whom tried or sentenced	Date(s)

NOTE

This form may be used to amend or amplify the original grounds set out in Form G. See notes on that form. This form must be signed by or on behalf of the appellant. Any person signing on behalf of the appellant must give his address and status. Further grounds are admitted only with the consent of the Court.

Continue overleaf if necessary.

| (Signed) (Appellant) | Date | SEE NOTE ABOVE |
| | **FG** | FOR USE IN THE CRIMINAL APPEAL OFFICE Received |

Form 1456 31429—4-5-70 XBD

FORM 4   R.3(1)(a)

CRIMINAL APPEAL ACT 1968

Notice of application for bail

To the Registrar,   Criminal Appeal Office
Criminal Appeal Office,
Royal Courts of Justice,   Reference number
Strand, London, W.C.2.

Particulars of appellant:
                    Forenames   Surname
Full names:
(Block letters)

Address:
(Where detained and, if
detained in prison, give
prison number)

Give the appellant's address if bail were granted

Address if granted bail

Give the names, addresses and occupations of two persons who might act as sureties
if bail were granted and the amounts of the recognizances in which they might agree
to be bound.

1st Surety:
Name, address, occupation
Amount of recognizance offered £.............................

2nd Surety:
Name, address, occupation
Amount of recognizance offered £.............................

If bail was granted before trial or sentence subject to the finding of sureties state:—
Amount of recognizances:

£............................. and £.............................   ....

Were the sureties the persons named above?
What, if any, conditions were imposed?

The appellant applies for bail pending, appeal (retrial) on the following grounds:—

Signed ....   For use in the Criminal Appeal
                    (Appellant)   Office

Date ....   Received

Notes
1. This form must accompany or follow Form 2. If this form follows Form 2 the Criminal
Appeal reference number must be given. An application for bail may be made whether or not
Form 2 contained an application for bail.
2. An application for bail pending appeal will be considered in the light of the grounds of
appeal or application for leave to appeal. Accordingly, it is usual for the application for bail
to be submitted to the court or judge together with the other applications and the transcript
of the proceedings at the trial. This imposes some delay. Generally, strong grounds of appeal
or application for leave to appeal have to be shown before bail is granted.
3. Do not repeat the grounds of appeal or application for leave to appeal as the grounds for
bail pending appeal. Mention any special other grounds which the judge or court might consider, e.g., medical reasons.
4. Time spent on bail does not count towards sentence.
5. This form must be signed by, or on behalf of, the appellant.

R.4(5) and (8)   FORM 11

CRIMINAL APPEAL ACT 1968

Certificate by Registrar of grant and of conditions of bail

R. v.

*Bail pending appeal to the Court of Appeal

*Bail pending appeal to the House of Lords

*Bail pending retrial or on order *venire de novo*.

I certify that on.............................the appellant was granted bail by ....
....subject to the condition(s) specified in Schedules I
and II hereto and with a duty to surrender to custody on such day and at such time and
place as may be notified to him by [the Registrar] [or the appropriate officer of the
House of Lords] [or the appropriate officer of the Crown Court].

Signed   ....
                         Registrar of Criminal Appeals

Dated   ....

SEE NOTES ON BACK	**CRIMINAL APPEAL ACT, 1968**	(See R 10 Form 14)

| COURT OF APPEAL CRIMINAL DIVISION **A** | NOTICE OF ABANDONMENT | To the Registrar, Criminal Appeal Office
REF. No.
Royal Courts of Justice, Strand, LONDON, W.C.2A 2LL |

Write legibly in black.

	FULL NAMES Block letters	FORENAMES	SURNAME
Particulars of APPELLANT	ADDRESS If detained give address where detained		INDEX NUMBER if detained

| COURT where tried and/or Sentenced | DATES of appearances at the Court including dates of conviction (if convicted at the Court) and sentence. | Name of Court |
| | | Name of Judge |

Leave Part 1 blank if Part 2 is completed.

Part 1 must be completed where ALL proceedings in the Court of Appeal whether under the above or any other Criminal Appeal Reference No. are abandoned.

PART 1

I ABANDON ALL PROCEEDINGS IN THE COURT OF APPEAL

	Date	Address of person signing on behalf of Appellant (See Note 3)
(Signed) Appellant		

A1 | FOR USE IN THE CRIMINAL APPEAL OFFICE
Received |

Leave Part 2 blank if Part 1 is completed.

Part 2 must be completed where the appellant is continuing with any proceeding in the Court of Appeal whether under the above or any other Criminal Appeal Reference No.

PART 2

The following are **ABANDONED**:—	The following are **NOT ABANDONED**:—

	Date	Address of person signing on behalf of Appellant (See Note 3)
(Signed) Appellant		

A2 | FOR USE IN THE CRIMINAL APPEAL OFFICE
Received |

FOR USE IN THE CRIMINAL APPEAL OFFICE.

To the Appellant

Copies to:

The Home Secretary

Clerk of the Court

The Governor

FORM 1454 31427—4-5-70 XBD

Form of Acknowledgment by the Registrar.

The Registrar acknowledges the receipt of the above form of abandonment on the date shown.

for REGISTRAR

DATE

CRIMINAL APPEAL ACT, 1968

(See R3 Form 5)

| COURT OF APPEAL CRIMINAL DIVISION **P** | NOTICE OF APPLICATION FOR LEAVE TO BE PRESENT | To the Registrar, Criminal Appeal Office
REF. No.
Royal Courts of Justice, Strand, LONDON, W.C.2A 2LL |

Write legibly in black

| Particulars of APPELLANT | FULL NAMES Block letters | FORENAMES | SURNAME |
| | ADDRESS Where detained | | INDEX NUMBER |

The appellant applies to be given leave by the Court of Appeal to be present at proceedings for which such leave is required. The special reasons for the application (see Note 4) are as follows:—

| (Signed)   (Appellant) | Date | Address of person signing on behalf of Appellant (See Note 6) |

| | **P** | FOR USE IN THE CRIMINAL APPEAL OFFICE
Received |

NOTES

1.   Form P is required for an application for leave to be present at the hearing of an application for leave to appeal or an appeal on grounds involving a question of law alone. This form must accompany or follow Form N. If it follows Form N the Criminal Appeal reference number must be given.

2.   Subject to note 3, Form P is not required, and the appellant if in custody is entitled to be present, on the hearing of an appeal by a certificate of the trial judge that the case is fit for appeal, on a reference by the Home Secretary, or by leave of the Court of Appeal.

3.   Form P is required in the case of an appellant detained in consequence of a verdict of not guilty by reason of insanity or a finding of disability. The appellant is not entitled to be present at the hearing of any proceedings unless leave to be present is given.

4.   The Court grants leave to be present only in exceptional cases.

5.   An appellant who is not in custody may attend a hearing before the full Court and need not apply for leave. Proceedings before a single Judge are in private.

6.   This form must be signed by or on behalf of the appellant. Any person signing on behalf of the appellant must give his address and status.

Form 1459   31432—4-5-70 XBD

COURT OF APPEAL CRIMINAL DIVISION	FORM O	REQUEST TO THE REGISTRAR	To the Registrar, Criminal Appeal Office REF. No. Royal Courts of Justice, Strand, LONDON, W.C.2A 2LL

Write legibly in black

Particulars of APPELLANT	FULL NAMES Block letters	FORENAMES	SURNAME
	ADDRESS If detained give address where detained		INDEX NUMBER if detained

PART 1
SEE NOTES ON BACK

Set out the request under the appropriate heading.
A separate form must be used for each request.

(Signed)	(Appellant)	Date	O	For Use in Criminal Appeal Office Received

PART 2
FOR USE IN THE CRIMINAL APPEAL OFFICE

Form 1461 31433—4-5-70 XBD

O

NOTES

Form O must be used by the appellant for the following requests to the Registrar.

1. To inform a witness in mitigation of sentence only, of the date of any hearing before the Full Court. The name and address of the witness must be given. (However, the Registrar is <u>not</u> responsible for the <u>attendance</u> of the witness). MITIGATION WITNESS

2. To delay the reference of the case to a Single Judge, or the hearing before the Full Court. DELAY REFERENCE TO JUDGE OR COURT

 The appellant must give reasons for the request and whenever possible the date when he will be ready. If he has been informed of the date of hearing before the Full Court he must mention that date. The request may be referred to the Judge or Court as an additional application. If the application is rejected the Judge or Court may proceed to deal with the case.

3. To treat as withdrawn until further notice an application for bail, for leave to be present, for leave to call a witness or for legal aid. SECONDARY APPLICATION WITHDRAWN

 This does <u>not</u> apply to application for extension of time or for leave to appeal. See Notes in Form A.

4. To inform the appellant of the cost of copies of the transcript ordered by the Registrar and/or specified documents. COPIES OF DOCUMENTS ETC. ON PAYMENT

 The Registrar will not be able to state the cost until he has received the transcript or documents.

5. To supply to the appellant, free of charge, copies of transcripts ordered by the Registrar and/or specified documents. COPIES OF DOCUMENTS ETC. FREE OF CHARGE

 All necessary copies of transcripts and documents are supplied free of charge to Solicitors and Council if acting in the Court of Appeal under legal aid. Save in exceptional circumstances they will not be supplied free of charge to the appellant as well.

6. Where an application for bail has been granted, to re-submit to a Judge as an application for variation of the conditions, e.g. reduction of the amount of recognisances. CONDITIONS OF BAIL

7. To add a notice of application for legal aid (where such notice has not been given in Form N, or has been withdrawn – see Note 3 above). LEGAL AID

8. NOT to arrange for the appellant, being in custody, to be brought to the Court for the hearing of any appeal. APPELLANT NOT TO BE BROUGHT UP

9. To place additional documents before a Judge or the Court. (A list of the documents should be given in Part 1, and the documents should be attached to Form O. When the application for leave to appeal is dealt with the documents will be included with the papers for the Judge or the Court). DOCUMENTS FOR THE JUDGE OR THE COURT

 Form O may also be used for other requests to the Registrar, but NOT for purposes for which other forms are provided, e.g. it must not be used to give notice of application, or grounds in support of applications, except that it may be used as explained in Note 7 above.

 A SEPARATE FORM MUST BE USED FOR EACH REQUEST.

SEE NOTES ON BACK	**CRIMINAL APPEAL ACT, 1968**	(See R3 Form 6)

COURT OF APPEAL CRIMINAL DIVISION **W**	NOTICE OF APPLICATION FOR WITNESS ORDER and/or LEAVE TO CALL A WITNESS	To the Registrar, Criminal Appeal Office REF. No. Royal Courts of Justice, Strand, LONDON, W.C.2A 2LL

Write legibly in black

Particulars of APPELLANT	FULL NAMES Block letters	FORENAMES	SURNAME
	ADDRESS If detained give address where detained		INDEX NUMBER if detained

Name and Address of witness:

Do you want a witness order?
(A witness order is not required if the witness would attend at the Court of Appeal voluntarily).

Was the witness called at the trial?

The witness can now give the following evidence (which he did NOT give at the trial):—

The evidence was not given at the trial for the following reasons:—

		DATE	Address of person signing on behalf of Appellant (See Note 5)
(Signed)	(Appellant)		
		W	FOR USE IN THE CRIMINAL APPEAL OFFICE Received

Form 1460   31571—18-9-70

SEE NOTES ON BACK	**CRIMINAL APPEAL ACT, 1968**	(See R23(1) Form 17)

| COURT OF APPEAL CRIMINAL DIVISION **HL** | NOTICE OF APPLICATION FOR LEAVE TO APPEAL TO THE HOUSE OF LORDS | To the Registrar, Criminal Appeal Office REF. No. Royal Courts of Justice, Strand, LONDON, W.C.2A 2LL |

Write legibly in black

PARTICULARS of DEFENDANT	FORENAME(S)	SURNAME (Block Letters)
	WHERE DETAINED Index Number	ADDRESS IF NOT DETAINED

DATE OF THE DECISION OF THE CRIMINAL DIVISION OF THE COURT OF APPEAL	

*Delete if inapplicable

The Defendant will apply to the Court of Appeal

* to certify that a point of law of general public importance is involved in the decision of the Court of Appeal

and if the Court so certifies

* for leave to appeal to the House of Lords against the decision of the Court of Appeal

* for legal aid

* to extend the time within which an application to the Court or the House of Lords for leave to appeal to the House of Lords may be made

* to be given leave to be present on the hearing of the appeal or any proceedings preliminary or incidental thereto

* to be admitted to bail pending the appeal

GROUNDS OF APPLICATION

	Date	Address of person signing on behalf of Defendant (See Note 4)
(Signed) (Appellant)		

HL	FOR USE IN THE CRIMINAL APPEAL OFFICE Received

Form 1462   31434—4-5-70   XBD

APPENDIX G
FORMS IN USE IN THE HOUSE OF LORDS
IN CRIMINAL APPEALS

Form of Criminal Petition for leave

[*The Petition should be typewritten on foolscap bookwise or A4 ISO on good quality service paper. The copies should be duplicated on paper of the same size.*]

IN THE HOUSE OF LORDS

ON APPEAL FROM
{ HER MAJESTY'S COURT OF APPEAL
(CRIMINAL DIVISION)
A DIVISIONAL COURT OF
THE QUEEN'S BENCH DIVISION*

BETWEEN   ‡   [name]   PETITIONER
or RESPONDENT

and

[name]   PETITIONER
or RESPONDENT

TO THE RIGHT HONOURABLE THE HOUSE OF LORDS

The Humble Petition of [name‡‡ and address] praying for leave to appeal in accordance with the provisions of the { Criminal Appeal Act 1968.
Administration of Justice Act 1960. †
Sheweth:—

1. That
    [Set out very briefly in numbered paragraphs the origin and facts of the action followed by a very short summary of the proceedings in the Courts below]

2. etc.

3. etc.

That on the [date] [State what action taken by the Court of Appeal or Divisional Court]*

Your Petitioner(s) humbly submit(s) that leave to appeal should be granted for the following amongst other

REASONS

1. [Give reasons as to why the Appeal is of sufficient public importance to be heard by the House of Lords]

2. etc.

3. etc.

---

* or the relevant Court.
† or the relevant Statute—see footnote on page 5.
‡ Petitions for leave to appeal to the House of Lords carry the same title as in the court of first instance. The prosecutor is therefore shown first in the title and on the Petition whether he is the Petitioner or the Respondent in the House of Lords. " Regina " is used in the title.
‡‡ If the Crown is Petitioner, insert here the words " Director of Public Prosecutions *or other prosecuting authority* (on behalf of Her Majesty) ".

Your Petitioner(s) therefore humbly pray(s) that Your Lordships will be pleased to grant leave to appeal from the said Order of
$\left\{ \begin{array}{l} \text{Her Majesty's Court of Appeal (Criminal Division)} \\ \text{a Divisional Court of the Queen's Bench Division*} \end{array} \right.$

And your Petitioner(s) will ever pray.

[Signature]

Form of Certificate of Service to be endorsed on the back of the original Petition

for Leave to Appeal

We, Messrs.   , of   , Agents for the
Petitioner(s) within-named, hereby certify that on the   day of
        we served Messrs.   , of   ,
Agents for   , the within-named Respondent(s) with a correct
copy of the aforegoing Petition, and with notice that on the
day of   , or as soon after as conveniently may be, the Petition
for leave to appeal would be presented to the House of Lords on behalf of the
Petitioner(s).

---

* or the relevant Court.

Form of Criminal Petition for leave out of time

[*The Petition should be typewritten on foolscap bookwise or A4 ISO on good quality service paper. The copies should be duplicated on paper of the same size.*]

IN THE HOUSE OF LORDS

ON APPEAL FROM { HER MAJESTY'S COURT OF APPEAL (CRIMINAL DIVISION)*
A DIVISIONAL COURT OF THE QUEEN'S BENCH DIVISION*

BETWEEN   ‡   [name]   PETITIONER or RESPONDENT

and

[name]   PETITIONER or RESPONDENT

TO THE RIGHT HONOURABLE THE HOUSE OF LORDS

The Humble Petition of [name‡and address] praying for leave to appeal in accordance with the provisions of the { Criminal Appeal Act 1968 / Administration of Justice Act 1960 notwithstanding that the time limited by { Section 34(1) / Section 2(1) of that Act has expired.

Your Petitioner(s) humbly pray(s) that in accordance with

Section 34(2) } of that Act, your Lordships will be pleased to
Section 2(3)

grant him (them) an extension of time to enable this Petition to be considered. The Petition is out of time for the following reasons:—

1. That . . .

2. etc. . . .

THE HUMBLE PETITION SHEWETH:

1. That

   [Set out very briefly in numbered paragraphs the origin and facts of the action followed by a very short summary of the proceedings in the Courts below]

2. etc.

3. etc.

---

* or relevent Court.

‡ See footnote on p. 17 for title of petition.

That on the [date] [State what action taken by the Court of Appeal or Divisional Court]*

Your Petitioner(s) humbly submit(s) that leave to appeal should be granted for the following amongst other

REASONS

1. [Give reasons as to why the Appeal is of sufficient public importance to be heard by the House of Lords]

2.

3. etc.

Your Petitioner(s) therefore humbly pray(s) that Your Lordships will be pleased

to grant leave to appeal from the said Order of ⎰ Her Majesty's Court of Appeal (Criminal Division) a Divisional Court of the Queen's Bench Division*

[Signature]

Form of Certificate of Service to be endorsed on the back of the original Petition

for Leave to Appeal

We, Messrs.   , of   , Agents for the Petitioner(s) within-named, hereby certify that on the   day of
            we served Messrs.   , of   ,
Agents for   , the within-named Respondent(s) with a correct copy of the aforegoing Petition, and with notice that on the
day of   , or as soon after as conveniently may be, the Petition for leave to appeal would be presented to the House of Lords on behalf of the Petitioner(s).

---

* or relevant Court.

APPENDIX G

Form of Petition of Appeal

IN THE HOUSE OF LORDS

ON APPEAL FROM (*a*) or (*b*)*

BETWEEN   †   [name]   APPELLANT
                                          or RESPONDENT
          and
                 [name]   APPELLANT
                                          or RESPONDENT

TO THE RIGHT HONOURABLE THE HOUSE OF LORDS

THE HUMBLE PETITION and APPEAL of (*c*)

YOUR PETITIONER(S) has/have, in pursuance of (*d*)/(*e*) obtained the Certificate set out in the Schedule hereto of (*a*)/(*b*)* that the decision of the Court hereinafter referred to involves a point of law of general public importance.

(*f*) The (*a*)/(*b*)* has on the day of 19 given your Petitioner leave to appeal against the said decision	(*g*) Your Lordships' House on the day of 19 gave your Petitioner leave to appeal against the said decision

(*h*)

Your Petitioner, in pursuance of his powers under the Prosecution of Offences Acts, 1879 to 1908, and the Prosecution of Offences Regulations 1946, has intervened to prosecute the Appeal to Your Lordships' House.

YOUR PETITIONER(S) HUMBLY PRAY(S) that the matter of the Order set forth in the Schedule hereto may be reviewed before Her Majesty the Queen in her Court of Parliament, and that the said Order may be reversed, varied or altered and that your Petitioner(s) may have such other relief in the premises as to Her Majesty the Queen, in her Court of Parliament may seem meet; and that (*i*) mentioned in the Schedule to this Appeal, may be ordered to lodge such Case as they may be advised, and the circumstances of the Case may require, in answer to this Appeal; and that service of such Order on the solicitors in the cause of the said Respondent(s) may be deemed good service.

(signed)

Agent(s) for the Appellant(s)

Address:

---

    * or the relevant Court.
    † Petitions of Appeal to the House of Lords carry the same title as that in the court of first instance. The prosecutor is therefore shown first in the title and on the Petition whether he is the Appellant or the Respondent in the House of Lords. " Regina " is used in the title.

Marginal Notes

(*a*) Divisional Court of the Queen's Bench Division of Her Majesty's High Court of Justice.

(*b*) Her Majesty's Court of Appeal (Criminal Division).

(*c*) Set out full name(s) and Address(es) of the Appellant(s) or if a Prosecutor, his name, rank, designation, Police Authority and address. followed by the words " (on behalf of Her Majesty) ".

(*d*) s. 1 of the Administration of Justice Act 1960.

(*e*) s. 33 of the Criminal Appeal Act 1968.

(*f*) or (*g*) Use one of these alternatives.

(*h*) This paragraph for the DPP's Office only.

(*i*) Set out full names of Respondent(s).

If the Respondent is a prosecuting authority, the words " (on behalf of Her Majesty) " should be inserted after the words (" such Case ").

THE SCHEDULE ABOVE REFERRED TO

From   (name Court)

FIRST SCHEDULE

In the matter of certain criminal proceedings wherein...............................

was the Prosecutor and...............................was the Defendant.

The Order of the   (name Court)   dated the   day of

19   appealed from, is in the words following:—

(here recite the Order)

SECOND SCHEDULE

In the matter of the   (name Court)

—and—

In the matter of an Appeal to the   (name Court)

by

Part of the said Order dated the   day of   19   and set out

in the First Schedule hereto is in the words following:—

(here recite the Certificate)

Form of Certificate of Service to be endorsed on the back of the original

Petition of Appeal

We, Messrs.   , of
Agents for the Appellant(s) within-named, hereby certify that on the
day of   we served Messrs.   of
, Agents for   , the
within-named Respondent(s) with a correct copy of the aforegoing Appeal, and
with a notice that on the   day of   , or as soon
after as conveniently may be, the Petition of Appeal would be presented to the
House of Lords on behalf of the Appellant(s).

Numbers of documents normally required for the hearing of an Appeal

(The numbers shown below are, apart from those specifically laid down in the Directions, given merely as a guide. Actual requirements must be subject to agreement and depend on the number of parties, Counsel and Agents concerned, and on the special circumstances of each Appeal.)

Appellants must provide:—	*For Judicial Office*	*For Respondents*	*For themselves*
(1) Petition of Appeal ...	Original and 4 on lodgment 12 in Record	2 on service	(as required)
(2) Records (with Red Covers)	12	(as arranged)	(as required)

Respondents do not normally provide any documents, but they should agree the list of documents which the Appellants consider necessary for inclusion in the Record (see Direction No. 22).

AUTHORITIES

(See Direction No. 33)

The House of Lords Library has five sets of the following Authorities:—

> LAW REPORTS FROM 1866
>
> THE ENGLISH REPORTS
>
> ALL ENGLAND REPORTS
>
> CRIMINAL APPEAL REPORTS
>
> REPORTS OF PATENT CASES
>
> SESSION CASES
>
> TAX CASES
>
> WEEKLY LAW REPORTS
>
> STATUTES

1. Where it is desired to refer to Reports shown on the above list, it will suffice to submit lists of authorities as has been done in the past.

2. In cases where it is desired to refer to Reports not shown on the above list, Counsel and Agents should set out these Reports separately on their lists of authorities, indicating clearly the particular passage to which reference is to be made.

3. If the House of Lords has one copy of these authorities, arrangements will be made for copies of these passages to be made at the House of Lords, and they will be available to their Lordships at the hearing of the Appeal.

4. When copies will be required, every effort should be made to lodge the list of authorities in the Judicial Office not less than seven days before the hearing of the Appeal.

5. If the House of Lords Library has no copy of these authorities, the London Agents will be informed, and it will then be their responsibility to produce the necessary copies (5 in number) at the hearing of the Appeal.

APPENDIX H
THE COSTS IN CRIMINAL CASES (CENTRAL FUNDS) (APPEALS) REGULATIONS

1977 No. 248

CRIMINAL PROCEDURE, ENGLAND AND WALES

**The Costs in Criminal Cases (Central Funds) (Appeals)
Regulations 1977**

Made - - - -   *15th February* 1977
Coming into Operation   *2nd May* 1977

In exercise of the powers conferred upon me by section 17 of the Costs in Criminal Cases Act 1973**(a)**, I hereby make the following Regulations:—

Citation and Commencement

1. These Regulations may be cited as the Costs in Criminal Cases (Central Funds) (Appeals) Regulations 1977 and shall come into operation on 2nd May 1977.

Interpretation

2.—(1) In these Regulations—
"the Act" means the Costs in Criminal Cases Act 1973;
"taxing authority" means—
  (*a*) in the case of proceedings in the Court of Appeal, the registrar of criminal appeals;
  (*b*) in the case of proceedings in the Crown Court, the appropriate officer of the Crown Court; and
  (*c*) in the case of proceedings in a Divisional Court of the Queen's Bench Division, the master of the Crown Office.
  "Taxing Master" means a Master of the Supreme Court (Taxing Office).

(2) In these Regulations any reference to a Regulation shall be construed as a reference to a Regulation contained in these Regulations.

(3) The Interpretation Act 1889**(b)** shall apply to the interpretation of these Regulations as it applies to the interpretation of an Act of Parliament.

Review by taxing authority

3.—(1) Where, after the coming into force of these Regulations, the costs of any person are ordered—
  (*a*) by the Court of Appeal under section 7(1) or (2) or 10(1) of the Act; or

(a) 1973 c. 14.   **(b)** 1889 c. 63.

(*b*) by the Crown Court under section 3(1) or (2) thereof (including those provisions as applied by any of the provisions of section 18 thereof); or

(*c*) by a Divisional Court of the Queen's Bench Division under section 5 (1) thereof,

to be paid out of central funds and that person is dissatisfied with the assessment by the taxing authority of the amount of costs due to him, he may, within 14 days of receiving notification thereof, apply to the taxing authority to review his decision.

(2) The application shall be made by giving notice in writing to the taxing authority, specifying the items in respect of which the application is made and the grounds of objection.

(3) The taxing authority shall permit oral representations to be made by or on behalf of the applicant in support of the objections specified in the notice given under paragraph (2) above, and shall notify the applicant (or his agents) of the time at which he is prepared to hear such representations.

(4) The taxing authority shall reconsider his taxation in the light of the objections specified as aforesaid and any oral representations made by or on behalf of the applicant and shall notify the applicant (or his agents) of the result of his review.

Appeals to Taxing Master

4.—(1) Any applicant dissatisfied with the result of a review of taxation under Regulation 3 may, within 14 days of receiving notification thereof, request the taxing authority to supply him with reasons in writing for his decision and may, within 14 days of the receipt of such reasons, appeal to the Chief Taxing Master.

(2) The appeal shall be instituted by giving notice in writing to the Chief Taxing Master stating whether or not the appellant wishes to appear or be represented, and shall be accompanied by a copy of the notice given under Regulation 3(2) and of the reasons given by the taxing authority for his decision, together with the bill of costs and full supporting documents.

(3) The appellant shall send a copy of the notice of appeal to the taxing authority.

(4) The Chief Taxing Master shall send to the Secretary of State a copy of the notice of appeal, of the notice given under Regulation 3(2), of the reasons given by the taxing authority for his decision and of the bill of costs and of such other supporting documents as may be requested by the Secretary of State.

(5) With a view to ensuring that all considerations relevant to the appeal are taken into account, whether they relate to the interests of central funds or of the appellant, the Secretary of State may arrange for written or oral representations to be made on his behalf; and the Secretary of State shall send a copy of any such written representations to the appellant (or his agents) who shall be permitted a reasonable opportunity to make written representations in reply.

(6) If it is intended that oral representations be made on behalf of the Secretary of State, the Chief Taxing Master and the appellant (or his agents) shall be given written notice of such intention by or on behalf of the Secretary of State and such notice shall specify the grounds on which the representations will be founded.

(7) The appeal shall be conducted by a Taxing Master and, if the appellant has given notice of his intention to appear or be represented or notice has been given under paragraph (6) above by or on behalf of the Secretary of State, the Taxing Master shall inform the appellant (or his agents) and the Secretary of State of the date on which the hearing of the appeal will take place.

(8) On hearing an appeal, the Taxing Master shall permit oral representations to be made by or on behalf of the appellant and if notice under paragraph (6) above has been given, on behalf of the Secretary of State but, unless the Taxing Master otherwise directs,—

    (*a*) no further evidence on the part of the appellant shall be received on hearing an appeal; and

    (*b*) no ground of objection on the part of the appellant shall be valid which was not raised on the review under Regulation 3.

(9) Before reaching his decision the Taxing Master may consult the presiding judge who made the order for the payment of costs and the taxing authority.

(10) On an appeal, the Taxing Master may allow or disallow any item and may alter the assessment of the taxing authority in respect of any sum allowed, whether by increase or decrease.

(11) The Taxing Master shall communicate the result of the appeal to the appellant (or his agents), to the Secretary of State and to the taxing authority.

Appeals to the High Court

5.—(1) If the appellant or the Secretary of State is dissatisfied with the result of an appeal under Regulation 4 he may, within 14 days of receiving notification thereof, appeal by originating summons to a judge of the Queen's Bench Division of the High Court:

Provided that the appellant shall not be entitled to appeal under this Regulation unless the Taxing Master certifies that the question to be decided involves a point of principle of general importance.

(2) On the hearing of the appeal the judge may reverse, affirm or amend the decision appealed against.

Payment and repayment of costs

6.—(1) Where an assessment is increased on a review or on appeal under these Regulations the taxing authority shall pay the amount of the increase to the person entitled thereto.

(2) Where an assessment is decreased on such a review or appeal, any person who has received payment in respect of the assessment shall repay any excess paid to him to the taxing authority.

Extension of time limits

7.—(1) The period of time prescribed by Regulation 3(2) or 4(1) for giving notice to or requesting reasons from the taxing authority may be extended by him on such terms as he thinks just.

(2) The period of time prescribed by Regulation 4(1) for appealing to the Chief Taxing Master may be extended by him on such terms as he thinks just.

(3) The period of time prescribed by Regulation 5(1) for appealing to a judge of the Queen's Bench Division of the High Court may be extended by such a judge or the Taxing Master against whose decision the appeal is brought on such terms as he thinks just.

Merlyn Rees,
One of Her Majesty's Principal
Secretaries of State.

Home Office,
  Whitehall.
15th February 1977.

INDEX

Judicial Review—*cont.*
  application for—*cont.*
    interrogatories on, 51
    lodging order in case of certiorari, 51
    representation of justices on, 51–52
    statements and affidavits, 50
Justices,
  representation of,
    case stated, on appeal by, 36
    Crown Court on appeal to, 15, 16
    judicial review, on application for, 51,
      52
Juvenile Court,
  definition of, 2
  remittal to, 3
  rights of appeal from, 3

Legal Aid,
  case stated, on appeal, by,
    Crown Court, 34
    magistrates' court, 31
  Criminal Division, on appeal to, 74–78
  Crown Court, on appeal to, 13, 14
  House of Lords, on appeal to, 105, 107
  judicial review, on application for, 49

Magistrates' Courts,
  appeals from,
    Crown Court, to, 1–23
    High Court, to, by way of case stated,
      24–38
  control of, by judicial review, 39–53
Mandamus, 40–42

Official Solicitor,
  assignment of in bail applications,
    Crown Court, to, 11
    judge in chambers, to, 55

Plea of Guilty,
  appeal after,
    Criminal Division, to, 61
    Crown Court, to, 1, 3–5
      equivocal plea, 3–5
      mistake or misapprehension, 4
    certiorari not normally lying after, 45
Prerogative Orders, 39–53
Probation Order,
  appeal against,
    Criminal Division, to, 59, 93
    Crown Court, to, 1, 5, 7
  breach, sentence imposed on,
    Criminal Division, appeal to, 93
    Crown Court, appeal to, 1
Prohibition, 45

Recognisances,
  appeal from binding-over order, 2
    forfeiture of not appealable, 6, 92
  default sentence in respect of, not
    appealable, 6, 92
Registrar of Criminal Appeals,
  duties of, 67–69
Remittal,
  juvenile court to,
    rights of appeal on, 3
  other magistrate's court to,
    after change of plea, 5
  other magistrate's court to,
    rights of appeal on, 1
Respited Judgment,
  bind-over on,
    appeal to Criminal Division, 59
Retrial,
  Criminal Division, ordered by, 99–101

"Schedule," Offence,
  no appeal in respect of value,
    Criminal Division, to, 58
    Crown Court, to, 1
Sentence,
  appeals in respect of, to Criminal Division,
    91–97
    to Crown Court, 5–7
  case stated in respect of, 24–26, 37
  definition of,
    in respect of appeals, to Criminal
      Division, 92, 93
    to Crown Court, 5–6
  judicial review, challenge by, 53
Separate Trials,
  judge's discretion in ordering,
    appeal against, 59
Special Verdict,
  powers of Criminal Division,
    in respect of, 84
Supervision Order,
  appeal to Crown Court,
    in respect of, 3

Trial Judge,
  bail, no power to grant pending appeal, 71
  certificate of, in appeal to Criminal
    Division, 60, 61
  exercise of discretion by,
    bail during trial, 59
    discharge of jury, 59
    separate trials, 59

Venire de Novo, 101

Witness Summons,
  appeal against issue of, 43
  certiorari to quash, 43